The Prime Target

by Sopa B. A. Princewill

A Manager reflects on serial killer Jeffrey Dahmer
Inside the Oxford Apartments

Perfect Publishers Ltd

ISBN 978-1-905399-32-1

Cover Design by Duncan Bamford
http://www.insightillustration.co.uk

Edited by Jan Andersen
http://www.creativecopywriter.org

PERFECT PUBLISHERS LTD
23 Maitland Avenue
Cambridge
CB4 1TA
England
http://www.perfectpublishers.co.uk

Table of Contents

Dedications

God Almighty
Mr Bessy Atanga Princewill, Dad
Mrs Vida J. B. Horsfall Princewill, Mom
Mr Abbot B. H. Princewill, Bro
Mr Akidiye B. H. Princewill, Bro
Mrs Ann Somiari Amachree, Sis
Ms. Harrisonba B. H. Princewill, Sis
Mrs Nderiya Harry Princewill, Sis
Mr James D. Ogoye-Atanga, Cous
Navy Capt. **Ibim E. Princewill,** *(Rtd), Cous*
Statesman **Mr Albert Dabipi,** *Pal*
Comrade **Chief Okorie Okpara** *& Vicki, Pals*
Companion **Mr Amadu Bangura** *& Paulette*

Many great miracles have happened throughout my life; I survived a civil war while in high school, had an opportunity for higher education in the United States of America and acquired a job that put me in the spotlight. The greatest miracle that happened on this job was the one that saved me from a serial killer. The credit goes to almighty God.

Acknowledgements

Since the trial of Jeffrey Dahmer vs. The State of Wisconsin regarding the murder of fifteen victims, I hadn't had an opportunity for an interview regarding the serial killer until Jon McKnight of Two-Four Productions from England called me up to schedule an interview for May 23, 2005. It was The Prime Target and, with a literary agent in mind whom Jon had recommended, I decided to start immediately. As a first time writer, everything was new to me. I was discovering the process through trial and error and I obtained help from many.

I therefore acknowledge Mr Jon McKnight for the interview that triggered my motivation to write the story, which is already in demand for publication.

In appreciation for their assistance in compiling my exciting story, I wish to acknowledge Ms Antoinette Andino. I met Antoinette through her ex-boyfriend who was a very good friend of mine. Even though she is very busy teaching and practicing local entrepreneurship, she had made important referrals connecting me to Mr Craig Lewis, who offered support by recommending and providing the appropriate writing software. Antoinette also referred me to Ms Crystal B. for her skills in data processing. Crystal was readily available for any little changes that I needed to make in the document at any time at the Milwaukee Enterprise Center North.

At a time when I encountered the most difficult problem in moving sections of the document around to create the chapters, the unforgettable Leticia Williams brought her computer keyboard skills to organize the document in the correct sequence for a smooth reading experience. She was fantastic. Leticia is an intern, teaching kindergarten kids. She is very busy too, but she always finds time to help me out when I call upon her. I was fortunate to meet this young lady at the Milwaukee Public

Library East.

Next, I wish to acknowledge Dr A. Obuoforibo from whom I learnt my first lesson in document submission. He advised that the document be submitted on a CD-RW disk for easier editing and that I should engage a professional copy editor for the document before submission. Dr Obuoforibo is a lecturer of Econometrics at the Milwaukee Area Technical College South Campus.

I also acknowledge the clerks, especially Jesse Gastelum, who worked with FedexKinko Copy Shop in the neighborhood where I always went to make copies of the document. These guys were wonderful. They showed me how to make savings from the large volume of materials I had to copy when I did it by myself on a special copier.

For the abundant library resources and the able clerks, I acknowledge the Milwaukee Public Library where I always learnt something new about the publishing process. I found informative books about the publishing game, literary agents and publishers specializing in true crime, fiction and nonfiction articles for publication. Some books taught me how to be my own literary agent, how to negotiate with publisher's editors for an advance and royalties, and the rights of the author relative to the publisher at the time of entering into a contract. It was amazing to find out that much through the Milwaukee Public Library. It was awesome working with the well-trained library staff, who help to arm people with the necessary knowledge required to accomplish a particular task, like writing the story and understanding the publishing process.

Preface

The Preface hereon is the introduction or synopsis of the book "The Prime Target," which covers the chain of miracles that occurred to save my life while I worked as a new resident manager at the Oxford Apartments. Before I commenced employment, one of the residents in the building was Jeffrey Dahmer, the man rated as the most twisted sex serial killer. My arrival as the new manger caused him to feel threatened by exposure, since I was the person most likely to have access to his apartment when he was away. He therefore made me his prime target and made several attempts to stalk me and murder me, but failed.

It is a narrative of several encounters that I had with Jeffrey Dahmer, both inside and outside the Oxford Apartments, his final residence. What only became known afterwards was the fact Jeffrey Dahmer murdered twelve minor and adult males in his apartment and made three desperate, but failed attempts, to murder me too. I therefore consider myself as a live victim, because I lost my job as resident manager of the building when he was caught. I also suffered the consequential psychological trauma following the tragedy. I have had a flash temperament since the exposure and arrest of this serial killer and the aftermath of this terrifying experience will remain with me forever.

I recall the encounters with Jeffrey Dahmer, along with other residents who were equally under the threat of exposure for some illegal or criminal activities in which they were engaged. Even then, I was unaware that my job was in a valley of death. Some of the things that happened during the year could have been fatal to me, but I was saved by the Grace. I wasn't aware of anything sinister taking place in the building until the serial killer was exposed and arrested. I did have experiences with others who felt my presence as a threat and so put themselves as my adversaries and set me up, framed, intimidated and threatened me while I was resident manager of the building. I didn't know what it was all about at the time, but I was always protected by God through the miracles that saved me.

The Oxford Apartments addressed as 924 North 25th Street on the westside of the City of Milwaukee, Wisconsin, in the United States of America was a building with attractive amenities, but it was also a silent valley of death because of the crimes that were committed in it by a dangerous serial killer. The former manager still lived in the building.

I was completely unaware that such a killer resided in the building. The miracles started right from when I obtained the job. My job required me to move into and live in the building, which I did. From everything I could remember during the time that I worked as the new resident manager of Jeffrey Dahmer's last residence, it felt as though I was in the middle of an ocean of evil. I believed in miracles already, because of other incidents that had taken place in my life before the Dahmer incident. Now I have an even stronger belief in miracles after my life was saved from the serial killer and other dangerous individuals whom I encountered in that job.

I was not aware of Dahmer's heinous activities occurring at the time, because I was so focused on my job. My awareness came only after Dahmer's arrest. I was able to survive it all through these God-given miracles that enabled me to trust my instinct and make the right decision and show the right attitude and the right action at the right times.

The book "Prime Target" has valuable new information that is authentic, original and complete from inside Dahmer's last residence in the Oxford Apartments. This book is therefore loaded with the thrilling episodes that I had with Jeffrey Dahmer himself. Full of action, the book has brand new revelations about the serial killer that have never before been told, because it is part of the inside information unbeknownst to others. "Prime Target" is therefore the only book currently on the market that offers the complete story about this serial killer.

I write it from the viewpoint of the building's new Resident Manager, a role I held at the time of the atrocities. I had been in frequent eye to eye contact with Jeffrey Dahmer for twelve out of the fourteen months that he lived in the building. I testified at Dahmer's trial and had even more to tell out of court. On this job I became an instant threat to Jeffrey Dahmer's secret life and thus also became his prime target, whilst being blissfully unaware of it at the time.

Jeffrey Dahmer made three failed attempts on my life. He was arrested following the escape of one of his victims, who subsequently brought the police back to Dahmer's apartment. The arrest and aftermath eventually brought the job to an end. When the job was terminated, all the other adversaries who were seeking to eliminate me from the job were also being eliminated themselves, because when Dahmer was arrested everyone had the choice to go. An incredible 92% of the residents moved out following the tragedy. My adversaries had to be moved out of there because a great anarchy had been dropped upon the building by the deeds of the serial killer. The tragedy indeed cleaned out all the illicit activities taking place inside the building, but it didn't end there. The building itself couldn't be left to stand, either as a monument or a memorial; it had to be demolished as another victim of the serial killer.

I now have a new lease of life and the opportunity to tell the world my compelling story. Since the Jeffrey Dahmer's real life mass murder story hit the media, only a privileged few had the chance to talk with me directly for details of the story from inside the Oxford Apartments. I feel so grateful to have been saved and I am happy to be alive.

Immediately after the serial killer was exposed and arrested, everyone involved with management was duty bound to be diplomatic. I was still employed and a witness at the trial for the prosecution, so I was not permitted to give any interviews before the trial. This book now covers it all; the story that has already been told by previous authors, plus the inside story as told by the Manager of Dahmer's last residence in the outside world.

The Prime Target will give readers an insight into Jeffrey Dahmer, the person. He was not just a serial killer, but an aspiring politician and more.

When I was a young man I received the wise advice not to yield to temptation. I have applied the wisdom of that advice at all times and especially since working at the Oxford Apartments. It was tempting to make extra money for doing nothing, with knowledge that a crime was being committed. I previously had an offer of money to turn my head the other way for any drug activities that were taking place in the building. However, I refused to yield to that temptation because it was not an official job order, nor was it in my job description. I was not going to subject myself to the consequences of failed drug deals.

It is good to have money if the negative results do not outweigh the positive. For as much as I walked the straight and narrow, I feared no evil. And even though I was totally unaware of the extent of evil surrounding me in my job, I was steered out of harm's way by my guardian angels who would push, pull or drag me any time when evil was about to strike. I held on to the job for a year and five months after Jeffrey Dahmer's exposure.

Chapter 1

Employed as Resident Manager

My employment as Resident Manager of the Oxford Apartments came with a bundle of surprises. First there was a four-step application process involving one application scan and three interviews. I was taken into a cubicle and provided with a personal computer for the application scan. I was required to input identical biographical data and other information that I had provided in my original application, which was hand scripted. After a positive output was obtained from the scan, I was invited for an interview.

I had my first job interview with Mr Don Gregory who was then the building supervisor and my future boss. He told me amicably at the end of the interview how he remembered one of my referees as a resident of one of the buildings he used to manage. He wished me well and scheduled the next interview to take place at the main office at 1123 North Astor Street, with Steven Hauptly who was the vice president of the company.

At the end of the second interview I was told to await the interview results from the office. I waited for two weeks and was invited for a third interview at the job site, the Oxford Apartments, located at 924 North 25th Street. Present at my final interview were Mr Hauptly the vice president, Mr Gregory the building supervisor and Mr Marion, the outgoing building manager.

I recall the last question in my last interview was "How would you react if you noticed a drug activity in the building? (a) call the police, (b) confront the individual(s), or (c) just look the other way as if you didn't see anything?" While it raised my eyebrows, this last three-pronged question sounded as if the hiring decision was heavily based upon the answer to it. So I gave an elaborate

1

answer, which happened to be appropriate.

My answer demonstrated that each of the options would be acceptable. In conclusion, I suggested approaching the individual(s) to give a warning that such activity should be taken to someplace else. As a result, I was employed to be the new manager of the building.

Considering the size and reputation of my employers, Metropolitan Associates, I hoped to work my way up. I was poised to pursue a career in property management, but my hope soon melted away twelve months later when Jeffrey Dahmer was exposed and arrested in the building for mass murder in his own apartment.

Jeffrey Dahmer lived in the apartment #213 inside the Oxford Apartments for fourteen months and it was there that he murdered twelve victims. The building was structurally sound to continue as a rental apartment building, but following the arrest of Jeffrey Dahmer and the discovery of body parts in his apartment, the Oxford Apartments became infamous. It was a building that offered the best of amenities to all of its residents. For example, the Oxford Apartments offered clean, fully carpeted apartments with air conditioners in the living rooms and garbage disposers in the kitchens. These amenities were uncommon to find in many of the buildings in the neighborhood where the Oxford stood. An especially impressive feature in the bathroom was the exhaust fan that was installed to air out bad odors.

It was a gigantic three story building of masonry structure seating on three acres of land. For a building of this kind, the Oxford Apartments had a flat composition or built-up roof of asphalt and gravels. Protruding through the roof were the main vent pipes of the plumbing and heating systems. A cable-television antenna was also installed near the northwest corner of the rectangular flat roof.

The Oxford was also equipped with an elevator of a 10-person capacity. The elevator had beautifully polished wood paneling and it was located across from the main building entrance. A few steps across the lobby, the elevator opened up to gain access to the higher floors of the building. A building directory that listed the names of current residents was mounted on the outside wall to the left of the entrance door. There was a basement about half the size of the main floor to provide ample storage bins and a clean laundry room. There were three washers and three dryers in the laundry room.

Next to the laundry room was the boiler room, which was out of bounds to all residents. Part of the basement was also the manager's apartment. This was the only apartment unit in the building with two bedrooms, a large living room and a separate kitchen. It was the apartment that I was supposed to occupy as manager of the Oxford Apartments. However, the former manager didn't move out of it and he assigned to me the apartment #215 next to Jeffrey Dahmer's apartment #213. I refused to take it.

There were a total of 49 apartment units inside the Oxford Apartments. These had recently been renovated with modern amenities in the form of name-brand appliances such as GE refrigerators, stoves and garbage disposal units in the kitchen. There were beautiful vanities, drapes and exhaust fans in the bathroom and "Carrier" brand air conditioners in the living rooms.

Each apartment unit was fully carpeted and boasted a beautiful shinny oak cabinet. The building entry door comprised of a metal frame with glass panes. It was equipped with intercom and electric catch. Each apartment entry door was made of solid oak wood with deadbolt locks. The hallways or corridors of the building, which ran in the east-west direction, were extra long - about fifty yards on all three floors. Thus it was easier for the residents who lived near the back of the building to use the rear exit as an entrance.

A side entrance midway between the front and the back

of the building had a hollow core metal door on the south face of the building. This entrance provided more convenient access for residents whose apartments were too far from the main entrance in front of the building. It was cumbersome to walk the entire length of the hallway to an apartment located around the rear end of the building, like Dahmer's apartment. This was Dahmer's favorite entrance.

The alley, paved with cobblestones and running alongside the south face of the building, led to the side or middle entrance. Cars usually drove over this alley to the parking stalls in the rear of the building.

Perhaps Dahmer used the side or middle entrance to bring the big plastic barrel he kept for the vats of acid he used to melt down his victims' flesh into sludge. This was the same barrel he opened for me to see during the second inspection. Something like acid evaporating hit my face and was irritating to my eyes and nose. I am glad I didn't inhale it. He set me up and failed to knock me unconscious. After the inspection, I asked him to dump that barrel.

Sometimes, for easier access, the residents would prop open the rear exit door, thereby also giving access to strangers. This was a practice that could hurt some residents when dangerous strangers entered into the building, especially at night, because an unchecked traffic developed and even street people took advantage to come through to change clothes.

One day, when I took the stairway leading to the roof of the building, I saw a used condom. It showed that the strangers who entered the building not only come to change clothes, but also had sex. Once I caught a guy in the building who explained that he just wanted to change his clothes and leave.

As part of the problems the Oxford Apartments experienced, some of these strange guys were drug peddlers. It was not easy to monitor them because the traffic flow continued 24/7, evidence of the restless mode

4

of the neighborhood. The rear exit opened out into the parking lot, providing stalls for only eight cars and space for two dumpsters. Therefore, a great deal of shady and illicit type of activities took place at night in and around the Oxford Apartments.

The building's main entrance door opened up into an attractive lobby where the mailboxes were located. Next to these mailboxes was the elevator on the north wall. All the walls to the west end of each of the two lobbies on the higher floors were fully covered with wall size mirrors. It was visually delightful inside the lobbies of the Oxford Apartments. There was also a table in each of the three lobbies. Flowers were displayed in exquisite vases, which stood tall on the centre of each table.

The only apartment in the building having two bedrooms was the manager's apartment, located next to the main entrance at front of the building. The entrance was below ground level, so a stairway running up to the first floor was provided. It was so beautiful that I couldn't believe that so much horrific activity was taking place in the building.

The Oxford Apartments' Leasing Office was a model apartment. This was where most business transactions were handled. It was a model one bedroom apartment set up as a marketing tool, located next to the lobby on the first floor. The office was the apartment unit #101, which was open to the public. Therefore, the office was simply another comparable apartment unit to show to the apartment shoppers looking to lease. This model was a one bedroom 400 sq ft apartment unit consisting of a tastefully carpeted living room, bedroom and a short hallway from the living room, which led to the bathroom.

The kitchen was located at the near end of the living room next to the apartment unit's entrance door. It was a combined living room and kitchen arrangement. The kitchen had a nice counter into which a full size aluminum sink fitted with garbage disposer was installed. It also had a modern GE brand refrigerator and a stove, which had the special feature of an electronic ignition system. Oak wooden cabinets were conveniently installed above the refrigerator and stove. Designed for convenience, the cabinets were placed within reach of most people of an average height.

For the office, there was a large walk-in closet that swung open to the hall across from bedroom entry door. This contained office supplies that were awaiting immediate use.

The bathroom had a ceramic tile floor and a shower installed over a sparkling tub. As usual, the bathroom had the combination of a mirror and medicine cab hung to the wall above a vanity and sink. One special feature in the bathroom was the exhaust fan to help remove any lingering aromas. All areas in each apartment unit were equipped with modern lighting fixtures.

The living room generally doubled as the reception area where I attended to the guests for business. This area was furnished with some stylish black leather seats, a shinny oak wooden desk and a metal swivel chair. Flanking each end of the desk was a straight metal chair. In addition to the air conditioner, there was a 48 inch ceiling fan in this reception area.

The one and only window, which was approximately 16 sq ft in size and about 3 ft above the floor, had sliding glass panes to open or close as required. The only entry door was made of solid core mahogany wood. It was fitted with a Schlage brand deadbolt lock. One bright ceiling globe light provided ample lighting in addition to an ancillary desk lamp. On the southeast corner of the living room stood the filing cabinet with four drawers. These drawers contained files relating to individual residents, past and present, some lease agreements and application blanks.

This on-site office acted as a liaison to the main office.

One of the duties undertaken here was the compilation of a weekly rental traffic report. Other duties included showing apartments to potential residents, taking new applications and fees, answering the telephone and packaging the documents for pick up by Ms Lynel Mandel from the main office.

The Oxford Apartments had a lot to offer its residents. It was located near a major college, the Marquette University in the City of Milwaukee. It was owned and operated by Metropolitan Associates, an experienced major property management firm providing professional management services in Milwaukee and the suburbs. It was conveniently located near the downtown in a major transportation arterial and it was loaded with modern amenities, as described earlier.

It was unthinkable to imagine a mystery man in such a neighborhood, operating unnoticed and committing unspeakable crimes in a building like the Oxford Apartments. It was not in the worst neighborhood and was located next to a University Campus. However, it was close to downtown Milwaukee, a neighborhood that had mainly rental apartments with high turnover ratios, because the majority of residents were in the low income bracket. They moved frequently and made rental revenues unstable. As a result, some of the residents engaged themselves in criminal or illegal activities in order to survive. In these situations, the need to survive outweighs the fear of the law. People understood that they had only one life to live and if they were lacking in one area, it was no excuse to sit back and be stranded. They would go out and get what they needed to survive by any means necessary. These people felt that the law was made to protect the rich people, who have no interest in the survival of those less fortunate individuals.

I observed every Friday when the police van would drive up into the neighborhood and load the van with any black male they found on the street, escorting them downtown to the County Jail. When asked why the police officers were doing that, a neighborhood resident said that the officers of the district had to meet their quota of the number of people they jailed each week. Some of the guys who were arrested had no choice. They knew that it was part of the survival process, because at least they would be given two hots and a cot for the weekend.

For most of the residents who remained in the Oxford Apartments after the arrest of Jeffrey Dahmer, life had returned to normal. People got used to living there again as memories of the tragedy gradually faded.

I had reduced the vacancies by re-renting ten more apartments, using every opportunity I had to promote it. I used my television interviews to advertise the property to potential renters. I was able to hold on to my job for another one year and five months after Jeffrey Dahmer's arrest.

Chapter 2

Welcome to the Oxford Apartments

If anyone can imagine how it feels to walk through a valley of death, then it would be easy to understand how I felt whilst working inside the Oxford Apartments. There were chilling discoveries, but without any clues to answer some nagging questions.

Just one month from signing the employment contract with the company, the summer heat drove out the smell of the decaying corpses into the surrounding air, affecting an area of about a three mile radius. It was mysterious, as the residents of the Oxford Apartments did not know the source of this nauseating smell. Many residents were concerned for their health, while I had the added concern for rental shoppers. I was working hard to maintain a nice curb appeal to enhance traffic for the building. By the time I completed the clean up, I was shocked to discover some whole bones on the north ground of the building.

The unsightly discovery was chilling. These were fresh, complete bones with the knuckles on both ends, partially covered with cartilage. The bones looked fresh enough to unnerve me and make me question whether something strange might have been going on, but I had no clue as to what it might be. The first thought that occurred to me was, "Was anyone making an animal sacrifice in the immediate vicinity?" If it was true, I wouldn't have suspected that person to be living in my building, on my job site. When I contemplated the possibility of an individual making animal sacrifice in order for those bones to be there, my skin immediately broke out in goose pimples.

I wasn't an anatomical expert, so I was unable to decipher from what creature the bones were, neither did I have any clue as to who might have left them there. At first sight the bones were so unusual; they were not cut up and there was no clue to connect such bones with anyone in a building that was 82% occupied. There had to be definite evidence that the bones were human and, obviously, a suspect in order to start an investigation.

The Oxford stood in a high crime neighborhood and most of the people I saw and observed seemed to live with a "watch out" syndrome. Almost everyone you met would decline to give out any information for fear of reprisals. Consequently, all residents of the neighborhood had to be responsible to watch their own backs.

I remember one resident of the Oxford Apartments by the name of Joe, who often shared a peculiar joke with me whenever he met me in the building. Joe would say to me, "Watch out Sopa" and I would reply him saying, "Watch out Joe". This joke sounds funny, doesn't it? It was a joke from which to learn. One day, Joe's woman Leuvenia asked me whether I was tired of watching out. As a continuation of the joke, I told her that everyone was in a survival mode and that anyone who could not afford to lose should not get tired of watching out. My explanation to her pointed to the fact that the need to survive in this neighborhood was stronger than fear. To relent isn't the answer for survival. My job was located in a valley of death and yet I only realized this after Jeffrey Dahmer's arrest.

There are some people who might not believe in miracles, even though they happen every day. I am a living testament to the power of miracles. Life itself is a miracle. Miracles open up mysteries and that is why I was saved by the Grace. A chain of miracles guided me to safety while I was on that job with an unbeknownst hazard.

In July of 1990 I started my job as the Oxford manager. My initial experience on the job was the deprivation of the apartment that should have been assigned to me as manager. However, the former manager was allowed to continue living in the building in this apartment. He then assigned an apartment to me that was next to that of Jeffrey Dahmer at the rear end of the building. Even though I didn't know who Jeffrey Dahmer was at that time, I rejected the apartment unit #215 assigned to me because I didn't want to live in the back of the building as manager. I told my boss to let me choose my own apartment, or I would rather commute to work from my personal residence at 1807 West State Street. My boss agreed and allowed me to choose my own apartment. He said that the job required the manager to live in the Oxford Apartments, so I chose a different apartment, unit #309 on the third floor, one above that of Jeffrey Dahmer. This was the very first miracle.

I had been curious about why the former manager still lived in the building after I had been employed, so I spoke with Mr Stephen Hauptly who was the president of the property management company Metropolitan Associates. I asked him why they gave me an apartment at the back of the building when I was the manager. He explained it as an arrangement for the former manager to watch the front of the building, while I looked after the back of the building. In other words, I was also a security guard looking out for activity that he hadn't told me about. If they had knowledge of an existing or imminent danger, they didn't let me know. I was not comfortable with their arrangement. There must have been a potential danger I felt. I was not going to carry out any duty that was not specified in my job description. I made it clear to him that I was a manager, not a security guard. Later the former manager accused me of having an attitude.

My attitude towards the perceived dissatisfaction was clear. I rejected the apartment he assigned to me and picked an apartment of my choice. It was my rejection of his offers that saved me from Jeffrey Dahmer. If I had accepted the apartment assigned to me by the former manager, Dahmer would have had an easier access to harm me. Even the street gangs who had signs on the building as their territory would have sought to eliminate me, because they viewed me as a threat. Thank God I feared no evil.

I had to show them that I believed I deserved better when I rejected the apartment. I was welcomed as if aboard a boat with two captains on this job. To me it was an awkward arrangement that signaled the conflicts that I might have later down the road. It was the first job of the kind that I ever had, but I knew that this arrangement was not good for me.

In this neighborhood people lived with fear and nobody ever saw any crime. The fear of reprisals for giving out information to investigating officers kept most people tight-lipped. I was alert and observing the plots against me by the adversaries in the building. Their intent was to drive me away from my job. They framed me, intimidated me, threatened me and boldly assaulted me physically during the time that I held the post.

There was an elderly couple in the building who lived in the apartment next to my office. The lady usually came to the office in her night gown at about 9.00 am, as soon as I opened the office. During one such visit she discussed her experience in senior citizen apartment management. She claimed to have come from Chicago in the State of Illinois where she did that kind of work. This old lady wanted my job and she was willing to do anything to get me out. One day, the old lady volunteered to vacuum clean the hallway, stating that since we all lived there, we should take care of it too. She was a friend of the former manager who engaged her in a long conversation in the lobby 'til late at night. At about 2:00 am one morning, the old lady's telephone started ringing. I was with them in the lobby that night. She ran to take the call in her apartment and returned to tell us that the call came from some friend lady of hers who lived in a house across the alley.

She said that her lady friend had invited her to come

for a visit at that time of the night. She asked the former manager to accompany her to visit her friend. Then they asked me to join them. I declined the offer, because I thought that it was too late to go into alleys. I also hated to lose my sleep as it was the only thing I got for free. Thus I offered them what we call a "rain check," meaning "till next time".

I had used a lot of common sense in dealing with these people successfully from July 10, 1990, when I started working, to November 2, 1992 when I officially moved out of the Oxford Apartments alive. I was the last person to move out of the building because I had no fear of anything after Jeffrey Dahmer was gone. Also as manager I wanted to see that every resident was moved before I move. After my first physical fight with a resident who I evicted from the apartment I immediately sent a general message through another resident. The message told them that I was not afraid of anybody; that if they had guns and knives, I had a missile that could blow up the entire building and that I would not hesitate to act immediately I feel the threat.

The next morning before we woke up the old lady packed up her few belongings and skipped. She did not pay the rent or give any notice to vacate, as required by her lease. She must have had some evil intentions against me and she was scared to remain in the building after I sent the message.

I heard people say, "An evil man runs when no one pursues." The old lady shouldn't have skipped after I sent the message if she had no evil plot against me. This type of person made my job even more difficult, because in addition to all my other tasks, I was constantly watching out for them. This first experience showed me that the company employed me to use my services, but control was beyond its reach. However, I wasn't going to let the arrangement become abusive. I already felt that such an arrangement was offensive to me. Therefore I had put my guard up to balance any ulterior motive for such arrangement that was equivalent to putting two captains in the same boat.

The arrangement put me at odds with the former manager of the building. His continued presence in the building therefore made my job harder because most of the residents seemed to be his loyalists. They were the adversaries that I was up against. If he were no longer in the building, I would have had more of their cooperation. I didn't take his orders, nor did I give him any of mine. I don't know why he continued to live there after he had ceased to be manager. I tried to be the manager at all times. I suspected that something was not right, because of the arrangement that allowed him to remain in the building, but I didn't know what it was.

Only God knows how I made it out alive. I never really lived in fear, even though I knew that the Oxford Apartments was in a tough neighborhood and the chances of being a victim of crime were higher than in some other areas. However, I was totally unsuspecting of anything as heinous as mass murder happening in a place like this. So many things happened that perhaps were regarded as commonplace in such neighborhoods, so I just went with the flow like everyone else. Nobody needed to be nosey or inquisitive about anybody. In my position, I needed to promote good resident relationship among all people.

My success on this job required the full cooperation of all the residents. Sometimes information was received only after the incident, by which time there would be little or nothing that anyone could do about it. A typical example was this horrible case of Jeffrey Dahmer. It was very bad for the business, yet I didn't know about it at the time it was occurring.

Being new to the job, I didn't know anything except that I had a job in a tough neighborhood. There had been some incident reports of domestic violence in this neighborhood and there had been illegal activities, gang violence on the streets and other unlawful activities that constantly drew the focus and attention of the police and kept them constantly on their toes.

In my position I observed several police responses to the calls coming out of this building along with other buildings next door. For Jeffrey Dahmer, this neighborhood was "it". His apartment was like the roach motel. Most who checked in never checked out.

In such a restless community, it felt like everyone was always concerned with watching out for their personal, private or family security. Jeffrey Dahmer therefore took advantage of the general attitude of the people who tried to mind their own business. The people in this neighborhood did not like to meddle with others and turned a blind eye to what others were doing. Most of the people avoided getting involved with the police. In other words, they wanted to stay out of trouble.

There are good people in bad neighborhoods, depending upon their individual life circumstances. Jeffrey Dahmer knew that under the cold mood of the neighborhood residents and the "mind your own business" attitude of the people nobody would care to observe what he was doing in his own apartment. Nobody seemed to be paying attention to what might be going on even if it was happening under their noses. Dahmer told the detectives that he continued to dispose of his victims by dumping their mutilated body parts.

He used the dumpster behind the building because nobody seemed to care about it. As long as they were not the potential victim of a crime, these residents turned their head the other way to ignore it. Dahmer was sure that nobody would interfere with his privacy at this location. That was why it was a surprise to him when I was brought to the building as a new manager. He was worried and assumed that I was employed to catch him. He therefore saw my presence as a serious threat to his murderous secret life.

If any crime was being investigated by the officers of law enforcement, it often turned out that nobody saw or heard anything. There were reprisals if anybody became a "snitch," either talking to the police or other undercover agents. Under such conditions, Jeffrey Dahmer was sure of the security of his secret life. But that assurance changed when he had a new manager to deal with. Although it was not a requirement for the job, I had a bachelor's degree in business administration. I also had a license as real estate broker. I was excited to get this job because I finally had a chance to put some of my academic knowledge into practice.

At the beginning of my employment, I didn't know that there was the element of a hazard on my job. Jeffrey Dahmer was stalking me as his prime target because he felt my presence as a threat to the security of his secret life. He felt a threat of exposure and the "watch out Sopa" joke was nothing short of a warning. I thought at first that it was indeed an indirect warning from my adversaries in the building. I didn't know exactly who they were, but I suspect they might be those who were uncomfortable with the change of manager. Thank God I had some good people who were friendly to me in the building. These were the residents who didn't worry about the change of manager, because they had no illegal activities to conceal.

One female resident, the late Dana Curry, who occupied the apartment #107, saw me when I first moved into the Oxford Apartments. She warned not to bring my stereo system to the building. The warning was a mystery to me, but it wouldn't be long before I found out why. Within one week of moving into the Oxford Apartments, Daryl Elliot lost his television set and a VCR to a thief who broke into his apartment #208 on March 16, 1991.

There were frequent incidents of theft. At about

midnight one Friday, a security guard chased a lady from Ricky's, a nearby Gentlemen's Night Club located on West State at North 26th Street. The security guard traced the lady to an apartment inside the Oxford Apartments, accusing her of stealing audio cassette tapes from a car. He was lucky to recover them. The lady did not live in the building, but was simply using her connection to a resident for her illicit activities. In addition to being a thief, she may also have been a prostitute.

On one occasion, I was framed by someone who had the master key like I did. As a result, one resident who was disgruntled over a missing television set physically assaulted me. At the end of the fight I reported him to the police and also evicted him for being disrespectful to the manager. Soon after this encounter a homicide was discovered.

In apartment #308, the resident Dean Vaughn was strangled to death. It was a murder mystery that happened in the apartment unit across from mine at #309. We didn't know who to suspect in this tragedy, but the law enforcement officers were called in to investigate. With this unsolved murder mystery, the shockwave of fear temporarily broke through the little trust that everybody enjoyed in the building. Under such circumstances, people felt more grateful to the Creator and appreciated life every time they breathed the air. The building residents now discovered that anything could take life at any time and it could happen to anyone. Sometimes the culprit remained a mystery, as in the tragic case of Dean Vaughn in apartment # 308.

Sounds of gunfire were common in this neighborhood especially at night. Sometimes we would wake up in the morning to find a body in the alley or street lying dead from gunshot wounds, not far from the Oxford Apartments. We usually reflected on the sounds of gunfire from the previous night as the moment that this unnamed person had been shot.

Such battles on the street were often motivated by the rivalry among likely drug dealers for trading territory. I remember one morning when we discovered blood splattered across the ground in the parking lot behind the Oxford Apartments. We could not tell what might have happened on the previous night, but I discovered that the blood was from one of Dahmer's victims who tried to escape naked and bleeding from wounds. Neighbors had called the police to help that victim, but Jeffrey Dahmer convinced the police officers to return the boy to him, claiming to be his guardian.

The highly drugged boy could not understand what was going on, even as the police officers were there. Dahmer did all the talking and the boy didn't respond in dispute to Dahmer's claims. The ill fated boy was thus left behind with the serial killer who confessed to murdering him as soon as the police officers left the building. Jeffrey Dahmer told the detectives that the little boy, Konerak, was so disoriented from the drug that he forgot how to speak English. He was only speaking his native Laotian language when the police officers were in the apartment. The Police officers could not understand the Laotian language. They didn't bother seeking the assistance of an interpreter to make their decision on this particular case. It was only the serial killer speaking for the little Laotian boy. So Dahmer slipped through the net again when he convinced the officers to leave the boy with him.

Only one man, Tracy Edwards, escaped from the building with Dahmer's handcuffs dangling from his left arm. It was a close call for Mr Edwards. His escape was not as miraculous as escaping totally unaware of the serial killer. Mr Edwards fought his way out just before Dahmer was ready to kill him. He was conscious of his ordeal before he escaped, whereas I was not conscious that Dahmer was a killer in all the contacts I had with him during the time that I worked in the building. Time and time again, Dahmer made failed attempts to annihilate me. His last attempt on my life was just five hours before his arrest. Following his failure, he went for the guy that eventually escaped and had him arrested. Jeffrey Dahmer himself had made it through several narrow escapes over the period he had been a serial killer. He had excellent knowledge of how the legal system worked and smartly maneuvered his way through it.

The elevation of the Oxford Apartments was lower than that of an adjacent property to the north, so it was as if it really were in a valley. A valley of death, as I called it.

At the start of my job, when I made the early discovery of the whole and fresh bones, I almost suspected that they were thrown from the adjacent building.

Luckily, I was not at the Oxford Apartments when Jeffrey Dahmer was arrested. The arrest and the discoveries created an emergency and the first person that the residents looked for was the manager. I was nowhere to be found, so some of the residents thought that Jeffrey Dahmer might have got me. They didn't know that I had left the building earlier that night, something I hadn't done since I started working there a year previously. It was the final miracle that saved my life. It was funny to learn of some of the answers and gestures that one of the frightened residents gave when people asked to know where the new resident manager was following Dahmer's arrest. Ezra West was a senior resident who lived in apartment #101 across from the leasing office. He had no idea that I had left the Oxford Apartments the previous night to spend my next day off at my property on State Street.

I was regarded as missing, because I was nowhere to be found, not in the building and not anywhere else close by. Nobody knew what had happened to me. In speculation, they kept their fingers crossed praying for my safety. I was safe in my personal residence at 1807, West State Street

19

that night. I was in a remote place as I planned just for that night and the only night in the time that I had held the post as resident manager. The tragedy that hit The Oxford was like a storm that had missed me, or from which I had escaped unscathed. Nobody knew where I was at the time of Dahmer's exposure.

Following his arrest, the police had discovered fresh and old body parts from his apartment and they were gathered at a spot awaiting shipment to the laboratory for examination. Among the other objects seized were some cartons, boxes, huge kettles and garbage bags, not to mention the freezer and a huge plastic barrel. These were still in Dahmer's apartment waiting to be hauled by a company that handles hazardous waste materials. Some of the boxes and cartons had been marked with labels of specific body parts such as head, heart, bicep etc. When the residents asked "Where is the Manager?" they were naturally concerned because one of the heads discovered in the apartment was fresh. Mr Ezra West would point his protruded mouth towards the heap of recoveries as if to say, "There's the manager".

I was still unaware of Dahmer's arrest until about 7.00am the next morning, on Tuesday July 23, 1991. The former manager of the Oxford Apartments knocked on my door and broke the news of the arrest to me. At that time he told me, "Jeff is in jail; six bodies found in his apartment." The former manager continued, "Everyone was asking about you, so you go and show your face." He then returned to the Oxford Apartments. The stigma of Dahmer's deeds on my job would become a definite hazard to my future chances of securing another job in a similar position.

The Exodus II was expeditiously completed and all the residents were safely relocated to various destinations throughout the city of Milwaukee. Now reality began to set in, as I realized I would have to seek another job. As usual,

I filed the job applications, sent out the resumes, used word of mouth and networking to attempt to find another position. The responses to my applications were good, because they were selected for an interview, but unfortunately the interview results were regrets.

One lady in charge of employment at a Title Insurance Company who invited me for an interview said, "We have a celebrity among us," within earshot of everyone in the conference room, but she didn't employ me.

I had previously tried a property management company for a job, but they had reservations because of where I worked last, the now stigmatized Oxford Apartments. I could therefore imagine that the arrest of Jeffrey Dahmer had a negative impact on my chances for employment in similar positions. In fact Dahmer's presence and his criminal activities inside the building were hazardous to my future career, because subsequent potential employers could not understand how I was totally unaware of the serial killer's secret life.

I was only a new manager starting to learn how to work with these apartments. Without knowing it, Jeffrey Dahmer had stalked me from August of 1990 through to the time he was arrested on the night of July 22, 1991. I was lucky that he continued to miss me as his prime target even though he tried very hard. As accidental as it was, his arrest was a blessing to me because he had no more chance to continue his attempts to harm me. There was the psychological trauma of the crime that affected some of the residents who had gotten treated by psychological counseling. I was not seriously affected, because I was not present at the time of Dahmer's arrest to see the gruesome discoveries in his apartment.

Even though they were in shock about the arrest of the serial killer, many of the residents still went close enough to look at the body parts. Some of the body parts were very fresh and bloody and caused the trauma to those who saw them.

Everyone watching the television when the news of Dahmer's arrest was broadcast had their first shock. I remembered the street fights, the gunshots out on the streets, the dead bodies on the sidewalks and the constant police interrogations. There was always something to keep the police busy in this neighborhood. I just didn't know that there was something more frightening that was happening in the Oxford Apartments.

Jeffrey Dahmer was using his apartment as a human slaughterhouse. He had murdered two males in the building before I started the job. Things didn't seem to be right when I started working there, so I never felt complacent with the job. Firstly, I was dissatisfied with the arrangement that allowed the former manager to remain in the building after I had started working as manager. This arrangement made my job difficult. I experienced all the set up, the lures and the intimidations that were staged to oust me out of my job. Nevertheless, but I was keen to gain the experience in the management aspect of real estate so I was determined to remain where I was. I made sure that I always worked as a professional showing the distinction between myself as manager and others. I was framed with theft and set up for disaster, but I didn't yield to the temptations and most importantly of all, I was saved by the Grace.

The Oxford Apartments' building was bounded; on the west by the building façade, which faced 25th Street and was also the location of the main entrance. The building was also bounded on the south side by an alleyway paved with cobblestone and on the east and rear by another alleyway paved with concrete. Both alleyways were pleasant to drive on and there was space for eight parking stalls and a steel dumpster. On the north side, the building was bounded by a six-foot high cyclone wire fence, which ran along the lot line from the front to the back of the building. Without regular care, perennials and runners in the summer time covered the fence so that the view to or from an adjacent property was totally eclipsed. This was the side of the building where Jeffrey Dahmer lived.

Towards the rear end of the building there was a tall tree with its branches hanging down and almost touching the ground. Thus it formed a canopy, shading that part of the building from view. The ground was fully covered with weeds and plants. It was like an enclave for rodents before I started to work as the new manager.

Jeffrey Dahmer's bedroom was right under the branches of the tall tree. There was less traffic, less attention and it appeared secure for offenders or criminals like him. With a twisted secret life, he was very smart to pick such a spot because it offered him everything he needed. Thus he continued murdering his guests one after another in his apartment, until one of his victims escaped. When the apartment next to him was assigned to me, I turned it down, even though I didn't know who Jeffrey Dahmer was at the time. As manager of the building, I was not comfortable with living next to an exit. I also didn't feel that I deserved to live in the rear as manager. I didn't know what was going on before I refused this apartment, nor did I realize that Jeffrey Dahmer had marked me as a primary target until after his arrest.

Dahmer's arrest heralded the start of prank calls from people who pretended to be interested in renting apartments. When I picked up the phone and after describing what the apartment looked like and what was included with the rent, they would stop me there and say "I cannot pay an arm and a leg for your apartment," and would hang up. There was another instance when the caller pretended to be Jeffrey Dahmer himself and when I answered the phone he said, "This is Jeffrey Dahmer. I want your head in my fucking freezer" and hung up.

There were many other Dahmer jokes that came out at that period in time. A friend of mine who was commuting to work in Chicago once told me that he heard somebody saying, "Anyone could easily pay for human body part like the limb; the radius and ulna that could easily be folded into a briefcase and move on if you go to " Dahmertown, Milwaukee, Wisconsin."

When I complained to Dahmer about a resident who also lived across from him, he told me that the same resident owed him $25.00. I was not interested in settling financial disputes between residents. So I didn't ask Jeffrey Dahmer why that resident owed him the $25.00. It was this resident who broke my trust and who might have stolen the furniture from an apartment in the building. I allowed that resident to use the bathroom of a vacant apartment when his apartment had a plumbing problem. The problem was to be fixed in a few days, at which time he would return the keys. In fact, it only took two days, but by then all the furniture in that apartment had gone. Thus that apartment unit was no longer a furnished one. I was very upset about it. I reported the incident to my boss who took action from there. I think the management company Metropolitan Associates filed a theft complaint with the police.

I remember the same resident in question trying to sell me steak once before, but I didn't buy it because I didn't know how he acquired it. I knew for sure that he was not a grocer operating a store, so I told him that I had no money. On that particular day I had fresh fish on my mind, so I told him that I didn't want the steak. The resident insisted upon selling the steak to me saying, "Steak for seven dollars?" as if it were a big meat deal. I wanted to discourage him from trying to sell me meat from wherever he might be obtaining it. He might have been stealing it from somewhere and if he was, I at least wanted to discourage him from doing so.

On another occasion, the same resident came to me with a pair of shoes he wanted to sell for five dollars only. The shoes were new, but were not in a box. I didn't want them, so I told him so. Another day he came again to sell the same pair of shoes to me, this time for two dollars only. I then gave him the financial relief that he needed. I didn't know where he got those shoes from, but he didn't try to sell me anything more after that.

When the residents first began to complain about the bad smell in the building, I went to inspect Jeffrey Dahmer's apartment. He said that his freezer had broken and that the meat he had in there was getting spoilt. The inspections were only minimally intrusive, so as not to delve into somebody's privacy. I had no suspicions that the smell was the result of decaying human body parts and I couldn't smell it when I was in his apartment for the two inspections I conducted without prejudice. Both inspections were for specific items that became problematic in his apartment. There was the broken freezer during the first inspection and the aquarium during the second inspection. My friend Amadu Bangura was with me when I went again for the second inspection and he didn't smell anything unpleasant while we were there either.

No one would have suspected anything sinister, because mass murders in such apartments were unheard of. Nobody expected such a crime to occur in a 49 apartment unit located right in the middle of a glaring metropolis.

Dahmer was familiar with this neighborhood where he committed a child molestation crime and was sentenced to five years on probation in the house of corrections. After he was released from confinement, he returned to the same neighborhood because he felt more secure with his secret life of committing mass murders.

Jeffrey was smart enough to know that residing in a high crime neighborhood where people pay more attention to the open crimes would shield his heinous acts. Again, he cleverly picked an apartment located in the back of the building, where there is literally no traffic, hence affording him more security. He had always done his best to elude detection by law enforcement.

Chapter 3

Resident Manager for Positive Change

Eventually, when I accepted the job as the new resident manager of the building, Jeffrey Dahmer showed some concern. He was interested in finding out about me and was also wondering why a new manager has been brought in at that time. He had only been living there for two months before I took up my post. It was at this time that he must have started to feel the threat of exposure, because he had already killed two victims prior to my employment.

There may also have been others in the building who were also concerned with the change of manager. I knew that one of them was interested in being the manager and there were others who needed the cover for some criminal activities that they were engaged in. From the beginning of my employment, some of the residents were already violating the terms of their lease by having more occupants than were allowed in an apartment. All these people showed their concern with the change of manager.

A nauseating smell surrounded the building, the source of which was a mystery. Nobody could have imagined the true reason behind the odor. Approximately one month into the job, in August of 1990, the building was engulfed in a nauseating smell about which the residents started to complain. I was not sure whether there had been any similar complaint about any smell before I started to work. It was like the smell of decomposing meat. I was not sure whether anyone in the building was familiar with a smell of dead humans, but most of them would almost certainly have likened it to the smell of a dead animal or something relating to rotten meat.

Despite the complaints, Jeffrey Dahmer continued his secret life of mass murder and went on to fortify his apartment from detection. I received a tip from a neighbor that the smell was coming from Dahmer's apartment, so as part of my duty to follow up on such complaints, I went to inspect his apartment for the first time.

My first inspection of Dahmer's apartment resulted in no clues. I didn't notice the bad smell while I was in his apartment and it looked quite clean. He opened the freezer that he said was broken and causing the bad smell in the building. In retrospect, I think at that time the stench must have been emanating from those body parts he deposited outside in the dumpster behind the building.

Dahmer's first cover up effort was evident after the inspection. Consequently, he installed a security alarm system that cost around $400 and continued to murder his victims. He had also earmarked me as one of his future victims, because he knew that I was the most likely person to enter into his apartment unit when he was not at home. He knew that I might see what he was attempting to keep hidden. The building manager must have access to any apartment unit during an emergency, usually via a master key. Even though it was only in August 1990 that the residents complained about the smell in the building, in September of 1990 Jeffrey Dahmer went on to murder Ernest Miller, a 24-year-old black male of Chicago Illinois. Miller was his third victim inside the Oxford Apartments, the sixth victim in Wisconsin and the seventh victim in Dahmer's murder history.

Next, in September 1990, Dahmer murdered David C Thomas, a 22-year-old black male of Milwaukee, Wisconsin. At this point, the smell in the building disappeared because Dahmer disposed of his last victim entirely.

In December 1990, Dahmer brought a six pack of beer to my apartment as a 'treat'. It was part of a cunning plan to eradicate me, but this first attempt failed. When I heard a knock at the door, I knew that it must be someone from within the building, because people who entered the building from the outside generally used the intercom in order to be buzzed in. On this particular day when I looked through the pinhole, I saw Jeffrey Dahmer standing in front of my door holding a six pack of beer. I opened the door and let him in. He appeared very disappointed to see someone with me when he came in, my friend Amadu Bangura. I believe he came to commit a premeditated homicide, but failed because I was not alone at that moment. It was a divine intervention by my Creator, the Supreme Being.

Dahmer knew that I lived alone and obviously felt that he had a good chance of getting me once I had allowed him into my apartment. It was a close call for me, because he would have had a good chance if I hadn't had a visitor with me. He immediately left us after he had finished a bottle of our beer that we offered him when he came. When he left my apartment, he took the six pack of beer with him.

Amadu could have come to visit at a different time, but fate intervened so that he came exactly when Dahmer was planning to harm me.

It was that same Christmas in 1990 that a few of the residents decided to cook out on a grill. They contributed some money to buy some beef ribs, chicken, some hot dogs, beer and other items of entertainment. Nobody knew what Jeffrey Dahmer was doing and the residents were trying to set the mood of Christmas in the building. In a cookout party like that, everyone was invited to come around and enjoy the fellowship. The party would continue as long as there was food and booze. Someone was in charge with the cooking on the grill. It was great, but little did we know that there would be no more Christmas parties in the building after that one.

Just as it was Christmas for the residents who had organized the party, it was also Christmas for the petty thieves who stalk out such parties to do their thing. When most of the cooking was done, almost everyone was inside to enjoy the party while some meat was left, still cooking on the grill. Not only did the petty thieves steal the whole grill with whatever was cooking on it, but they stole some of the Christmas decorations, including the statue of Jesus Christ. The stealing the statue of Christ was the funny part of the complaint about the theft. The thieves stole the statue of Christ because they loved him, but the paradox is that his teachings forbade theft as a sin. The thieves probably ignored that teaching for a different reason. The need to survive may have been their motivation. Those thieves loved and feared God, but obviously felt they needed to steal in order to survive.

Jeffrey Dahmer's next victim was Curtis Straughter, an 18-year-old black male from Milwaukee, Wisconsin. In March 1991, Straughter became Dahmer's fifth victim inside the Oxford Apartments, the eighth victim in Wisconsin and the ninth victim in his murder history. From this point on, Jeffrey Dahmer accelerated his murderous pace.

The first telephone call from his mother in five years made him realize that he might not hear from her again for a long time. His mother, Joyce Flint, had abandoned him when he was about 17-years-old and he started drinking heavily as consolation. From then on he was not able to connect socially amongst young people of his age and so he became a loner. In adulthood, Jeffrey Dahmer had been a mass murderer and his mother didn't yet know it. He only revealed his homosexuality to his mother during that phone conversation. She loved him and so she accepted him as her son, regardless of his sexual orientation. She didn't know that his homosexuality was laced with necrophilia, the mental disease that caused the sufferer to be obsessed with having sex with the dead.

Dahmer went for his next victim after the phone conversation with his mother, who lived in California. Around April 1991, Errol Lindsey, a 19-year-old black male from Milwaukee became Jeffrey Dahmer's sixth victim.

Another shock came when a mysterious death was discovered in the building. It was the first time a homicide had occurred when everyone knew about it. The killer was unknown. The residents were upset, but what they didn't know was that this one mystery was only like the tip of an iceberg.

There had been a mysterious murder in apartment #308 inside the Oxford Apartments. The resident of that apartment, Dean Vaughn, was found strangled. His larynx was crushed and he had also been sodomized. The investigation of this homicide took place two months before Jeffrey Dahmer's exposure and arrest. At the time of the investigation, Dahmer denied being responsible for it. After Dean Vaughn was found strangled to death, the little love and trust we enjoyed in the building ceased. It was as though everyone in the building was now a suspect in that murder. We didn't know who did it and we were too terrified to trust anyone.

Dahmer's next victim was Anthony Hughes, a 31-year-old black man from Milwaukee. Dahmer killed him in May 1991, his seventh victim in the Oxford Apartments and his eleventh victim overall. Deaf and mute, Anthony communicated with Jeffrey Dahmer by writing and exchanging short notes.

While the last victim's body was still lying in the bedroom, Jeffrey Dahmer brought Konerak Sinthasomphone to his apartment. Sinthasamphone was a 14-year-old Laotian living in Milwaukee. In May 1991, Sinthasomphone became Dahmer's eighth victim inside the Oxford Apartments. This young boy was an aspiring soccer star and his murder was the most tragic of all, because Jeffrey Dahmer had victimized this same family twice. The sexual molestation of one child and the murder of another child was too much for a family that fled their country in

Cambodia to the United States for safety.

Some residents of the apartment building said that they had seen the young Laotian boy with Jeffrey Dahmer in the building before. So this boy was another person whom Dahmer had befriended before killing him. The boy didn't know that it was going to be fatal for him to go to Dahmer's apartment that night and he tried to escape even after Dahmer had drugged him. He was so unlucky that even the police officers who came could not save him. The entire story relating to this boy and his fate with Jeffrey Dahmer is continued in Chapter 9, "A 911 Good Samaritan".

Jeffrey Dahmer continued his killing spree as if he were really obeying the command of the ghosts, "One more time!" after each murder. He had become more comfortable doing it and he could not stop himself. He lived to kill people or killed people to live. Despite the burden of disposing of the bodies, he still felt compelled to target his next victim.

In June 1991, Dahmer murdered Matthew Turner, a 20-year-old black male of Flint, Michigan, his ninth victim inside the Oxford Apartments.

The summer arrived once more and the nauseating smell of the previous summer returned, this time with even greater intensity.

Jeffrey Dahmer was still very concerned by my presence and therefore made desperate attempts to eliminate the threat in three episodes that I considered to be my closest calls with the serial killer.

Dahmer's Independence Day "Cookout" took place as usual on 4 July, 1991. Many families and friends celebrate this festive occasion by cooking out at any convenient location. Some do the cookout on the beach at the Lake front, whilst others cook out in their front porches, backyards or at the parks. Magnificent displays of fireworks conclude this nationwide celebration during the night at Milwaukee's Lakefront.

On that Independence Day, 4 July 1991, the weather was mild. I saw Jeffrey Dahmer cooking out behind the building. He set his grill on the ground directly below the window of his living room. At that time, I also saw a few black males standing around his grill. I remember sighting a former resident of the building who had previously been evicted for defaulting on rent payment. They were drinking some beer and liquor while chewing on meat that had been cooked on the grill. There were various brands of beer, including Budweiser, Miller Highlife and Old Style. Jeffrey Dahmer himself did the cooking. I was not sure what type of meat he was cooking. He looked a little drunk and he seemed to be enjoying whatever it was he was chewing on. It looked like a piece of steak. The cookout lasted several hours into the late evening.

I believe that one of Jeffrey Dahmer's guests that night eventually became his next murder victim. He often organized similar drinking parties, cookouts and visitations in order to make new acquaintances. Darryl Payton, who knew Anthony (Tony) Hughes, remembered a party Jeffrey Dahmer attended at Tony Hughes' home back in the summer of 1990. The party was held in a predominantly black neighborhood and Jeffrey Dahmer was the only white person at the party. As mentioned earlier, Tony Hughes became the serial killer's eighth victim right inside the Oxford Apartments. There were live victims who would remember the tragedy for the rest of their lives.

The deaf and mute, but handsome Tony Hughes had been Jeffrey Dahmer's companion for two years, as revealed by Darryl Payton who was assigned to work as a security officer at the Oxford Apartments after Jeffrey Dahmer had been arrested.

This building needed protective services as the turmoil raged on in the City of Milwaukee. Mr Payton indicated that Jeffrey Dahmer must have killed Tony Hughes because of what Tony might have discovered in Dahmer's apartment. This discovery may have been body part, the head of his last victim or something equally disturbing. Jeffrey Dahmer didn't put his house in order before he invited Tony back that last fateful time. Tony had been familiar with Jeffrey Dahmer's shrine in which skulls were displayed, but he was made to believe that they were artificial. At least they looked artificial, because Dahmer painted them in different colors.

After Tony saw what Dahmer didn't want him to see, Dahmer felt that it was risky to let Tony go this time. Thus, Dahmer immediately gave Tony a drugged drink that knocked him down. Whilst Tony was unconscious, Dahmer strangled him. Dahmer kept Tony's dead body in the bedroom and when his next opportunity to target another victim arose, he went and grabbed it immediately. That was the young Laotian boy whose encounter with Jeffrey Dahmer brought the police to his apartment.

Meanwhile, I was experiencing adversity from some problem residents who began an intimidation campaign against me. This happened when I ignored some unnecessary orders from the former manager who continued to live in the building. I ignored any order from him that was not part of my job description. I had asked my boss to do the right thing and not let two captains work in the same boat. In other words I wanted my employers to move the former manager from the building. I waited to see it happen within the following sixty days, but it didn't. The former manager was at my office so frequently that I had to ask him to move out his belongings from my office. He had a television and some personal effects. I felt that he should come to my office only on official business. I already knew that his stay in the building was detrimental to me.

One vacant apartment unit had a lot of personal belongings. I observed items such as stereos, a VCR, a set of dishes, television sets and other electronics when I started to work as the new manager. Only about a week after this conflict with the former manager, a new resident who rented the apartment #208 complained about a theft from his apartment. Daryl Elliot, who moved in just a week earlier, lost his VCR and his 19" color television set to a thief who lived in the building. The note from Daryl to my boss Don, dated March 25, 1991, explained that he lost those things when some unknown person broke into his apartment in his absence. I was not in the building at the time of the theft. I reported the incident to my boss who made no comment. This was a potentially dangerous situation for an employee in my position. It was a set up, but it failed, because I had an alibi.

There was always someone trying to frame me, but I was never around when the crimes occurred. It would have put me in a very volatile situation if I had been around at the point when the residents discovered the theft of their property. Some of these residents had the potential to become violent. I had a physical altercation with the boyfriend of a lady who lived in the apartment unit #207. The resident of that particular apartment, Edith, claimed that someone had stolen her television set and that people had told her that it was the manager. Another resident, Mr Lindsey, who occupied apartment #112, told me that he heard a rumor about that. He also personally told me that he knew they were framing me. Mr Lindsey knew me and had worked with me on my property.

One night, after about 10.00pm, the resident of apartment #209, Luvenia, complained about loud music coming from apartment #207, so I went to investigate. Before I arrived at the apartment in question, I saw three men and two ladies coming out of it. Edith said, "This is the manager," pointing at me. I asked her who told her that I took her television set, but before she could answer, her brawny boyfriend landed an unexpected punch on my face. I felt dizzy and looked down, thinking that I might fall to the ground. However, within in a few seconds I regained full consciousness. When I looked up, I saw a second punch heading in my direction, but this time I dodged. As his second punch missed me, he lost his balance and I gave him my first punch, which took him down on his knees. I immediately charged closer and drilled two more punches on his neck. In the vulnerable position that he was in, I did consider kicking his mouth so that he would lose a few teeth. Nevertheless, I didn't wish to harm him further and his friends then came to break up the fight.

There are fewer physical fights in America because nobody likes to have a swollen face or a black eye or scratches on their skin. Therefore, people just shoot at their opponents either during or after an altercation. It was a potentially dangerous situation for me. The urge to win escalates the battle. I was lucky that the guy didn't have a weapon at the time of our quarrel. He would have used it if he had it, because he was losing the fist fight at that point. Though he was the aggressor, he lost so he would have had a good reason to use his weapon to avoid the embarrassment of a defeat.

At the end of this encounter I called the police to file a complaint. I also instructed the girlfriend, Edith, to start packing, because I didn't want her as a resident there anymore. The police didn't arrive until the boyfriend returned from obtaining some drugs an hour and a half later. I was talking with the former manager in the lobby when the "strongman" returned from drugs' trip. As soon as he saw me, he wanted to fight again. The former manager was telling him not to fight, but I told him to bring it on if he thought he was bad. I was going to show him what he hadn't seen before in fist fighting. However, just before we started the second round of the fight, the police officers arrived. The strongman was in possession of the drugs he had just acquired, so he was hiding them with his hands behind his back.

The police officers asked him to bring out his hands, because they thought that he was reaching for a gun. They were going to shoot at him if he did not obey their order, an action that would be justified in such a situation. Those of us who were present at the scene were scared of police shooting, so we shouted at him to obey their order. When he brought out his hands the bag of drugs fell on the floor. The female police officer picked it up while the male police officer put handcuffs on the offender. As the female officer opened the bag to see what was inside, the strongman stretched out his leg and kicked her hands so that the powder went flying in the air. At least he would not be charged for the felony of drug possession.

As the police officers were taking the culprit away, he told me that he would deal squarely with me when he was released. I wished him good luck, but added that I would be right here as the manager waiting for him. A couple of days later he came out and apologized. He pleaded with me not to evict his girlfriend. He was disappointed when I told him that the eviction had unfortunately started immediately and that it was beyond my jurisdiction to stop it. They moved out and when he saw me out there again later, he was friendly.

The nauseating smell, a second time around, became a primary concern among the residents. The heat of the New Year 1991 forced the smell to come out again. This time I knew that it might be Jeffrey Dahmer, so I went to his apartment for a second inspection. As usual, I summoned him to the office and asked him what was wrong with his apartment again. This time his excuse was different. His two fish had died in his aquarium. I told him that he should dump the fish the moment they die. I told him that he didn't have to wait till they start to decompose before he disposed of them. As usual, he apologized for the inconveniences that the smell had caused and then he promised to dump the dead fish.

About a couple of hours later I went to inspect the aquarium that had been emptied. This was a close call for me. Jeffrey Dahmer exposed me to some acid vapor that irritated my nose and eyes. I made sure that I didn't inhale the vapor. This reaction on my part was contrary to what Dahmer might have expected during this second inspection. He thought that I would inhale the vapor when it first hit me directly in my face. If I had inhaled the vapor, I might have been rendered unconscious and then Dahmer could have taken advantage. He was cowardly and didn't want any resistance when he strangled his victims.

Again, my friend Amadu Bangura was with me when I went for the second inspection. He heard me when I told Dahmer that the barrel containing the acid vapor must go. Dahmer later called to show me that the barrel was in the dumpster behind the building. He went back later to the dumpster and retrieved the barrel. From then on, Jeffrey Dahmer used that barrel to dispose of his victims' bodies, using several vats of acid to soak and melt the flesh into a mucous sludge to be flushed out in the toilet.

In July 1991, Dahmer lured his tenth victim, Jeremiah Weinberger, to his apartment. Weinberger was a 23-year-old Hispanic male from Chicago, Illinois. Again, in July 1991, Dahmer murdered his eleventh victim, Oliver Lacy, a 23-year-old black male from Oak Park, Illinois.

Finally, in the same month, Dahmer murdered Joseph Bradehoft, a 25-year-old white male from St. Paul, Minnesota. Bradehoft was Dahmer's twelfth victim inside the Oxford Apartments, the fifteenth victim in Wisconsin and the seventeenth victim in Dahmer's murder history.

At this point, Jeffrey Dahmer was not aware that his days of committing murder were numbered. As the dates show, Jeffrey Dahmer killed more people within the year prior to his arrest than he did in his entire murder history. The period between September 1990 and July 1991 was the most prolific. This was also the time period during which

Dahmer fantasized about his own death, as his probation notes indicated. He had suicide fantasies about jumping off a tall building.

The real change in the Oxford Apartments came when Jeffrey Dahmer was arrested on July 22, 1991 and there was a mass exodus of the residents, approximately 92%, which also resulted in a cessation of crime incidents. After the tragedy that cleaned out the now infamous Oxford Apartments, I returned to business as usual and re-rented ten more apartment units before we were all evicted prior to demolition of the building. The following sixteen months I enjoyed the change, because all the current residents were those to whom I rented the apartments, so they were my loyalists as opposed to those residents who already lived in the building when I took up my position. The new residents did not gang up on me.

Another change that I considered to be necessary at the time was the use of security guards for the protection of both the residents and the building. Although this was an extra cost to the management company, it was a necessity under such traumatic circumstances. We were living with the threat of bombing by the families of Jeffrey Dahmer's victims. We were also living with the stigma of the tragedy that had occurred there. Some of the new residents complained that their friends refused to come to the building. This was an irony of the stigma. Some members of the public came to the building out of morbid curiosity, trying to obtain a photo of Dahmer's apartment, whilst others did not want to have anything to do with it.

I enjoyed those curiosity seekers who would obtain my permission to enter the infamous apartment unit #213 for a few bucks. There were also the mystery hunters who were more interested in keeping any part of the property as a souvenir. It became a building in the spotlight, unlike before when it was just like any other apartment complex. People traveled long distances to come to see it.

Chapter 4

Close Encounters and Confrontations

During the time I worked at the Oxford Apartments as resident manager, I had more than a dozen contacts with Jeffrey Dahmer, but I was totally unaware of him as a serial killer. Three of these contacts could so easily have been fatal, so I narrate these episodes as close calls.

The incident in which he brought some beer to my apartment happened, as mentioned in chapter three, during the Christmas of 1990 and it was my first close call with Jeffrey Dahmer but he didn't have the chance to start his rituals on me because someone else, Amadu Bangura was visiting with me when he came. Amadu and I were drinking Guinness, the dark beer from Ireland and indeed we offered him a bottle of ours, which he accepted and emptied very fast before leaving with his unopened six pack of the local beer. He at least created the impression that I could go to him for some beer anytime I might need some.

Unfortunately for him, I don't go to people for beer. I'm able to buy my own beer. Jeffrey Dahmer used alcohol as one of the lures for the victims. He didn't have anything that would tempt me.

This first attempt to get me didn't seem to be the ideal occasion he was looking for - when he and the intended victim were alone, one on one.

Meanwhile, Dahmer continued to murder the victims in his one bedroom apartment. His freezers were full, so he was forced to leave some body parts out and actually forgot where he had left them in the apartment. Despite this, the smell disappeared for a while in the colder Fall air and the aroma in and around the building was pleasant again.

When the hot weather arrived again the following year, the nauseating smell returned. There were too many body parts decomposing and releasing such a pungent smell from Dahmer's apartment. Outside, he had dumped some of the flesh wrapped in plastic garbage bags into the dumpster behind the building. I remember seeing a heap of clothes right next to the dumpster. It was nothing unusual for anyone to see such a waste of clothes in the USA. Many people either donated old clothes to the charities or just dumped them.

The nauseating smell added to Dahmer's worry about exposure and the fact that the body parts were outside in the dumpster for discovery. Disposing of the body after each murder was a major task, because he did not want any evidence around. It was at this point that he decided to dissolve the body parts in a barrel of acid placed in his bedroom. Dahmer obviously didn't consider the disadvantage of using this barrel.

The source of the stench remained a mystery, because nobody would ever have considered the possibility that the odor was coming from decomposing murder victims. This time the repulsive smell was much stronger than that of the first time, when I was only one month into the job. It fouled a three mile radius and became the main topic of conversation of the black neighborhood. Jeffrey Dahmer was very concerned with what the stench might provoke this time among the other residents of the Oxford Apartments, especially when the complaints began again. Dahmer was also worried about me having authority to enter his apartment, even when he was not there. Every resident was angry about the smell, so I had to do something about it.

This time I knew where the stench was coming from, so I immediately confronted Jeffrey Dahmer about it and this time his excuse was that two fish died in his aquarium. Again, I asked him to dump them as soon as they die. I expressed my annoyance at the fact that he didn't seem to be keeping up his apartment, because I knew that it was bad for business.

Luckily by this time I had achieved the level of occupancy desired, but then a second inspection of Dahmer's apartment became necessary. This was the inspection during which I had my second close call with the serial killer. He didn't expect anyone to come with me for the second inspection. He had put something in a plastic barrel that he kept in his closet; vats of acid, some chloroform and whatever else could be harmful if one were exposed to it. Very fortunately Amadu was again visiting me, so I asked him to accompany me for the second inspection.

Again, I had no suspicion of any crime and neither did my friend Amadu after we saw the emptied aquarium, which Dahmer claimed contained the dead fish. Amadu and I didn't smell anything while we were in Dahmer's apartment. As we were about to leave, Dahmer came into the hallway leading to the bathroom and showed me a tall plastic barrel in the closet, which he said he had used to empty the aquarium. He exposed me to the barrel's contents by opening it. When he opened the lid and I looked in, there was nothing in it, but a very strong vapor hit my face and I jerked backwards. I told him, "That must go," while I pointed at the barrel. The vapor came from the acid, the chloroform or whatever he had put in the barrel to try and render me unconscious. I didn't know what Dahmer would have done if my friend Amadu Bangura was not there with me during the second inspection. The vapor was strong enough to knockout someone if inhaled and it was also irritating to the eyes and nose.

Amadu and I left the apartment after the inspection and Dahmer later called me to show that he had dumped the tall plastic barrel in the dumpster behind the building. He later retrieved the barrel for further use, something that became clear at the time of his arrest. Jeffrey Dahmer also gave me a liquid deodorant in a small plastic bottle to give to the residents to use in their apartments to clear the air. The unpleasant smell remained in the building for a short time before his arrest, following the discovery of body parts when Tracy Edwards escaped and called the police to the apartment.

On July 22, 1991, when the summer heat was more intense, I met Dahmer in the hallway next to his apartment. He was holding a can of beer in a brown paper bag and he said to me, "Do you have a few minutes? I'd like to talk to you." Then he drank the beer in my face. He hoped that I would come to his apartment as it looked like his best chance to eliminate me. I replied, "Yes I do, please come to the office." Then I hurried down to the office and waited for him for about half an hour, but he didn't show up. I had planned to go to my alternative property for the night, so I did just that. I felt that since it was he who wanted to talk to me about something, I shouldn't have to go looking for him.

Dahmer's attempt to get his prime target this time was my third close call with the serial killer. I was only about six feet from his apartment in the hallway when he tried, once again, to lure me into his abode with the offer of beer. He must have felt more confident about getting me this time, because I was alone. I didn't know at this time that he was a serial killer, but I knew that he was a filthy resident to whose apartment we had traced the nauseating smell in the building. I did not wish to hang around with someone I considered to be so unhygienic, so he didn't have a chance with me on this third attempt. Besides, it wasn't my custom to go into residents' apartments unofficially and I didn't socialize with any of the residents. In other words, I knew the limits to which I associated on a personal level with individuals in the building. An old quotation in the Bible goes, "My son, if sinners entice thee, consent thou not." I did not and thus I was saved by the Grace.

I left the Oxford Apartments that Monday night to go

to my residence at 1807 W. State Street. This was the first and the only night in one year that I had ever been away from the building. Thus, it was a miracle that happened for my safety.

"After darkness comes a glorious dawn," was a statement by the late Chief Obafemi Awolowo, a former Nigerian Federal Minister of Finance. After all the darkness on my job in the valley of death, the glorious dawn hadn't yet arrived.

I was not in the building when Dahmer was arrested. Anne Schwartz, a TV news' reporter with Channel 12, an ABC news' affiliate here in Milwaukee, broke the news of the serial killer's arrest for mass murder inside the Oxford Apartments. This lady didn't talk to me at all before writing about me in her book, "The Man who could not kill enough". In her book, she referred to me as an African immigrant. I really expected her to speak with me before writing about me or my story. It was more evidence of the prejudice and lack of respect for others that we see so much in journalism and the media.

Schwartz's statement that I "cleaned out Dahmer's freezer" was incorrect. After my first inspection of Dahmer's apartment, I told some residents that I had offered to help with dumping the rotten meat that he claimed was causing the bad smell. I told them that he declined my offer and promised to do it by himself. My offer to him was an effort to alleviate the bad smell in the entire building, because it was detrimental to the rental business. He declined my offer, apologized for the inconvenience it had caused to the other residents and the business and then he promised to dump the meat by himself.

Ms Schwartz didn't bother to obtain that information directly from me, because she was evidently in a hurry to publish her book. She really missed out on the inside information, but through this book she now has the chance to read about the true events that are missing in hers.

For all who believe in God and in miracles, I declare my survival on this hazardous job as a living testament of the power of miracles. Since Dahmer's arrest, I have constantly asked myself, "If my survival weren't attributed to miracles, then what was it that saved me from him, or others, when I accepted the task of managing the building?" I didn't know that my job would be that hazardous when my boss welcomed me aboard. Following a report that someone was shooting in the hallway of the first floor, I found an expired bullet there. We had a resident whose son was a Korean War veteran and it was he who had fired the bullet from his handgun.

Although the building became associated with Dahmer's crimes, there were others too who were committing other offenses in and around the building. There were incidents of theft, drugs and prostitution that we knew about, but we weren't aware that mass murder was being committed in the building. It would be the least expected type of crime to happen there, because it was situated in the middle of town. It had never been heard of before, at least not in the way it happened. This is where Jeffrey Dahmer filled the gap. Situated in a depressed neighborhood, the building was infested with criminal activities.

Apparently, the change of manager raised a concern among the perpetrators of these crimes. They had to set up lures to obliterate the new manager, but I didn't yield to temptation. I continued to elude many other attempts by these criminals living there to eliminate me. I kept my distance from all residents to show the distinction between a resident and a manager. The residents of the building with a criminal mindset didn't like me, but they could not hurt me, because I was protected by the chain of events that I call miracles, which took place to save me each and every time they attempted to hurt me.

46

Although I was not consciously aware of their intentions at the time, from what I observed of their behavior I was able to use my common sense to be wary of them, but with no fear. When I was a boy my father told me not to fear any man that was evil unless he had two heads.

After the first mystery murder of Dean Vaughn in apartment #308 in May 1991, everyone in the building became a suspect and while investigations were still being carried out, Jeffrey Dahmer was arrested for mass murder. He had denied responsibility for Dean Vaughn's murder during the investigation and still denied it after being arrested for multiple murders. At this point, we residents were wondering who could have strangled Dean in his own apartment. We started to think that there might be another killer in the building. If so, who might that be? We didn't know, thus the panic in the building escalated and every resident wanted to move out.

If I had been present in the building on the night when Dahmer was first arrested, I wonder whether people would have believed that I had no knowledge about what was taking place inside his apartment. People might have thought that I was supposed to know what Dahmer, or any resident for that matter, was doing in their apartment, just because I was manager of the building. Such assumptions could have been damaging to me at the time when the tragedy had inflicted such a shock on the city in general and the victims' families in particular. I was not employed to manage the private affairs of residents. I was employed to manage the building for profit, which I made my primary obligation. The people who think that a manager was supposed to know what residents were doing in their apartments might want to put the blame on me. They did not know that there was a former manager who continued to live in the building, even after I was employed as manager.

I had been promised money to turn my head the other

way if drug activity was going on. I had been framed for theft of a television set, which resulted in a physical altercation with the boyfriend of the owner. I had been intimidated by the former manager who told me that I had two strikes against me and that the job did not require a college degree. He didn't explain what the two strikes against me were, but I guess he meant that I was black and alien, so he could rightfully abuse me. He did not realize the strikes against him until the serial killer to whom he rented the apartment was arrested. I was away from the building at the time of Dahmer's arrest, so he had to explain why he was still living in the building after he had been replaced as manager. I didn't mind him at that point, because I had learned how to deal with such prejudice.

Some other residents had intimidated me by threatening to shoot through the window of my office. They wanted to run me off my job, but I didn't budge because the need to survive was stronger than fear. Thus the miracles were happening to keep me alive and around on my job. After surviving all of the above encounters I still didn't know that there was even a greater hazard on this job, the serial killer I didn't know about living in the building. Jeffrey Dahmer was the worst hazard that existed in the building. He continued to stalk me with no luck to hurt me. The job was not good for me as manager under such adverse circumstances so the final miracle took place to end it for my safety. I thank God.

It is important to note that there is valuable new information about Jeffrey Dahmer that until the publication of this book was still unknown to the world. The experiences on my job are a combination of mysteries and miracles. The mysteries kept me wondering about the what, who, the why and the when of occurrences around me. When I started the job, I wondered from what creature the fresh whole bones lying on the green slope behind the building came. At that time, I had no clue to suspect or to

48

confirm that those bones belonged to a human. It was unusual to find whole bones in the middle of the city. I didn't know what they were, so I didn't worry about them. In my mind, I believed that finding uncut and fresh bones in the middle of town was obscene. I was then speculating the possibility of the existence of a mystery man who might be making an animal sacrifice in the vicinity.

Another mystery was why I turned down or rejected an apartment unit that was assigned to me by the former manager of the building. At that time, I did not know that happened to be the apartment next to that of a serial killer. I rejected it because I knew that I deserved better and that I was not going to settle for anything less.

The miracles in this story were how I escaped unaware after each of my contacts with Jeffrey Dahmer. I had many contacts with him between July 1990 and July 1991.It was miraculous how I escaped the three most near fatal contacts that I had with him. I was totally unaware that he was a serial killer and that he was stalking me as his prime target. I was Jeffrey Dahmer's prime target not for sexual tendencies, but for the prevention of his exposure.

The next miracle was how I was away from the Oxford Apartments on the night of Dahmer's arrest, the only night that I hadn't been in the building since I took the job a year previously. I was very glad to have left the building that night. This one was the greatest of all the miracles.

These miracles assured me of the ultimate existence of a Supreme Being that's still in control of all the activities taking place in the world. Although there is so much evil happening everywhere in the world, the Supreme Being sometimes intervenes from above. He protects the innocent by a divine and timely intervention. I was not meant to be Dahmer's victim, so he came with his beer at the same time that my friend was visiting me.

The story finally shows how an accident for Dahmer also turned out to be a blessing for me in particular and for all the other residents. The escape of a victim who had already felt the knifepoint of the serial killer was the accident. There had been an unsolved murder of a resident two months before Dahmer was arrested. Dahmer was not a suspect in that homicide before his arrest and denied being responsible even after his arrest. However, the evidence showed a Dahmer style killing, because it was so similar to the others.

There were more eye to eye contacts and episodes while I was on the job inside the Oxford Apartments. I installed a lock on Dahmer's mailbox after he came to my office and made a request for the lock. That was my first contact with the serial killer. I remember at that time the cool expression on his face. He looked clean and sounded responsible. I observed a man with a meek and humble appearance, speaking in clear English and using polished grammar. I also observed that he didn't look straight into my eyes. His eyes often crossed mine, but the contact was only fleeting and never steady. He looked down momentarily while I was discussing his request for action. I didn't know either that he was the only Caucasian male resident in the building. I knew of a Caucasian female who was sharing a one bedroom apartment unit with an African American male.

While I continued to work as the Oxford manager, I often saw Jeffrey Dahmer in the building either coming in or going out of the building, or walking to the store at West Kilbourn Avenue at North 27th Street. On occasions like that, Dahmer and I often exchanged the natural greetings like, "Hi, how are you?" or "What's happening?" On other occasions when I met him out there, we exchanged the standard "Good Morning" or the appropriate greeting for the time of day. You would never know that Jeffrey Dahmer was a serial killer by just looking at him.

My property on West State Street at North 18th Street was located on the route to Dahmer's job at the Ambrosia

Chocolate Company, so my route to the Oxford Apartments from my property often crossed his. Sometimes when he was on his way to work while I was on my way back to the Oxford Apartments, we met and chatted briefly. On one such evening, I met him on his way to work while I was returning to the Oxford Apartments. I was a little late returning to the Oxford that evening because I had some friends that stopped by. This time he made a joke that I didn't take seriously at the time, but I was stunned when I thought about it after he was arrested. Then I started to reflect upon my other contacts with him prior to his arrest. He responded to my joke when I told him that he was working the graveyard shift.

He worked in a third shift on his job. A graveyard shift is the late shift, which is often called a third shift at work. It is during the quietest time of the night, usually between 11.00pm and 7.00am. The graveyard has an absolute quietness that is comparable to the quietness of the third shift at work.

"The graveyard is not too far from anyone," was Dahmer's remark in response.

I really didn't think of anything at that time except the graveyards in the city, so his response to my joke raised no red flag. At that time I was thinking that he meant the graveyards or cemeteries that are always common to see when driving up some streets in the city. I didn't know that he meant that there was one graveyard right in the Oxford Apartments where we lived. Only he knew about it and he owned that one illegal graveyard for his victims on death row behind his closed door at apartment #213. He did not look like a psychopath.

At the times I was in contact with him, I was blissfully unaware that he might have just killed someone in the last hour. He was always calm and polite, so nobody could tell that he was a severely disturbed person hiding a dark secret.

Another conversation I had with Jeffrey Dahmer was at

a McDonald's restaurant around the early spring of 1991. I usually start working from 9.00am, so on this particular morning I went to the Mc Donald's restaurant on West Wisconsin Avenue at North 26th Street to pick up one of my favorite breakfasts, (sausage biscuit with egg meal and a medium orange juice). When I got there, I saw Dahmer seated by himself at one of the tables and having a cup of coffee. After I received my order from the servers at the counter, I decided to join him at his table. I was expecting him to walk back to the building with me after he finished his coffee. He was very slow while drinking up and he didn't have any much of a smile on his face. In retrospect, he was probably thinking that I was out to get him. Dahmer had a nonchalant posture that morning. I complained to him about vandalism on my own property, which was a project for restoration that I was hoping he would be interested in investing in. It was a good investment opportunity for someone with the finance. I was trying to raise some investment capital to finish the project.

As of that time, I knew that he had a computer and he had installed a security alarm system. His apartment looked cleaner than most others I had seen in the building. From these attributes I observed of the man, I thought that Dahmer was a person I could approach for some investment like that. Following his arrest, it was discovered that he was complaining to his probation agent about his finances.

"This is a high crime neighborhood," was his remark in response to my pitch for capital. I understood that we had incidents of petty crimes in this neighborhood, but not the crimes as high as he was committing in his own apartment. I didn't know him then and I didn't know that he actually knew the neighborhood better than I did, hence he chose to live there in order to operate unnoticed.

When he finished his coffee, we walked out of the restaurant together, but he didn't go back to the building with me as I had expected. Instead, he told me that he was going downtown, so we went our separate ways. He boarded a bus that was going east on Wisconsin Avenue, while I walked back to the building alone, just two blocks north of the restaurant on 25th Street.

At that time, he then must be very protective of his apartment from any intruder. One day, I walked up to a serious verbal altercation between Dahmer and a young black male in the building. When they saw me coming in their direction they cooled it down, but I still asked them to be peaceful saying, "Knock it off guys." The young black male's sister lived in the apartment #215, which was the apartment next to that of Dahmer, the same one that I turned down when I first moved to the building. I was not sure of the origin of the argument between Dahmer and the young black neighbor, but I heard the young man threatening to buy a gun. When a gun is mentioned during a verbal altercation, the assumption is that the dispute must be a very serious one. Maybe the black male was feeling the racist pressure in Milwaukee that had suppressed aspiring young black men in the neighborhood.

Apparently, the young black male knew what he was talking about. Dahmer might have propositioned him that day, something he did not like. The serial killer didn't always get everyone that he propositioned for his needs. Most of Dahmer's victims must have been lured with something they could not resist. He said he approached each of them in the same way. It was the offer of money, video and sex. He learnt to look for the most vulnerable people who saw him as a sex partner for money. They thought that he would give them his money as he promised them at the time of contact. The only return they got was a premature death.

Most of the black people in Milwaukee do not trust the system that deprived them of opportunity and protection. A lot of them have difficulty respecting the law enforcement officers who often didn't respect their human rights. There

53

had been incidents in which clashes resulted between police and minority citizens who decided to fire the shots back at the police, killing them too. As Dahmer's neighborhood was restless, most people didn't pay attention to what others were doing and he took advantage of it committing homicides unnoticed for a long time.

I remember one Friday night when a security guard chased a lady from a strip club to the Oxford Apartments for alleged stolen cassette tapes. The lady didn't live here, but had an accomplice. The security guard was lucky to retrieve the tapes. Perhaps the most obscene circumstance was the presence of the former manager of the building, because a conflict of opinions might occur. I had quite a few cold conflicts while doing my job. On one occasion, I had to ask the former manager to vacate my office because I thought that he was there too frequently. I asked him to remove anything in my office that belonged to him, which he did.

On attending a seminar at the Waukesha County Technical College, the company had no seminar package for me, but they had one for the former manager. I was furious and I demanded to get my own seminar package for building management. Something was not right on that job the way I perceived it, but I didn't know what it was.

Some residents of the building were there when I started my job. It was a job that I didn't expect to control my life, so I had resisted some imposition that came from the former manager when I thought it to be unfair.

One resident came to my office one day boasting of terror, talking about shooting in a way to intimidate me. This was 1991, the same time when Desert Storm - the war to liberate Kuwait - was going on. I reminded the young man what it meant to be real man with a gun. I told him that only the men who went to Kuwait were the real men with guns. I told him that Kuwait was where men with guns were expected to be, not here where men with guns terrorize neighborhoods at home. He felt embarrassed and dropped the idea.

Another resident also threatened to shoot through the window of my office and I told him that shootings don't always get the target. I gave him an example of what I meant. I told him that the frontline in a battle or a war is probably where there are more bullets and shells flying in all directions. Even in those conditions, there are soldiers who still returned alive after it was over. He knew that his intimidation instilled no fear in me and he went on his way. One other resident in a furious mood intruded into my office the next day. He had no appointment and I didn't know what his problem was. I ordered him to leave my office immediately and he did, because he knew that he was not intimidating me. As an alternative plan, they framed me in connection with the television set that had allegedly been stolen from one of the resident's apartments.

Chapter 5

Behind Closed Doors

My job began on July 10, 1990 when I actually signed a contract with my boss to manage the Oxford Apartments. The job terminated on November 2, 1992. I remember it was also the US Presidential Election Day, coined "Decision 92". On this historic day, all the residents of the Oxford Apartments were finally moved out to make way for demolition of the building.

The chronology of events on the job follows with respect to all the eye to eye, day to day encounters that I had with Jeffrey Dahmer inside the Oxford Apartments. Some of these contacts could have been fatal, were it not for divine intervention. All the murders he committed before he came to the Oxford Apartments are narrated in this chapter. His apartment inside the Oxford Apartments was the next best place to where he committed his first murder. He was younger then and he had a whole family ranch home to himself in Bath Township, Ohio.

Jeffrey Dahmer as a child, as an adolescent and as an adult had the experience of growing up in a broken home. He had little or no attention from his parents, as they were consumed in a storm of divorce. However, that was no excuse for what he did. As consolation, he turned to alcohol. He was very scared of the harsh experience of loneliness and vowed not to let anyone to leave him alone again.

Jeffrey Dahmer was enraged to know that he had no friends, so he made an effort to acquire them, dead or alive. In 1978, with his murderous rage and endless stalking stunts, Dahmer picked up and boldly murdered Steven Mark Hicks, an 18-year-old from Bath, Ohio in 1978. Still a teenager himself, Dahmer buried Mr Hicks' mutilated body in a shallow grave on the Dahmer family property. He then returned and exhumed it after two weeks to break up the bones with a sledgehammer. He scattered the bone fragments in various directions and left them there for thirteen years while he went on to college, dropped out after a freshman quarter, joined the military, discharged early, returned home to Ohio, to Wisconsin and started his murder spree.

After his arrest, Dahmer provided the custodian detectives with the details of Steven Hicks' homicide. The ghost of his first victim haunted him perpetually with "Ghostworks". The intensity of the effect of "Ghostworks" on Dahmer's mind increased as the number of victims increased, such that he could not stop himself.

Just completing one quarter at the University of Ohio in Columbus, Dahmer dropped out. He then joined the military. He was assigned to serve in Germany beginning in January of 1979, but was discharged in March of 1981 early because of excessive drinking of alcohol. He initially returned to his boyhood home in Bath, Ohio. No one in the Dahmer family was aware of the first murder on their property. Jeffrey Dahmer was now harnessing his boldness into an ambition, an insatiable desire and courage that would lead to the death of sixteen more victims over thirteen years.

After he returned home from the military, he moved to Wisconsin from Ohio. Wisconsin was a State where he would not receive the death penalty if he were caught. The State of Ohio had the death penalty in place back in 1981, so he completely avoided living there. This was another smart move by the murderer who wished to avoid being caught. However, it was another ten years before Dahmer began killing again and he accelerated his pace when he became more skilled doing it. In his own words to the sheriff detectives while he was in custody, he said that he "began getting quicker at cutting up the bodies" after his third victim.

His homosexual tendencies were intertwined with his fantasies of murdering and dismembering humans. At the same time, his social problem needed a solution too. His desires could only be gratified by the death of a sex partner (necrophilia). Jeffrey Dahmer did not get an erection when his partner was awake or conscious, so in order to have control of his victims, Jeffrey Dahmer experimented with several different drugs to come up with a most effective sleeping potion. He found some prescription drugs, over-the-counter drugs and street drugs. Equipped with these, Dahmer was ready to formulate a lethal concoction to gratify his fantasies and his necrophilia desires.

Jeffrey Dahmer was not yet a serial killer before he met Steven Tuomi, a 24-year-old white man from Ontonagon, Michigan. Tuomi became Dahmer's first victim in Wisconsin back in 1987. Dahmer told police that he did not know how Mr Tuomi died because both of them were heavily drunk on hard rum and passed out. He said that he woke up and found Mr Tuomi dead, with blood flowing from his mouth.

There wasn't enough evidence to charge Jeffrey Dahmer on this death because there was no other evidence. Dahmer disposed of the entire body, so he could not be charged with the death of Mr Steven Tuomi even if he had confessed to the crime. At the time, Jeffrey Dahmer did not report Steven Tuomi's death, because he was naturally afraid of the police. He had murdered Steven Hicks and not yet been apprehended and now this is another death for which he was responsible. Instead, he went to the Grand Avenue Mall, which is located in downtown Milwaukee, bought a large suitcase from one of the stores and returned to the room at the Ambassador Hotel.

Dahmer recalled how he disposed of his first victim's body. Like in his first murder, he didn't plan it so he wasn't prepared. He was even in the wrong place to dispose of a body. That's when he decided to move the body to his grandma's house where he was living at the time.

Jeffrey Dahmer then stuffed the suitcase with Mr Tuomi's body and called a taxi cab to take the body to his grandma's house in West Allis. The cab driver had no idea that the cargo he was transporting was a dead body. He even helped to unload the trunk. Dahmer then took the body down to the basement, cut it up and disposed of it entirely.

Starting with Steven Tuomi, a new serial killer named Jeffrey Dahmer was on the loose in the City of Milwaukee, Wisconsin. Of course, no one was alarmed about it, because nobody knew what he was doing.

Jeffrey Dahmer murdered two more victims at his grandma's house before he really became independent in 1988. At that time, he had a job, his own one bedroomed apartment and absolute privacy, because of his choice of location in the building. Before his independence, it all happened at his grandma's house in the City of West Allis, just south west of the City of Milwaukee. Jeffrey Dahmer had become bolder after each murder.

He had learned from the experience of his first murder a decade previously. He had his first close call with the police in Bath, Ohio, just a few hours after the act on his way to dispose of Mr Hicks' body, his first victim. When the police officers stopped and asked him about the cargo on the back seat of the car, he told them that it was garbage on its way to the dump. He was so cool and calculated, giving the officers convincing responses, that they believed him without any suspicion and let him go. He didn't show any signs of being nervous as he answered the officers' questions. They observed no red flags, so they didn't bother checking the cargo. He learnt early on how to interact under pressure with law enforcement officers.

The demeanor that he presented to convince the officers that he was an innocent, law-abiding citizen gave

Jeffrey Dahmer the confidence to use the same technique many times in the future. He learnt to be polite and not be nervous when in contact with the police. In other words, he could operate under any form of pressure. Ms Shelton who prosecuted his child molestation case indicated this talent that he possessed. In fact, it was the same manipulative skill that the police officers expressed about him when they were in contact with him during his involvement with a Laotian boy. Dahmer was in the process of murdering the 14-year-old when the police officers arrived in response to a 911 emergency call. Dahmer was able to manipulate the officers who left the boy with him as his next victim. At that time, Ms Shelton indicated that Dahmer was very manipulative. He was able to show the appropriate reactions to authority, irrespective of what he was feeling inside.

In 1988, James Doxtator, a 14-year-old Native American from Milwaukee, Wisconsin became Jeffrey Dahmer's second victim at his grandma's house in the city of West Allis, Wisconsin.

Next was Anthony Sears, a 26-year-old black male from Milwaukee, Wisconsin who became Dahmer's third victim in 1989 at his grandmother's house. Finally, Grandma, who was in her late seventies, couldn't handle his problems anymore and asked him to find his own place. Reports say that she asked him to move out after he was arrested for exposing himself in public.

Jeffrey Dahmer returned to a familiar neighborhood, the City of Milwaukee's Avenues West Neighborhood. It is the area surrounding Marquette University, a major Catholic University in the State of Wisconsin. The boundaries are the freeway I-94 West on the south, State Street on the north, 12th Street on the east and 27th Street on the west. Before moving to the apartment unit #213 inside the Oxford Apartments, Jeffrey Dahmer had lived in an apartment at 808 North 24th Street where he committed a crime involving the molestation of a child. He was given suspended sentence and was placed on probation. When he was released from prison he returned to grandma's house from where he moved to the Oxford Apartments. Thus the Avenues West was a familiar neighborhood to him.

Jeffrey Dahmer completed an application dated May 9, 1990 with Larry Marion, the previous resident manager of the Oxford Apartments. Just four days later, on May 13, 1990, Jeffrey Dahmer moved into apartment #213, his choice location where he would enjoy his independence and security to continue the secret murders.

Dahmer was familiar with this neighborhood. This would be the last place on anyone's mind to suspect such a crime as mass murder.

When I was finally employed in July of 1990 as manager of the building, Jeffrey Dahmer had settled comfortably into his apartment at the rear end of the building, a quiet location near the exit for his convenience. The rear door was usually propped open with a wedge and so it was easier for Jeffrey Dahmer to come and go via that entrance. It was closer to his apartment than the main entrance at the front of the building and people rarely paid attention to what others were doing, as long as it did not involve them.

About two weeks into the job, when Dahmer came to my office and made a request to install a lock on his mailbox, I didn't know that I had just met and shaken hands with a serial killer. However, although our eyes crossed many times, he never held my gaze while we discussed his request and frequently looked down. Nevertheless, I did not see him as a crazy man.

Dahmer was not scared to live in a neighborhood where most white people would be afraid to dwell.

After his arrest, the shockwaves were felt for the next sixteen months, during which time the building experienced two exoduses of residents. As narrated in Chapter 9, the first move out was voluntary and in panic following Dahmer's exposure and arrest. The residents felt the threat from the victims' families in addition to the horror that haunted the building. We received bomb threats and also observed drive-by shootings at the building, because the families claimed that the residents could have stopped Jeffrey Dahmer from killing their loved ones.

The second exodus was involuntary and occurred because the people of Milwaukee demanded that the building be demolished, as a way of "wiping out the memory of the tragedy." I wouldn't forget it, neither would any of the residents and our lives would never be the same again. The truth is that nothing can really wipe out the memory of the deeds of a mass murderer who took away the lives of families' loved ones. The idea of tearing down the building was only part of the effort to forget about the tragedy.

Another consequence of the same tragedy was the negative effect it had on the management company's profits. Enormous operating loss was an obvious reason for demolishing the building as it had a vacancy rate of 92%, coupled with the added cost of security services to protect the residents who continued to live in the building. In effect we were live victims. I had been told by some of my friends that I had developed a quick temper that reared its ugly head whenever I talked about the experiences on my job at the Oxford Apartments.

After Dahmer's arrest, I looked back and recalled all the contacts that I had with him, both inside and outside of the Oxford Apartments. I was disturbed by the fact that my job had been a death trap. Anybody in my position would have been angry to know that a job was hazardous without their prior knowledge. Thank God Jeffrey Dahmer missed me during all three close calls that could have been fatal for me.

As many as thirty-six out of the thirty-nine residents in

the building moved out after the serial killer was arrested. I was able to rent ten more apartments during the one year following the first mass move out. As you can imagine, it was no longer business as usual to continue rental management of the building.

Dahmer had certainly done his homework and knew how to operate silently in the way he did. He knew what to offer to each victim in order to gain their cooperation. As long as they went home with him, he would keep them with him dead or alive. When the victims went back to his apartment, they would make that obvious mistake later of trying to leave. He hated to be alone and would rather have them dead for company than to allow them to leave.

In May 1990, about two weeks after moving into the building, Dahmer murdered Raymond Smith, aka Ricky Beeks or Raymond Lamont, a 33-year-old black male from Rockford, Illinois, his first victim at the Oxford Apartments, the fourth victim in Wisconsin and the fifth victim in Dahmer's murder history.

Next, in June 1990, Jeffrey Dahmer killed Edward Smith, a 28-year-old black male from Milwaukee, Wisconsin, his second victim at the Oxford Apartments. In effect, Dahmer had set up an anonymous death roll behind the closed door at apartment #213. Many more guests would come through that door of evil, make the mistake of showing a desire to leave and consequently become victims.

Jeffrey Dahmer was a very smart murderer. He carefully chose that particular apartment because of the attributes of its location that were helpful to his secret life. His apartment on the north side of the building faced a high fence and no traffic. The six foot high cyclone wire fence marked the lot line between the Oxford Apartments and the building on the adjacent lot to the north. The fence was covered with summertime plants like runners and climbers, which obscured the view from the adjacent property. There was also a tall tree towards the back of the building on the fence side. The tree had branches that were hanging down almost touching the ground. Thus it formed a canopy that shielded Dahmer's bedroom in an aerial view to the adjacent property. It made it so secure for his secret and murderous lifestyle inside the Oxford Apartments.

Chapter 6

Tricked in the Act

Jeffrey Dahmer needed a body on that night like on many other nights. His desperate attempt to get me had failed just an hour previously. He therefore went out to one of his hunting grounds located in the heart of downtown Milwaukee. From there, Dahmer picked up a man, Tracy Edwards, who was in the company of two other male friends. After a small talk with Edwards, they decided to let Edwards' friends meet them at Dahmer's apartment later for a party. Knowing that he wanted to be with Edwards one on one, Dahmer gave the friends a note with the wrong address to his apartment. He also gave them some money for some beer in the hope that they might not come back to the party. Either way, Dahmer was able to elude Edwards' friends.

In the City of Milwaukee, Wisconsin, strange events were occurring. We had the news about missing persons, a nauseating smell permeated the building, there was an unsolved murder in apartment #308 of the Oxford Apartments and, finally, a miracle happened when Tracy Edwards tricked Jeffrey Dahmer and escaped from the apartment. The serial killer in the building was about to be exposed.

Tracy Edwards had no idea that he had just met a serial killer and was marked for Dahmer's murder rituals that night. He had no reason to suspect Jeffrey Dahmer and he only expected to have a good time at the party, especially after his friends arrived. Dahmer hoped to continue his murder spree long into the future. He didn't expect his old plan of action to fail. The old plan was the routine drugging to render the victim unconscious so he could have sex, then to strangle them so he could have more sex and take photos

67

and, finally, dismembering the victim, so he could collect parts of their body and then dispose of the remains.

This was going to be the last time Dahmer would ever attempt to murder anyone again, although he wasn't aware of it at the time. The party started when both Dahmer and his intended victim Tracy Edwards arrived at the apartment. When Dahmer routinely began the DSSM (drug, strangle, sex, mutilate) procedure on Edwards, he was unsuccessful. The ordeal lasted four hours. Dahmer was frustrated with Edwards' uncompromising attitude, but still didn't want him to get away, because that would create a serious security risk for Dahmer's secret lifestyle. Perhaps Dahmer himself strictly analyzed Edwards' conversations in comparison to the conversations he had with previous victims. Dahmer then realized that Edwards was not like most of the earlier victims who were in an adventure to obtain money from Dahmer. He knew that Edwards was much more street wise than previous victims.

Edwards was not going to be alone with Dahmer for too long because he was waiting for the arrival of his two friends who were supposed to join the party in Dahmer's apartment. Perhaps Edwards didn't want to be drunk before their arrival. He had seen Dahmer in the neighborhood, but they had never been alone together in one apartment.

Edwards was unaware that Dahmer had given the two friends the wrong address to his apartment. Dahmer didn't want Edwards to know about this, so instead of verbally giving his friends the address, he wrote it on a piece of paper. Edwards became frantic as time passed without his friends showing up at the party. At the same time, Dahmer felt that it was taking too long for the drug to take effect on Edwards. By this time, Dahmer was already angry with Edwards, because he was feeling more inebriated than his intended victim. Whatever might have happened, the drug was ineffective on Edwards and Dahmer kept asking him how he was feeling every few minutes.

Dahmer should have aborted the plan to kill at this time, but he was compelled by the killer instinct that turned him into a monster. Edwards had also seen the Polaroid pictures of men who had been slaughtered in that apartment. Dahmer took photos of the victims in dismemberment. Edwards was also disgusted by the foul smell in the apartment.

Edwards became bored and started walking back and forth to the bathroom, trying to find an escape route. To Dahmer, this was an indication of Edwards' desire to leave the apartment. For Dahmer, this guest was abiding by his desired routine and so he must now come up with a backup plan to keep him as one of his victims. Edwards was not a good candidate for Dahmer's murder rituals that night, but the serial killer wouldn't let go. The drug didn't work and Dahmer had no backup plan. There appeared to be no other way to get Edwards than go to extreme measures and cut him down using the butcher's knife he had in the apartment. So whether Edwards was conscious or not, Dahmer decided to slaughter him anyway.

After Dahmer slapped the handcuffs onto Edwards' left hand, a struggle ensued while he was pressing to get the cuffs on the other hand. Dahmer then pulled out his sharp butcher's knife that he hid under his bed. At this point Edwards was ready to fight for his life, but then Dahmer put down the knife to take a few photos of Edwards' lean body before attempting to butcher him. Fortunately for Edwards, this became the only window of opportunity and he used it. He mustered all his energy into a single punch of his right fist into Dahmer's face, which brought Dahmer to the floor. Dahmer's first victim, Hicks, was not drugged either. Dahmer killed him by fist fighting and using a barbell as a weapon, so he thought he could do the same thing with Edwards. He wanted to kill by any means necessary.

Now that Edwards had derived the maximum benefit

of that first and preemptive punch, he went on to give a few more kicks to Dahmer's stomach to keep him incapacitated on the floor. Edwards then headed quickly to the door after and escaped unharmed as a victor from the apartment of victims.

While in custody, Dahmer told detectives that he did not know when Tracy Edwards left the apartment. He told detectives that the handcuffs on Edwards' hand were for a bondage photo that he had requested. Dahmer said that he had wanted to take the handcuffs off, but that Edwards was reluctant. Apparently, Dahmer was the one who was too drunk to know when his victim escaped. He was the one who may have consumed the drugged drink, because the glasses could have been switched. Dahmer explained to the detectives that he was very drunk during the time that he was with Edwards and that he had probably blacked out. He said that the only thing that he remembered was the police officers at his door with Edwards standing behind them. Dahmer was expecting to add Edwards to his inventory of body parts, but fortunately Edwards was aware of the danger before he made a conscious escape. My escape on the other hand, was more of a miracle, because I was not aware of the danger, or that I was Dahmer's prime target.

The police officers were already in the neighborhood on a different assignment. Tracy Edwards was lucky to see them following his escape. Again, this was the blessing for all the good residents in the Oxford Apartments, including me and any others who might have been potential victims of the serial murderer. Edwards ran to the police officers with Dahmer's handcuffs dangling from his left hand and told them that a guy wanted to kill him in that building, pointing at the Oxford Apartments. The police officers didn't believe what they saw as they watched a man in a single handcuff running to them. They wondered whether that was one of their handcuffs or someone else's. When Edwards initially told them his story they didn't take him seriously, but nevertheless agreed to go and investigate. Tracy Edwards then led the police officers back to the apartment and arrested Jeffrey Dahmer who was expecting this action as soon as Tracy escaped. It was not looking good for Dahmer, but he was ready for whatever would happen to him now. Dahmer had no choice but to face justice.

Just before this ill fated night, Jeffrey Dahmer was tired of everything happening in his gruesome little apartment. There were decaying body parts of the victims emitting a vile odor that was difficult to breathe. Then there was the additional problem of his recent job loss. He was restless and confused by his current circumstances. He knew that it didn't look good for him.

Dahmer made a mistake, either deliberately or not, by not adhering to the proper sequence of the stages of his routine. May be Dahmer didn't wait long enough for the drug to take effect on Tracy Edwards. A prerequisite to the strangling is that the victim must be unconscious, yet Dahmer didn't want to let Edwards go. He had seen too much in the photos that conveyed what Dahmer did in his apartment. Therefore, Edwards had become a "must die" guest to the serial killer. Edwards probably learnt from the photos he had seen and was wondering why those victims did not fight back. Edwards figured that these victims must have been too drunk, or that they have been drugged. Edwards had street experience, so he could easily have put two and two together. Every few minutes Dahmer asked Edwards how he was feeling, trying to ascertain when he would become unconscious.

My speculation is that Edwards did not consume the drugged drink that Dahmer usually gave his victims. Either Dahmer didn't yet have the chance to slip the drug into Edwards' drink, or Edwards switched the drink so that Dahmer drank the drugged one. Another assumption is that Edwards only pretended to drink each time he lifted the drink to his mouth. Why Edwards was not affected by Dahmer's sleeping pills might be because he had some anti-sleeping, anti-intoxication pills that Edwards might have brought with him and used along with the drink. Some men who expect to drink heavily on a night out sometimes take some drugs with them to neutralize the effect of drinking too much alcohol. Maybe Tracy Edwards was one such man.

For Jeffrey Dahmer, this drugging procedure had worked perfectly well on all his previous victims, but not Edwards. There were deadly consequences for anyone who attempted to leave the apartment willfully without Dahmer's permission. The mystery of Tracy Edwards' escape made me wonder how he actually managed it. Edwards had given the stories about his ordeal with Dahmer. He was inconsistent with his claims of what really happened as revealed later by his national television appearances.

As manager of the Oxford Apartments, I had a 24/7 duty at the site. Prior to my job as the manager of the building, I was engaged in the restoration of a property that I had recently acquired. In fact I had no time to do any work on it. I had worked so hard on this job that I was always too tired to carry out any more work at the end of each day. My property restoration project began to suffer, so on that Monday night, July 22, 1991, I had decided to leave the Oxford Apartments to go to work on my property. I was under pressure from the City of Milwaukee Building Inspection. There must be progress in all projects as required by permits issued on those projects. It was the only night in one year of work that I had been away from the building. I was hoping to do a lot of work on my property starting from that Monday night. I was planning to work all day the following day, before returning to the Oxford Apartments on Wednesday. It turned out that the project on property restoration was the saving grace for me.

Immediately I arrived at my property at approximately 6.00pm Central Standard Time, I began with dismantling some old frozen pipes in the plumbing system. This was hard work because some of the frozen piping was difficult to twist off or cut through. Sometimes I had to apply some heat on them with a flame torch before I was able to twist them apart. If the pipes didn't come apart after the heat had been applied, then I had to use a hacksaw to cut through them. I was so tired after four hours of intensive work that I needed to sleep.

Jeffrey Dahmer's murder spree ended in the final hour of Monday, July 22, 1991 when he was arrested by the officers of the Milwaukee Police Department, Robert Rauth and Rolf Mueller.

The decaying body parts in the apartment fouled the air. Dahmer was also terribly overwhelmed with the weight of the contents of the 57 gallon blue barrel in which he left the torsos of his victims soaking and melting in acid. The content of the blue barrel was the main source of the stench in the entire building. The bones, the flesh, the blood and the body fluids were all being melted by vats of acid into a stinking sludge, which sat in his bedroom. Dahmer could not empty it, because its enormous weight prevented him from hauling it out of the apartment by himself. He didn't foresee the potential problem that the use of the barrel would create.

Prior to his arrest, Dahmer had lost his job and was about to face eviction from the apartment. Before then, he was planning to commit suicide as revealed by the notes of his probation agent Donna Chester. Thus, Jeffrey Dahmer was wondering how to move all the things he had in the apartment, including the body parts, if he were to be evicted. Maybe this was what he wanted to talk to me about just a few hours before his arrest the same night.

Tracy Edwards was on both the "Geraldo" and the "America's Most Wanted" television talk shows. Dahmer himself disputed part of Edwards' story. Edwards claimed that Dahmer issued a warning during the ordeal saying, "You die if you don't do what I say." However, experts said that serial murderers do not reveal their intentions to their victims in advance. They just do it. If Edwards could tell the truth as to how he managed to foil Dahmer's plan to drug him, it would be a very interesting lesson for the public. Nobody really knows the truth about what actually happened during Edwards' long ordeal with Jeffrey Dahmer before he escaped. The only obvious thing was that the punch of Edwards' right fist in Dahmer's face was the punch that put an end to his life as a serial killer.

Dahmer should have aborted his plan when he realized that Edwards was not affected by the drug, but he knew that Edwards had seen the Polaroid pictures of men who had been slaughtered in that apartment.

During interviews while in custody, Dahmer was asked why he did not provide the key to the handcuffs. He said that he didn't lock the cuffs because he had lost the key in the trash can earlier. He would have had to remove Edwards' hand from his body to remove the cuffs if he had locked them.

After the arrest, media activity began and thus placed the Oxford in the spotlight for the world to view. As of then, the Oxford became infamous. Consequently, the building itself became one of the victims of the sex serial killer. The building formed the backdrop of news' conferences and the site for candlelight vigils. Private individuals visited, curious to know anything about Jeffrey Dahmer and the murders he committed. They wondered how this could have happened there and unnoticed for so long.

Sometimes members of the victims' families came into the building just to see the door behind which their loved ones were killed. Some of them touched the door, as though they felt the spirits of their loved ones in the apartment.

These curiosity seekers and victim families were asking questions when they had a chance to get into the building. Any resident they found would answer their questions as best as they could with any shred of knowledge that they possessed. They asked questions such as, "Didn't you hear anything?" When the resident said, "No," they then asked "Didn't you smell something?" Then the resident would say, "Yes, but we didn't know that it was the smell of dead people."

From that point on, the residents of the Oxford Apartments faced threats from the public outcry. On their way to the store, the residents would encounter people who spoke to them impolitely or made a joke about them in connection with the tragedy. They also encountered similar abuse in their jobs and wherever else they were known as residents of the Oxford Apartments at the time of the tragedy.

John Batchelor, who had appeared on several television interviews, was nervous when he realized that he had become the spokesperson for the Oxford Apartments. As a result, he was unable to walk out unaccompanied for fear of the harassment that he endured whenever he left the Oxford Apartments. Later, bomb threats were directed at the building. That was when the residents became so terrified that they cried out loud for their security. Mr Batchelor didn't mean any harm when he let the police officers into the building, because he didn't know which apartment they were heading for. That's exemplary of someone who is not a criminal. He had nothing to fear when the police arrived, so he let them into the building. He didn't know what was going on in Dahmer's apartment.

The insignia of a gang on the building marked it as their territory, but they were still members of society under the law and must answer to the enforcement officers. Mr Batchelor simply let the officers in, because they told him who they were and at that point he had no choice but do what they said.

As the threats loomed over the building, all the residents wanted protection until they moved out of the place. It was not going to be an easy task. There was little that the police could do other than advise the residents to call them if the threats continued. There was an incident of a drive-by shooting at the building and the Oxford Apartments became more popularly known in the neighborhood as the "Dahmer Building".

The curiosity about these murders was so strong that crowds of people came from out of town or State and sometimes even from out of country to see the building and the site where Jeffrey Dahmer lived and committed these atrocities. I remember some crowds that came from the local suburbs as well as those who came all the way from Germany, France, England and Canada to name just a few. The Dahmer murder story was very special to many news' reporters and they wanted to get a piece of information, however small. It felt almost like a human circus there. There were just too many people to talk to, so we tried to avoid communicating with them simply because we had no idea what was happening in Dahmer's apartment.

The part of the crowd who were not news' reporters came to hunt for souvenirs. They were seriously aggressive and often attempted to enter the building by force. They even disabled the back exit door closest to Dahmer's apartment. Some of them climbed the ladder of the balcony escape to enter the building. We were constantly locking them out. Those who were not able to enter the building would decide to take anything from the surroundings of the Oxford Apartments. This tragedy seemed to have become an opportunity for treasure hunters, no matter how crazy it sounds.

It was amazing to find that the tragedy that angered so many people also seemed to have signs of glory associated with it in this society. At least one police detective asked

Jeffrey Dahmer for his autograph while he was in custody. Even now, seventeen years on, I still receive calls from abroad from people trying to get the Jeffrey Dahmer story. From Plymouth, England, a communications' production company named as Twofour Productions Ltd had a program on serial killers entitled, "Before They Were Infamous." I had an exclusive interview in May of 2005 about Jeffrey Dahmer in that program. The interview crew sent by Jon McKnight arrived as scheduled and conducted the interview with me about the serial killer.

The general public felt that the residents who lived in the building had a better chance of stopping Dahmer before he killed as many as twelve victims. However, none of these victims ever lived at the Oxford Apartments, so no one ever mysteriously disappeared. There was only one unsolved murder inside the Oxford Apartments, but Dahmer denied being responsible for it, despite there being a Dahmer style about the crime (drug, sex, strangle, mutilate). This was the only murder in the building that every resident knew about. It instilled such fear in the building at that time that nobody trusted anyone, because everyone was a suspect.

After Dahmer's arrest, the residents were in shock and panicked as they tried to move out as quickly as they could. However, this was a housing emergency that would take at least a few days before a solution could be found. Thus, the residents were temporarily housed at the Hilton Hotel to avoid media harassment, in addition to that from the victims' families and the general public.

I was fortunate to miss the immediate consequences of the arrest, such as seeing the gory nature of body parts in the Dahmer's apartment. If I were present at the time of the arrest, perhaps people would not believe that I had no idea that Dahmer was committing these multiple murders in his apartment. They might have thought that, as the manager, I was supposed to know about everything that occurred in each apartment unit inside the building.

Chapter 7

Dahmer's Arrest

Not quite fifteen minutes after I had gone to bed, I began to hear the sound of an approaching fire truck with its sirens blasting, until it drove past street on which my property was located. The fire truck drove speedily past and headed west from my house. About three minutes later, I heard the sound of another fire truck headed west on State Street, like the first one. A third fire truck then came through the same way. I didn't know that they were heading for the Oxford Apartments, but I was worried about being away at that time from the job. I didn't know what had happened until the next morning when the former manager came to break the news of Jeffrey Dahmer's arrest to me.

Jeffrey Dahmer looked just like any other human being, so you would never have imagined that you were interacting with a serial killer. What you saw when looking at him was a mask of deceit. Mass murder in the way that Dahmer performed it was the least expected tragedy in an apartment building that stood in the middle of town.

I listened attentively and heard all three fire trucks stop at a distance that was about the location of the Oxford Apartments. I had left the building only about five hours ago after Jeffrey Dahmer had wanted to talk to me. In that encounter I asked him to see me in my office, but he did not show up so I left the building.

I went to sleep feeling slightly uneasy for not being at the Oxford Apartments. The question that struck my mind was, "Is the Oxford on fire?" I didn't know for sure to which building the fire trucks had gone. I hadn't had any experience of emergencies in apartment buildings and my immediate reaction was to return to the building, but I could not take the risk of walking back there at that time of the night in a touch neighborhood.

I was usually off duty on Tuesdays every week. I had planned to spend the next day off, which was Tuesday July 23, 1991, in my property. I planned to return to the Oxford Apartments on Wednesday July 24, 1991, but all that changed when Dahmer was arrested. The former manager of the building came to my residence the following morning and broke the news of Jeffrey Dahmer's arrest and informed me of all the discoveries by the police in his apartment.

Before the former manager came, I had no idea of what, if anything, had taken place in the building on my first and only night away. From the news' reports I realized that it was about five hours after I left the building. I began hearing the sounds of the huge fire trucks speeding up the street after Tracy Edwards' escape. Following one miracle after another, I escaped before Dahmer had a chance to try his routine on me.

As a matter of official duty, the manager is the one to whom all emergencies should be reported by any of the residents. However, when Tracy Edwards tricked, punched and escaped from Dahmer and brought the police to arrest him, I was missing from the building. People were curious to know what might have happened to me and were unaware that I had left the building after my third close call with the serial killer.

All the discoveries of body parts in Dahmer's apartment were gathered in a heap awaiting shipment to the Medical Examiner's Laboratory. It was really funny to hear about some of the answers and gestures one of the residents was giving to people who came to ask where the manager was. A senior resident, Mr Ezra West, would point his protruded mouth to the heap of recoveries as if to say, "That's where he is." It was a tragic moment, but it made people laugh.

Three hours into my sleep at about 3.00am, I was

disturbed by someone knocking on my door, but I didn't answer because not only was it too late into the night, but I was not expecting anyone at my place at that time of night. In fact, I thought it was someone trying to break into my house, so I picked up my baseball bat and took position at a corner next to the door to strike really hard on any intruder. It was Mr William Vance, one of my favorite residents, who must have come to tell me what had happened in the Oxford Apartments, or to be sure that I hadn't fallen victim to Jeffrey Dahmer. I was ready, holding my bat and waiting to strike on a possible intruder, when I heard the sound of an automobile started up, which I recognized to be that of Mr Vance. I regretted seeing him drive off before I could get his attention, because I knew right then that something must have happened and I was needed.

I went back to sleep wondering what the emergency might be at the Oxford Apartments. I knew that Mr Vance was a good man and we often called him the Preacher, because he was a Reverend. The following morning, the former manager came to break the news of Dahmer's arrest. In his own words he said "Jeff is in jail, six bodies found in his apartment."

I didn't know what explanation he gave to the public when the madding crowds converged on the site of the macabre murders. He asked me to go to the building and show my face. He said that everyone was worried when they didn't see me after Dahmer's arrest. They thought that he had murdered me.

Once I was employed, everyone involved in criminal activities was worried and these were the ones setting me up. So you could imagine what all these adversaries might have done to me if I had been in the building when Dahmer was arrested. This was the same minority neighborhood where white police officers were not trusted for the way they handled minority problems. Nobody would have believed me if I told them that I didn't know anything about what Jeffrey Dahmer was doing in his own apartment. Jeffrey Dahmer was living in the building for two months before I started my job as the new manager. I was not the manager that rented the apartment to him, so I actually inherited him in the pack of current residents in the building.

The trauma after the arrest was enormous because it affected everyone in the city of Milwaukee. The discoveries in Jeffrey Dahmer's apartment inside the Oxford Apartments sent a shockwave through the entire community and caused a rumble inside the building. Some furious members of the public who were not related in any way to the victims' families made their way into the building and sometimes uttered insulting statements. A resident once beat and chased one such person out of the building. The guy came into the building and said, "What are you fuckers here doing and why didn't you stop Dahmer from killing all these people." He didn't know that the residents were just as angry as he was, because they didn't know about it either.

Following Dahmer's arrest, every resident felt as though he was still hiding in the building. The residents were having nightmares. They could not go outside and so they assembled in the lobby of the first floor every night for comfort. Being fully carpeted, the lobby of about 450 sq ft was beautifully decorated with life size mirrors. Residents felt more comfortable there. They avoided being alone in their apartments. The residents whose apartments were nearest to Dahmer's, suffered the most because they had to walk past his door, which radiated an eerie feeling. These residents had no other way to get around it. Mr Vance who lived in apartment #210 hated walking past Dahmer's door to take his garbage out. He decided to take the stairway up to the third floor and then to the exit so that he could dispose of his garbage in the dumpster in the back of the building.

There were other residents who avoided walking past Dahmer's closed door after the tragedy. I remember how I avoided going into Dahmer's apartment when I first arrived at the building, because I was scared. After this tragedy, it felt like anything was possible here. So the "watch out" syndrome remains in everyone's mind.

The fear that permeated the building became worse when a bunch of hit letters were written and then addressed to the building residents as a whole. The letters had no contact details, so no explanations could be given to the senders. From the style of the handwriting it appeared as though the letters were written by two people in black and red ink. The colors of the ink used in the letter, I presume, meant red for blood and black for death. This was the point at which the residents could not take it anymore. The management company was concerned with the possible vacancies that would occur as a result of this tragedy.

The management company was duty bound to provide security guard services for the safety of the residents before they move out of the Oxford Apartments. This mass exodus was not healthy for the rental business. The records showed that it took five years to reach the previous occupancy level of 92%, which occurred in 1990 when I became the manager. I had put in long hours and loyal dedication to achieve that occupancy level. High turnover trends existed in this market, but I was creative in the way in which I applied the qualifying ratios for some of the applicants, who eventually met the requirements to move in. Most of such residents were grateful and tried to abide by the rules and regulations while they lived here. They were the residents who were most concerned with my absence at the time Jeffrey Dahmer was arrested.

Some of such marginal applicants were not so grateful and they made life difficult for everyone else after they moved in. These residents broke the house rules, which were part of their lease agreement. The house rules were simple to follow such as: (1) Keeping the building entrance locked after 10.00pm for the security and safety of the residents; (2) Wrapping up laundry activities before midnight so that the manager could lock up the laundry room at midnight; (3) Avoiding the playing of loud music after bedtime so that other neighbors could have quiet enjoyment in the building; (4) Avoiding property damage so that the company managing the property could impose minimal rent increase.

The reasons why these house rules were added to and made part of the lease had been clarified. They were simple rules that help with self discipline and those who follow them closely would have really appreciated the "Just do it" slogan by Nike. It couldn't be overemphasized that a stitch in time saves nine. There was a lesson to learn. The future belongs to those who are efficient. Whenever a handful of residents engaged in a combination of acts that broke the house rules, it made my job harder. It made it difficult to control and focus on the more important tasks of showing and renting. Any apartment community of residents with such unruly behavior looked carefree. Under such circumstances, the manager on site would find his job tiresome.

Dahmer was an expensive joker inside the Oxford Apartments as he cast an aura of fear and evil in the minds of the building residents. Practically every resident had expressed how they felt about their ordeal to the media. It was Dahmer and only Dahmer alone who committed the murders and no resident should be a victim for something that Dahmer committed without public knowledge in the privacy of his apartment. This was the truth that the residents wanted to get out to the public through the media.

Jeffrey Dahmer confessed to seventeen murders he committed over a period of thirteen years. His sexual deviance was a mental disorder that drove him to kill these young men for his own desires. The law enforcement community now had more extensive police work to carry out. They would conduct a thorough investigation of everything that Dahmer had told them during the confessions. It was now a State affair that involved the Sheriff's Department. They would employ the services of medical experts, psychology and psychiatric experts and acquire the legal support that was required to get the job done for the government. Firstly, the Medical Examiner would start doing the arduous work of identifying who was dead in Dahmer's apartment.

As manager most of my contacts with residents were strictly official, but I recall moments of eye to eye encounters with Jeffrey Dahmer both inside and outside the Oxford Apartments. I often saw him on his way to work at the Ambrosia Chocolate Company, located at North 6th Street at west Highland Blvd. in the City of Milwaukee.

I met him once at a Mc Donald's Restaurant during breakfast. Our conversation at this restaurant was part of my testimony in court during his trial, but I still had more to say about him out of court. Sometimes I saw him in the building and in his apartment when I went to inspect it for the nauseating smell that the residents complained about.

Jeffrey Dahmer was simply an ordinary person when you looked at him. You would never know that he might have killed someone just a few hours before. On other occasions I would pass him in the hallway or corridor. Sometimes I saw him down the street, but amazingly I was totally unaware that he was stalking me, even when he brought the beer to my apartment at Christmas of 1990.

About one month into the job in August of 1990, the building was engulfed in a stench that could be smelled three miles away. After a room by room search through all the vacant apartment units I found that nobody was dead in them. This was the stench from the decaying remains of Dahmer's first two victims that he murdered in his apartment before I started the job as new manager.

Therefore, the source of the smell was still unknown and I was not relaxed because it was bad for the business to present the apartments to potential residents. It meant that most shoppers might not return for a second tour of the apartment units. I was aiming at achieving a higher occupancy level, but the atmosphere inside the building hampered my efforts.

I received a hint from Pam who lived across from Jeffrey Dahmer that the smell was coming from his apartment. She was not specific, but this information triggered my first inspection of his apartment. Before the inspection, I called Dahmer to the office and asked him what the problem with his apartment was. He told me that his freezer had broken and all the meat in it, about $150 worth, was going rotten. I asked him why he didn't dump it if it was no longer edible. He honestly showed that he was sorry about the inconvenience the smell had caused in the building. He then apologized, giving the excuse that he did not have the time to do it because he worked on the third shift at his job. He said that as a result he slept all day, sometimes until it was time to go to work again. I could understand how it felt to work the night shift. He needed his rest in order to perform when he returned to work the next night.

My main concern at the time was the negative impact the stench would have on the business. It was a competitive business and the stench factor could make the difference between the decline or acceptance of an apartment by a customer. Comparable apartment units in a building with a pleasant atmosphere would be the choice over any apartment unit inside the Oxford Apartments. For a short period of time our traffic log indicated a down trend.

In all good faith, I offered to help Dahmer dump the rotten meat, so that there would be no more smell in and around the building. Jeffrey Dahmer declined my offer and promised to dump it by himself as soon as possible. Then I requested to come to inspect the freezer and he agreed, so we both headed to his apartment together. I had no idea what was going through his mind at that time, but he looked relaxed just like anyone else. When we arrived at his apartment, he opened the door and entered. As I stepped into his apartment for the inspection, the first thing Dahmer did was to draw my attention straight to the floor freezer, which he said was broken. He moved straight to it and opened it. I moved towards the direction of the freezer and looked from a close distance. I saw the freezer full to the rim with meat in plastic wraps. It looked like meat from the store. I was not suspecting any crime, so I didn't dig down below the top view. I didn't go looking into the nooks and crannies of Jeffrey Dahmer's apartment, because I did not suspect him of anything sinister. It was simply an inspection of a specific item.

If I had had any hint of a crime prior to the inspection, I would at least have looked into the taller refrigerator that came with the apartment. The taller refrigerator was next to the entrance and Dahmer almost certainly didn't want me to see what was in there.

He successfully manipulated my attention to focus on the freezer in question and nothing else. After this inspection of his broken freezer, I only thought of him as being a little slow to clean up the mess in his apartment. At that time, his unit was cleaner than an average apartment. I did not smell anything while I was there and he had a liquid deodorant, which I believe he used constantly. It was "Odor Away" contained in a clear plastic bottle. Following the first inspection, the air in and around the Oxford Apartments was pleasant again.

The serial killer needed a security alarm to keep him alert. Jeffrey Dahmer was so concerned with his security after the first inspection that he asked me if he needed the management company's permission to install a security alarm system in his apartment. I told him no, so he went and installed the alarm system in his apartment. I had seen elsewhere that some apartment residents had installed a security alarm system for their protection, so I didn't consider this to be unusual. The Badger security system would alert him in the event of someone intruding into his apartment. He would then rush back to the apartment to do whatever was necessary to maintain the security of his psychotic secret life.

It was still a risk for Dahmer to continue to murder his victims, even with the security alarm system to assist him, because an intruder might have seen what he didn't want to expose before he had time to reach his apartment. Dahmer could have made it easier for himself if he simply stopped murdering, but he was not able to do so because of the cumulative boost by the ghosts of his victims, which commanded him to do it "one more time" after each murder. Thus he had to continue killing until he was caught.

In an additional effort to protect his security, Jeffrey Dahmer also refused to take the incentive for lease renewal, even though he renewed his apartment lease when it was due. The incentive was a free carpet cleaning or a free painting of the apartment for any of the residents who renewed their apartment lease. The management also provided pest control maintenance for each apartment unit. His apartment was not yet scheduled for the fumigation before he was arrested. He might have declined the fumigation to avoid any intrusion into the graveyard in his apartment. As manager of the building, Dahmer's refusal to take the incentive was a cost saving. It enhanced the company's bottom line, so I saved it.

I would never have suspected that he refused to have his apartment cleaned, painted or fumigated for free because he was committing murders. He was playing the elusive game. He was too concerned with my presence as the person most likely to intrude into his apartment when he was not there. Taking this job therefore made me an instant threat to the man who had turned his apartment into a human slaughterhouse. I didn't know that my presence was a threat to him. I was only doing my job and not suspecting anyone of any crime.

I believe that Dahmer had wished to continue his murderous endeavors and had even hoped to stabilize it for the long term. The shrine of skulls that he was thinking of setting up where he lived at the Oxford Apartments was at the least not a temporary plan. Perhaps he even expected to find somebody to join him some day. He wanted to worship in that shrine as a revered person. But now with a new manager on site, Jeffrey Dahmer was not sure of his security on the crimes inside his apartment. He therefore made desperate attempts to eliminate the threat that I posed.

Dean Vaughn's murder in his own apartment inside the Oxford Apartments still remains a mystery. With everything that we now know Dahmer was capable of doing, do we believe that he was innocent of that murder? Remember that he lied on many occasions, so if Dahmer was not responsible for that murder, then who was? Is the person who did it still alive? If so, then there might be a small hope that Mr Vaughn's murder might be solved and the murderer brought to justice.

A dog named Cocaine, because she was completely white, resided in the adjacent property and often barked relentlessly late at night. Dogs have a sixth sense, so she may well have been trying to alert people to what Dahmer was doing in his apartment. Dahmer had chosen the north facing side of the building where there was no traffic at all, because the weed covering the ground had not been cleared for a long time. This was one of my job backlogs as manager of the building. In an effort to clean it up, I made eerie discoveries. It was only after the arrest that I had a gruesome notion of what the discoveries were.

Although I felt that I was shielded by divine protection,

I knew that I was working under an arrangement that I did not like. I wouldn't submit to blind obedience, because I felt that I could ignore any orders from anyone as long as they were not part of my job description. I had a copy of my "Job Description" in my desk at the office and I knew what was not in it. I considered anything outside of it as a distraction and I would not yield to the temptations that I understood were effective lures to disaster.

It was understood that Jeffrey Dahmer had lost his regular job as of the time of his arrest. He was not expecting to be arrested. Instead, he was expecting to be evicted when his rent became due in the coming month of August of 1991. Can you imagine what Jeffrey Dahmer would have done had he not been arrested? If Jeffrey Dahmer were to have moved all his belongings from his apartment after an eviction, he would have been overwhelmed. I think he may have left everything and simply walked away from it all.

If Dahmer had skipped after an eviction, the first person to have seen the gory nature of things in his apartment would have been me. It would have been the most sickening shock of my life. I would have been greatly traumatized. Fortunately, Jeffrey Dahmer was arrested before his time for eviction to avoid all the implications that might arise as a result. If the eviction scenario had occurred, it would have complicated matters for me as the manager of the building. I wonder what explanations I could have given to convince the world that I didn't know what Dahmer was doing in his own apartment.

If I were present in the building at the time of Dahmer's arrest, I believe that I would have been in serious trouble. Nobody would have believed that I had no knowledge of what Jeffrey Dahmer was doing in his own apartment. I believe that all those residents who felt threatened with my presence would have teamed up as my adversaries and falsely lied to incriminate me.

Getting away from the building totally unaware that something tragic was about to happen made it so miraculous. Imagine that you passed a point on the road just before a big tree fell behind you. That was how I felt about it.

Chapter 8

The Oxford as Characterized

At the point when the tragedy was uncovered, the consequences were so immense that everybody was affected in one way or another. The future of both the people currently living in the building as well as the business and the building itself was uncertain. I knew personally that my job as manager of the building would terminate. I knew that I would have to hang in there for as long as I could, or until something else came up.

On the morning following Dahmer's arrest, I didn't know what to expect on arrival at the Oxford Apartments. It was daunting, but I had to build the courage to return to the building on a day that I should have been off duty.

At the breaking of the news I couldn't imagine how that much of a tragedy struck my work site, the 49 unit apartment building that had the best of amenities to offer its residents. It was an attractive Apartment Complex, but as a result of what happened inside it, I started to characterize the Oxford Apartments as the "House of Horror and Sorrow," "The Valley of Death," "A Slaughterhouse" and "Frontline Property".

I was advised by my next door neighbors at my personal residence to be careful immediately after the arrest. They said that Jeffrey Dahmer had not yet been charged with the murders. The neighbors said that there was the possibility that Dahmer might name people in the building, so I needed to be careful.

To clarify it as I characterized the Oxford Apartments above; there in the House of Horror and Sorrow everyone suffered the horror of death except Dahmer the perpetrator. Every victim's loved ones were in sorrow.

Characterizing the Oxford Apartments as the Valley of Death draws from all the murders that were committed inside it, plus other deaths resulting from street violence around it. Some of the criminal activities taking place out there on the streets usually ended up around the Oxford Apartments; drugs, prostitution, thefts and gangs. All these activities sometimes involved conflicts in which guns were fired at rivals or snitches. Thus, many people were shot to death at one time or another in the neighborhood.

The Oxford Apartments was like a Slaughterhouse as I characterized it because the serial killer didn't just kill the victims and leave the bodies alone. He had further uses for the bodies, so he had to mutilate or chop up the bodies to separate the different parts, storing some and disposing of others. He cleaned and kept the skulls of his favorite victims. When asked how he cleaned the skulls recovered from his apartment, he said that he boiled them in Soilex and water solution for an hour in a large kettle.

Of course, there were always rumors. According to a news' reporter, there was one such rumor of a meat sale on the streets. At the start of investigations, a TV news' reporter, Mike Strehlow of CBS affiliate Channel 58, came to ask me whether I had any knowledge of meat being sold on the streets. I was surprised to know that such an activity like that went on in the building. It was something I could not imagine people doing.

In early spring of 1991, before Jeffrey Dahmer was arrested, I overheard a voice at the rear end of the building that shouted, "This is a Frontline Property". I was not sure to which property the voice was referring, but I walked to the back to see who might be there. Perhaps I could find out something from that voice. I found nobody when I looked out in the back. Could this be the voice of a ghost, or did someone really know what was going on in Dahmer's apartment? I remember a gang sign at the back or the east wall of the building. I didn't understand what it meant and I didn't worry about it. I reported it to my boss who asked me to paint over it and I did so.

As I viewed it, "Frontline Property" was the one on one single combat situation that each victim went through with the serial killer inside the building. It was not a combat in balance, because Dahmer rendered them unconscious before he continued with his routine. Dahmer was always the victor, until his encounter with Tracy Edwards.

When I finally arrived at the building, I found the crowds, many law enforcement vehicles, some unmarked and used by detectives and emergency vehicles completely surrounding the Oxford Apartments. I estimate that there were at least five hundred people crowded around. The crowds were so thick that if some sand were to be dropped on them from above, only a few grains would reach the ground. It took a great deal of effort to break through the thick crowd surrounding the apartment building. I then went into the office first and made a few phone calls. Then I went to my own apartment unit #309 before heading to the now infamous apartment unit #213.

I was apprehensive about going near the crime scene, so I initially walked passed Dahmer's apartment in the hallway. Initially, I didn't enter into Dahmer's apartment, even though all the discoveries of victims' body parts had been removed by the authorities for identification.

The crowd, a mix of curious on-lookers, seekers, victims' families, law enforcement people and their vehicles etc. jammed the site and made it look like a human circus. The mood inside the Oxford was one of uncertainty after the breaking news of these murders. The little love, trust and care that existed in the building was completely eclipsed by an overwhelming tension that made the entire City of Milwaukee feel like a balloon about to explode.

Nobody knew what was going to happen after the arrest and before the trial. The horror of what had occurred in the building kept many residents awake and weary in the first week of Dahmer's arrest. They abandoned their apartments and decided to flock together in one common area.

In the first floor lobby every night, the residents assembled close to the Leasing Office so that they could share the hope and warmth of one another until the City of Milwaukee Housing Authority moved them to a public housing complex. Almost every resident had expressed how they felt about their ordeal to the media. The "watch out" syndrome that had existed for a long time in the building just amplified the tension. Every resident was expecting the worst, but hoping for the best that could come out of this tragedy. We were intensely scared and couldn't wait to get out of the infamous building. The building entry door was kept locked at all times to prevent the entry by angered members of victims' families. Security was kept tight by armed guards of BMW Security Services. I remember some officers of this service provider like Tyrone, Derrick and Payton were among those who were in the line of fire one night from a drive-by automobile.

Everyone remained traumatized but alert until the Housing Authority of the City of Milwaukee completed its arrangements to relocate the live residents.

Immediately following the arrest, a joke was circulating the Chicago area. A friend of mine who commutes to work in Chicago told me about it. He quoted them as saying, "It's easy to buy a limb, like the radius and ulna of a hand, fold it into a brief case and walk if you go to Milwaukee. Some people made jokes about the residents, others made jokes about the building and others made jokes about Jeffrey Dahmer himself.

One day, we were sitting out the front of the building and some people on the sidewalk were talking, pointing at the Oxford Apartments and calling it the "Dahmer Building." Another day, some curiosity seekers pretended to be rental shoppers so that they could be allowed into the building. I later discovered that they were not serious renters, so I had to ask them to leave immediately. They didn't get what they wanted and from then on I learnt how to scan the people before letting them into the building. That didn't stop them. They then resorted to using the telephone to make prank calls to the Leasing Office of the Oxford Apartments to continue their jokes. I had to fill the vacancies, so I could not afford to miss any call coming to the office. Thus I continued to answer the phone whenever it rang.

Also, in order to work with the authorities at this time while the investigation was being conducted, I had to answer every call that came. Some of the calls might be from the main office or from the authorities. During one prank call, I discussed the rent amount and what was included and at the end the caller said, "I cannot pay an arm and a leg for your apartment." He laughed and then hung up the telephone.

Some callers asked for Jeffrey Dahmer, whilst others called pretending to be Jeffrey Dahmer himself. All the time that these prank calls were being made to the office, my job became very frustrating. However, the passing of time gradually wore down the frequency of these unwanted crass calls and comments. Likewise, the human traffic was significantly reduced and only a few visitors would stop at the Oxford Apartments and just look on.

I made an extra effort to obtain rental applications from some people who were serious about moving into the building. Housing was in great demand in Milwaukee at the time. More residents took occupancy after the macabre murders were discovered, but it took fifteen months to fill ten vacancies, as the renters came slowly for obvious reasons. In an effort to fill the vacancies, I used the publicity I had during my time on the witness stand to advertise the apartments as well as testify at Dahmer's trial.

My testimony at the trial later had a positive influence in marketing the rentals in the Oxford Apartments. Under a subpoena to appear at the trial, I appeared in court on February 11, 1992 to testify to Dahmer's sanity regarding the murders in his apartment. The trial was televised and many people who watched it saw me on television for the first time since Dahmer was arrested. Many people didn't know that this occasion was also one for the confirmation of my position as manager of the Oxford Apartments. There was a former manager that still lived in the manager's apartment and some residents to whom he rented the apartment still considered him to be the manager up to the point of Dahmer's arrest.

Since I was officially the manager of the building, I was the manager answering to the investigators and thus I was the one who was served with a subpoena to appear at the trial. Many people were surprised to see me testifying as the manager of the Oxford Apartments. The former manager now coveted the manager's position and even talked as manager over the phone to the Oprah Winfrey Show. One week after my testimony, I had another televised interview with senior reporter TV News Anchor, Bill Taylor of NBC affiliate Channel 4. Again, during that interview I positively advertised the Oxford Apartments for rentals.

From the time Dahmer was arrested for the murders he committed in his apartment inside the Oxford Apartments, the building was out of bounds to the general public. However, the law enforcement authorities were allowed access to conduct their investigative work on the case. Even the news media didn't have access after the night of the arrest. I personally turned down several television interviews at that time for two reasons. The first reason was because I was still employed and the second reason was because the trial was approaching. I wanted to talk only after the trial.

Among the law enforcement officers who had access to the building after it was out of bounds to the general public was the Lieutenant of Detectives, Ken Meuler, of the Milwaukee Police Department and a Special Agent, David L Collins, of the criminal investigation division of the Department of Justice of the State of Wisconsin. The two police officers who arrested Dahmer also came through the Oxford Apartments Office. They were curious about the missing manager when they arrested Jeffrey Dahmer.

After the first exodus, other members of the public and some news reporters were allowed access into the building. Among them was Mr Gerald J. Meyer, Director of Public Relations at Marquette University, located in the same neighborhood as the Oxford Apartments.

Barry Eggert of the United Press International stopped to talk to me about the tragedy in which we were caught. He referred me to Tracy Eggert, who was an attorney for the Fire and Police Union in the Milwaukee Police Department.

Civia Tamarkin, correspondent for People Magazine Weekly, Time Inc. Chicago, came to obtain some information from me. It was a screw up after she left and I didn't appear in the weekly magazine. Somehow, the reporter was confused as to who the real manager was, because the former manager was talking to the Oprah Winfrey TV Talk Show over the phone at about the same time. The former manager left the building during the first Exodus.

John Carpenter, a staff writer of the Daily Herald of Paddock Publications Inc., of Arlington Heights, Illinois, was one of the many newspaper writers who came to talk to me. I wasn't free to say very much to them because the Dahmer Trial was approaching and I didn't want to cause a liability to anyone. I thought it was best to testify first in court at the trial and then tell my story outside of court. Lee Bergquist, a reporter for the Milwaukee Sentinel, also came to the Oxford Apartments for a piece of information connecting the Dahmer murders. Arnaud Levy of the

France-Soir came from Paris but got nothing from me.

The editor in chief and Associate Publisher of the Milwaukee Community Journal, Mr Mikel Holt, along with Mr Art Kumbalek of The Shepherd Express, stopped by to seek original information. I recall that Art Kumbalek's slogan was, "Art for Art's sake". Both the Community Journal and the Shepherd Express are weekly news publications in Milwaukee. There was a discussion on the accuracy of information and the timely availability of such information regarding accurate reporting. They didn't get much from me since I could not afford to talk at that time because of the forthcoming trial. There might have been some people who knew something about Jeffrey Dahmer's activities and at this time they might have been watching out to cover themselves. I didn't want to have to tell anyone, "Don't say I told you." I preferred to wait for the trial before telling my story.

Jeff Fleming, news' reporter with NBC affiliate, WTMJ 4 TV, also stopped at the Oxford for the same information on the tragedy. We had a nice little chat, but I did not disclose much information, because the truth was that I really didn't know what had gone on in Dahmer's apartment prior to his arrest.

The building stood on North 25th Street without the name "Oxford Apartments" and the address "924" insignia on it, unlike before the arrest. The United States flag in front of the building was flying halfway up the sixty foot pole. While the main entry door was locked at all times, we still focused our attention on all entrances and exits. The rear exit on the second floor nearest to Dahmer's apartment was badly vandalized.

The remaining five families who didn't move during the first big exodus worked closely with the security guards to ensure that the building was safe and secure. The duty to fill the vacancies was a priority on my mind as manager, even though the odds had been raised by the recent tragedy and the consequent stigma attached to the building. In the immediate days following Dahmer's arrest, some of the people were so curious that they even parked their cars to walk to the building to ask for the permission to go and see Jeffrey Dahmer's apartment. They were serious about seeing the apartment, even though it was no different than any other comparable apartment. Such curiosity seekers were willing to give up a few bucks as a cover for a visit to the former home of the serial killer. When they got there, they would stare at the apartment door #213, feel it with their hands and sometimes weep or ask any of the residents who escorted them some really sensitive questions.

Meanwhile, Dahmer's trial was coming up. After preparations for Jeffrey Dahmer vs. The State of Wisconsin trial were completed, I received a Subpoena from the prosecution. The Subpoena was delivered personally to me to appear as witness for the prosecution in the trial. I was a little uneasy about it, because the only times I had been in court were for traffic tickets. I didn't know what this was all about. This court appearance requiring me to testify to what I might not know was a little too much for me, so I called my boss and expressed to him how bad I felt to be drawn into something relating to the trial of a serial killer. My boss reassured me and explained to me that it was normal procedure for a trial like this. He said I shouldn't worry about it.

Following the tragedy, my boss Don Gregory was expected to come to the building to show support from management, but he was unable to come until two days after Dahmer's arrest. This was a case of mass murder by a white man in the building under his supervision. My boss also happened to be a white man. Dahmer had killed more black men here in the building. I didn't blame my boss. It was such a sensitive situation where everyone had to be extra vigilant.

The City of Milwaukee was in shock from what had been revealed about these murders and the racist implications surrounding them. Mr Gregory rarely visited the building, because it was in the kind of neighborhood in which he did not feel comfortable. It was the same reason Dahmer's probation agent Donna Chester could not visit him, even when she was required to do so. It was explained later that the probation agent was overwhelmed with her workload. Many white people felt unsafe in that neighborhood, especially with the soaring crime rate. My boss was visibly shaken up when he first visited the building after Dahmer's arrest.

The residents could still feel the residual energy of Jeffrey Dahmer in the building, as though he were still living there and so continued to have nightmares. We knew that this was a terrible time for all the residents, but they needed to be more realistic about the tragedy. No condition was permanent in life anyway. I learnt that change was the only thing that had been permanent and this was one of those changes that we had to deal with.

Shit happens, as the saying goes, some of which we have no control over, such as this tragedy. Therefore we could ride through both the rough and smooth times with courage to overcome the resultant consequences, even in such dire circumstances. However, there was so much tension and fear amongst the residents that most of them could not wait to move out. It was very disappointing to experience such horror in a place that many of the residents called home. There was too much sorrow, too much fear and too much harassment to continue living in the Oxford Apartments at that time.

As a result of being blamed for what happened in Dahmer's apartment, the residents therefore launched a serious public relations campaign. The aim of the campaign was to convince the world that Jeffrey Dahmer alone was responsible for the murders in his apartment. He did not have a partner in crime, nor any association with anyone who had any knowledge of what was taking place in his apartment.

Metropolitan Associates, the property management company operating the Oxford Apartments, had to give some rental incentives to retain the current and terrified residents. As was typical of this type of business, such incentives might be in the form of rent reduction, lower qualifying ratios, waiver of security deposit or the first month rent free and so on. The management thus reduced the rent from $307 to $250 per month for one bedroomed units.

No Efficiency units were occupied immediately after the relocation of all the residents. Some were rented later for $200 per month, reduced from $250 per month. The added cost of security services in the light of reduced revenues just didn't make a good economic sense.

Many minority residents in the neighborhood felt that they didn't have to respect the law enforcement officers who didn't respect their rights. There had been incidents in which clashes resulted between police and minority citizens who decided to fire the shots back at the police, killing them too. Some police officers took the law into their hands. When they took their oath of office as law enforcement officers, they pledged to work according to that oath before they were given their badges.

Unfortunately, some of the police officers did not abide by the oath when they came into contact with some minority citizens in these rough neighborhoods. Consequently, there was some distrust between some residents and the police. I had observed police officers who were called to the Oxford Apartments for various reasons, who simply sat in the squad car in the front of the building. I would then go to them to let them into the building before they walked to the apartment unit from where the call for police assistance came.

In theory, the first of the two-part oath required the officer to faithfully enforce the constitution of the United States, the laws of the State of Wisconsin and the city of Milwaukee. The second part is an oath to a code of ethics which reads, in part, as follows:

As a law enforcement officer, my fundamental duty is to serve mankind; to safeguard lives and property; to protect the innocent against deception, the weak against violence or disorder, and to respect the constitutional right of all persons to liberty, equality and justice.

I will never act officiously or permit personal feelings, prejudices, animosities or friendships to influence my decisions. With no compromise for crime and with relentless prosecution and appropriately without fear or favor, malice or ill will, never employing unnecessary force or violence and never accepting gratuities.

I recognize the badge of my office as a symbol of public faith, and I accept it as a public trust to be held so long as I am true to the ethics of police service. I will constantly strive to achieve these ideals and objectives, dedicating myself to my chosen profession in law enforcement...

On the ground in practice, the officers face circumstances unanticipated by the requirements of the oath. The officer then has to decide quickly how best to handle the situation, especially if his life is in danger. The officer has the right to shoot at a subject or suspect in an incident if he feels that his life is in danger. There had been a few incidents of fatal shootings by police in the city, especially in the minority or inner city sections of Milwaukee.

Law Enforcement officers were usually brutal on minorities and they got away with it a lot of the time. The attitude on the part of the police officers was changing, but at a snail's pace.

In this neighborhood, the need to survive was stronger

than fear. Such minority residents would be in and out of jail again and again to do more crime if that was what it took to survive. In the neighborhood streets, the anger and frustration of the young black men showed on their faces. That was how the Justice System made them feel about their society. It had become so bad that some disgruntled citizens of the minority neighborhoods made bold statements such as, "I don't mind going to jail but you, you'll be dead."

An article from the Public Policy Forum indicated that unemployment in the black community stayed high in Milwaukee. This news was reported in the Metro section of the Milwaukee Journal of Thursday December 7, 2006. It is therefore apparent that this young black man threatening to buy a gun while talking tough to Jeffrey Dahmer knew what he was talking about. Dahmer might have told him something he didn't like. Dahmer didn't always get all the people he propositioned. Maybe Dahmer propositioned the young black male, who consequently felt angry at him. I believe that most of his victims were the kind that always liked to take from others for personal gain.

There might have been some people who didn't belong in that group whom Jeffrey Dahmer must have tried to lure to his apartment, but with no success. He learnt to look for the most vulnerable people who saw him as a sex partner in return for money. Dahmer's victims must have believed that he would give them his money as he promised them at the time of contact. It's always wise to remember that in America there's no such thing as a free lunch. I've never found one before.

The Oxford must have been a gang enclave of some sort because of a visible gang insignia marking their territory. I was not sure who belonged to the gang controlling the territory, but from the intimidations and physical altercation that I experienced, it was clear that they had no fear of the law. For instance, the guy who had the physical altercation with me actually kicked the hands of the female police officer who was holding and opening up a drugs' package that fell from his pocket as he attempted to conceal it. I was shocked somebody could do that. There is always the potential for violence when dealing with such people who have the audacity to attack a police officer. They were hardened by their membership in an organized gang of thugs, drug lords and bangers who terrorized the neighborhood. The dominant gang in the neighborhood was the Vice Lords.

Chapter 9

A 911 Good Samaritan

Jeffrey Dahmer had his own close calls when police came into contact with him. He was good at handling the moment even when he was under pressure, like the time when he encountered a police officer just after committing his first murder. He had the ability to skillfully conceal any signs of panic or guilt. He showed police a good face by the way he spoke and the way he looked to best present himself. He showed each time that he was quite a responsible person.

Police had been in his apartment a couple of times before he was finally arrested. They had been in Dahmer's small apartment for the investigation of the murder of Dean Vaughn who was found dead in his own apartment in the Oxford complex. Again, they visited Dahmer on May 26, 1991, following a 911 Emergency call by two good Samaritans after a 14-year-old Laotian boy had escaped from Dahmer after being drugged. The officers took the boy back to the apartment where Dahmer convinced them that the boy was his house guest. To the police officers the boy looked like an adult and claimed that they didn't suspect that anything untoward had occurred. Dahmer assumed his usual composed persona, successfully fooling the officers, even though a corpse lay in his bedroom. After the officers had left, Dahmer killed the boy.

The 911 call was made by two ladies in the neighborhood who saw a naked boy who was running, but kept falling to the ground as he tried to escape with his life. The boy was bruised, disoriented and could not speak English well. When Dahmer was in custody, he told the detectives that the boy was no longer speaking English. He kept speaking his native Laotian language, so the officers could not understand him. He was a Laotian whose family moved to the United States in 1980 for safety after the Communists invaded and won the war in Indochina. The people of Cambodia, Laos and Vietnam had to flee their countries to the United States for refuge. The boy, Konerak, was an aspiring soccer star on his way to a practice session, but stopped at the Grand Avenue Mall for a moment. The Mall was one of Dahmer's hunting grounds where he sighted the young boy that night.

Dahmer made his usual pitch that was hard to resist. He invited the boy to his apartment with the promise of money for posing in front of his camera, watching videos and having sex. The boy had been with Dahmer before this impromptu meeting, so it was fairly easy to convince him to do what Dahmer wanted.

The boy fell for Dahmer's charming enticement and accompanied Dahmer to his apartment. It was there that Dahmer who drugged him, had oral sex and left him in the apartment to buy more beer from a neighborhood tavern. Dahmer liked to drink a lot while he dismembered the body of his victim. While he went for the beer the boy woke up and tried to escape. The boy ran outside to the street without even thinking about putting his clothes on. He was naked and disoriented and kept falling as he tried to run for his life.

In the warm morning, following this boy's brush with Dahmer, one of the old residents of the Oxford Apartments called me. We walked to the rear exit where he showed me some blood splattered on the ground near the parking stalls behind the building. He also pointed to some blood stains on the rear exit door of the building. If anyone in the building knew about the little boy's brush with Dahmer, then perhaps they would have kept a close check on Dahmer. Sadly, nobody in the building knew about it.

108

The source of the blood remained a mystery, but we heard the sound of gun shots that were very common in the neighborhood at nights. We had seen the blood trails on the sidewalks and sometimes even a dead human on the street. These sightings were common trademarks of the tough and minority neighborhoods. There was nothing we could do about the blood behind the Oxford Apartments, because we didn't know what might have happened the night before. It was only later realized that it was the blood of the Laotian boy.

Anything can happen in a neighborhood where people simply mind their own business. In that neighborhood, some of the people did what they felt like doing, whether or not it was legal. There were usually no clues after something bad happened. They couldn't afford to become tired of watching out. Somehow it was part of their survival. They didn't trust anyone, including the police.

A lady who felt uneasy about what she had heard about the little Laotian boy made a follow up effort to contact the police, trying to find out what happened to the boy after the police left. She was expecting the police officers to have custody of the boy and felt that the little boy was not safe with Dahmer. Glenda Cleveland, a senior relative of the two ladies who made the first 911 Emergency, decided to follow up with her own phone call to the police. She made this effort with the hope of getting the police back to the Dahmer's apartment to check it again. She was positive that something had gone really wrong, but she got no attention because the officers didn't take her seriously.

She was a member of a minority group and black. She was sure of what had happened at the scene between the boy and Dahmer. She felt that leaving the boy in that condition with Dahmer was wrong. She thought that the boy might be in danger. And she was right.

The officers believed that they had done their job and that everything was in order to the best of their knowledge.

109

The officers were so impressed with Dahmer in the way he presented himself that they didn't go for a records' check on him. There was something about him they didn't know and didn't want to know. The officers were preoccupied with Dahmer's charisma, his polite demeanor and his polished English language, so they forgot to keep up the vigilance associated with street policing. If they had checked the record on this tall white man, those officers would have known that Jeffrey Dahmer was a convicted felon on probation after serving part of his sentence for molesting a boy. Tragically, this boy Konerak happened to be a younger brother of the boy Dahmer had molested in the previous incident. This was only a coincidence; Jeffrey Dahmer didn't know about their relationship.

In addition, the boy didn't show any desire to leave when the police were there. He was sitting on the sofa while the police talked to Dahmer. The boy didn't speak at all and he was still disoriented from the drugs Dahmer slipped into his drink. Perhaps the boy was afraid to let his family know about his own secret adventures for money; teenage prostitution.

Unfortunately, Dahmer was not going to forgive him for trying to get away. The victims became victims because they violated Dahmer's rule not to leave without his consent. This young boy's case was the most tragic of all the murders committed by the serial killer, because Dahmer had victimized the same family twice. The first was the most dreaded sexual molestation of one child and the second was the torture and killing of another, Konerak Sinthasomphone.

After midnight of May 26, 1991, Nicole Childress and her cousin Sandra Smith saw the boy in distress and while Sandra approached to help him directly, Nicole went to a pay phone and called 911 Emergency. What happened following this call would reveal how police protection applies to different communities in Milwaukee, Wisconsin.

The transcripts of the first 911 call to the police relating this little boy's brush with Jeffrey Dahmer were made available from the investigation. The call was anonymous because the caller didn't give their name. Maybe the lady making the call was so distressed by what she had seen that she was more intent on giving the operator details about the boy's condition and forgot to give her name. Maybe the operator didn't ask for her name. But either way the call was taken.

The **Operator 71** took the call as follows:

Childress:
Hi. I'm on 25th and State, and there is this young man. He's butt-naked. He has been beaten up. He is very bruised up. He can't stand up. He has no clothes on. He is really hurt. I got no coat on. I'd just seen him. He needs help.

Operator: Where--Where is he?

Childress: 25th and State. At the corner of 25th and State
Operator: He's just on the corner of the Street?

Childress: Yeah, he's in the middle of the street. He fell out. We are trying to help him.

Operator: Operator: Okay. And he's unconscious right now?

Childress: They're getting him. He's bruised up. Somebody must have jumped on him and stripped him or whatever.

Operator: Okay. Let me put the Fire Department on the line. They'll send an ambulance.

Just stay on the phone, okay?

Childress: Okay.

The **Fire Department** answered.

Childress: Can you send an ambulance to the corner of 25th and State?

Fire Operator: What's the problem?

Childress: This butt-naked young boy, or man, or whatever. He's butt-naked. He's been beaten up real bad and he's fell out and people are trying to help him stand up. He can't stand up. He is butt-naked. He has no clothes on. He is very hurt.

Fire Operator: Is he awake?

Childress: He ain't awake. They're trying to get him to walk. But he can't walk straight. He can't even see straight. Every time he stands up, he falls out.

Fire Operator: 25th and State?

Childress: Yeah, a one way.

Fire Operator: Okay

Childress: Okay. Bye.

While these ladies continued to help the boy on the ground, Jeffrey Dahmer returned from his trip to the tavern for more beer. He saw his escaping victim, the little boy on the street, now surrounded by these ladies. He intervened immediately, trying to get the boy. Sandra was yelling at Dahmer not to hurt the boy when the police car Squad 36 of the Milwaukee Police Department arrived at the scene just before the despatched Fire Truck. The personnel of the Fire Truck were trained to handle any medical emergency and so they provided a blanket to cover the little boy. Perhaps if they were allowed to give their input as to really helping this boy, they might have taken him to a detoxification center to purge him of the drug. They didn't. The Fire personnel were asked to leave as their services were no longer required. Since the police had the duty to enforce the law, they had more power in the community than the firemen. The order was obeyed and the firemen left the scene.

The police were already feeling sorry for Jeffrey Dahmer with the way they saw the two ladies double teamed him over this little boy. Dahmer, being a white man and living in the tough neighborhood where most of the residents were black, had the favor of the white police officers. Among other things, the officers already thought that Dahmer was going through hell for living among the black people who they viewed now as having a serious altercation with the white man. At this time, the police felt that those ladies who were yelling at Dahmer were hysterical and belligerent because they kept talking and yelling without listening to anything that the police officers had to say. These women knew about the minority experience with the police in the City of Milwaukee. They were yelling because in their mind this was one more untrusting encounter with the police. Hence the police officers dismissed them from the scene by merely threatening to take them downtown if they did not leave. The officers promised to deal with the incident in a professional manner, but like most other promises, this was not kept either.

These police officers were considered to be very capable officers in the police department, with extensive years of service. In fact these veteran officers were training new officers about the ropes of street policing. With all the notoriety that these officers gained from their department, the reality is that they hadn't seen anything yet if they hadn't encountered Jeffrey Dahmer. Jeffrey Dahmer was a man with a deliberate offensive at the justice system. He had told lies each time he encountered a law enforcement officer and got away quite easily because they were influenced by his looks. He was smart, he spoke intelligently and he was white, an advantage that gave him the best shield. The cool, calm and calculated Dahmer was able to distract their attention from doing their job properly on this particular incident of Konerak Sinthasomphone.

These ladies returned to their home frustrated with the police who disposed of them even before questioning them as witnesses of the incident. Sandra Smith told her mother, Glenda Cleveland, aunt of Nicole Childress who made the 911 Emergency to help that boy. These black women thought that it was unfair for the police to ignore them and yet still accept what the tall white man told them.

Those Good Samaritans felt that the boy was unsafe in the company of Jeffrey Dahmer in the condition that he was in. The story she heard from her relatives who witnessed everything about that little boy didn't sit well with Glenda. She was very concerned with what had transpired in her neighborhood that night. Hence, she was determined to follow up with her own phone calls to the police. After dismissing the women from the scene, the police officers turned to Dahmer who pleaded to look after his house guest. The police officers then escorted both Dahmer and boy back to the Oxford Apartments to ensure that this was simply a domestic squabble between homosexual lovers as Dahmer insisted.

Dahmer told the officers that his guest behaved like this whenever he'd drunk too much. He even gave the officers the wrong name of his guest. The police officers didn't make any checks, so nothing was uncovered. Once they all entered into the apartment, Jeffrey Dahmer showed the boy's photo when he was posing for Dahmer's Polaroid camera wearing bikini outfits. The boy's clothes were placed on the armrest of the sofa on which he was sitting quietly. He was still disoriented from the drug that Dahmer had put in his drink and he was not talking while the police officers were there. The boy did not say anything to dispute Dahmer's claims and whenever he did say anything, he was not speaking in English. Maybe he was scared about his family finding out about his secret adventure for money. He already had a police record for teenage prostitution, but nothing that the officers saw gave them any reason to disbelieve Dahmer's story.

The police officers returned to their squad car, from where they reported back to base that a mission had been accomplished. From police transcript, the report went as follows:

Officer: Intoxicated Asian, naked male, was returned to his sober boyfriend. Their duty on this assignment is completed and so they were ready for more calls.

Officer: 10-4 (Ten-Four.) It'll be a minute. My partner is going to get deloused at the station.

Some laughter followed each radio transmission.

Glenda Cleveland didn't like what her daughter and her niece who were present at the scene told her. They were not satisfied with the police returning the boy to Jeffrey Dahmer. Glenda then followed up with another 911 emergency phone call to the police department. She wanted to know what had happened with the boy.

Following an internal investigation of the case after Dahmer was arrested, the department released this transcript.

The **"911" Operator 55** took the call as follows:

Operator: Milwaukee Emergency Operator 55. May I help you?

Cleveland: Yes, yes. A moment ago.

Operator: How long ago was it?

Cleveland: About ten minutes ago, my daughter and my niece flagged down a police squad when they walked up on a young child being molested by a male guy and, uh, no information or anything was taken, but they were taken to downtown. I was wondering, I mean, I'm sure further information must be needed. The boy was naked and bleeding.

Operator: OK.

Cleveland: Have you had any reports of that? Anyone been brought down like that?

Operator: OK, you know where it happened at?

Cleveland: The squad car was #68 that they flagged down and they picked him up.

Operator: Um, huh.

Cleveland: And my daughter and my niece said, that you know, their names or nothing was taken down or whatnot, but the fact is that a crime was being committed. I'm sure you must need, you know, some kind of information based on it.

Operator: OK, let me get you someone to talk to.

Cleveland: OK. (She waited on hold till another operator answered)

(Operator 66 comes on the line)

Cleveland: I was calling to see if a squad car #68 brought someone in, a child being molested by an adult that was witnessed by my daughter and my niece?

Operator: Where was this?

Cleveland: 26th and Highland, Sandra? At 25th and State St. OK, they was the ones that witnessed it and flagged the policeman down, and you know, told about the situation, but their names or nothing was taken down and I'm wondering if this situation was being handled. Because what it indicated was, this was a male child being raped and molested by an adult. It was.

Operator: Where did this happen?

Cleveland: Around 25th and State.

Operator: OK. Now which district are you calling?

Cleveland: What district? They were flagged down. The policemen were flagged down.

Operator: OK. If that's where it happened, then they were in that district. Hang on one second.

Cleveland: Cleveland: OK. (She was put on hold again awaiting the next voice while the call is being transferred.)

Operator: District Three.

Cleveland: Yes, I was wondering earlier this evening about 15 minutes ago, my daughter and my niece flagged down a squad car, number 68, whereas they witnessed a young child being molested by an adult.

Operator: Um huh.

Cleveland: And has this been reported?

Operator: Where was this happening at?

Cleveland: 25th and State.

Operator: 25th and State.

Cleveland: Yes.

Operator: Hold on. Let me check.

Cleveland: OK. (For a third time she is again put on hold while the call is transferred to a specific police officer's telephone.)

Officer: Police.

Cleveland: Yes. There was a squad car number 68 that was flagged down here earlier this evening, about 15 minutes ago.

Officer: That was me.

Cleveland: Yeah. What happened? I mean my daughter and my niece witnessed what was going on. Was anything done about this situation? Do they need their names, or…

Officer: No, I don't need them.

Cleveland: Or information, or anything from them?

Officer: No, not at all.

Cleveland: You don't?

Officer: Nope. It was an intoxicated boyfriend of another boyfriend.

Cleveland: Well, how old was this child?

Officer: It wasn't a child. It was an adult.

Cleveland: Are you sure?

Officer: Yup.

Cleveland: Are you positive? That's because this child doesn't even speak English. My daughter has dealt with him before, seen him on the street, you know...

Officer: Yeah, No, uh, he's uh, he's.....it's all taken care of, Ma'am.

Cleveland: Isn't this... I mean, what if he's a child and not an adult? I mean, are you positive this is an adult?

Officer: Ma'am, Ma'am. Like I explained to you, it's as positive as I can be.

Cleveland: Oh. I see...

Officer: I can't do anything about someone's sexual

preferences in life, and if…

Cleveland: Well, no, I'm not saying anything about that, but it appeared to have been a child. This is why...

Officer: No.

Cleveland: No?

Officer: No, he's not.

Her effort to save a little boy in jeopardy failed. A few days later, she was reading a newspaper column about a missing child. Glenda Cleveland was touched by this news' information about a missing child and, reflecting upon what had transpired since the little boy's incident, her instinct moved her to make yet another phone call. This time she called the FBI instead of the police. The matter was local and therefore out of its jurisdiction. The FBI, however, called the police department concerning an incident of a 911 call and the lady that had been following up.

The police officer who talked with the FBI admitted to having knowledge of it and promised to contact the lady. Glenda said that she had no call by anyone from the police department regarding the incident. There was no police report on record about the incident of the 911 call that was made on behalf of the boy. Two months later, following Dahmer's arrest, everyone realized that the police officers involved in the incident of that little boy were wrong and that Glenda Cleveland and her daughter and niece were right. It was just a matter of time for the truth to be uncovered, at which time the police department would regret the way that incident was handled, but would naturally be on the defensive.

What was discovered in Dahmer's apartment, among others, was the skull of that young boy identified from dental records and the photo from which Dahmer himself identified his victim. Dahmer told police that he strangled the boy to death as soon as the police officers left the apartment building. He then had sex and took a few photos before and after dismemberment. He kept the skull as a trophy among other skulls and other unclean heads found in his personal freezer in the apartment.

Glenda Cleveland, despite her efforts, never got the attention she intended for the young boy, but she was commended by the head of the FBI in Milwaukee and from the mayor of Milwaukee, John Norquist, for her role as a good citizen in that incident. The mayor then advised other citizens to do likewise. In other words, the mayor wanted all citizens to follow Glenda's example in watching out for one another. People must depart from the attitude of not caring, because it is not happening to them. Minding one's own business could result in another Dahmer-like tragedy.

Dahmer took advantage. Nobody paid enough attention to be able to detect a crime that was happening right under their noses, even though they smelled the smell and complained about it. When my boss and I were walking through the hallway of the second floor, I told him that there was this awful smell that the residents had complained about. I told him that this was the second time the smell had been noticed and that it was coming from the apartment #213. So my boss asked me, "Did you smell it?" I answered yes and asked him, "Didn't you smell it?" It sounded funny, but it was real. This interaction with my boss took place four days before Dahmer's arrest. The boss was not as relaxed when he came to the property in this neighborhood as when he was at a property out in the suburbs. He didn't want to be there for too long, so he didn't do anything about the complaint of the smell.

It was for the same reason that Dahmer's probation agent did not visit him, even though that was a requirement of the maximum supervision that Dahmer was supposed to have. She was scared to come to the neighborhood. Between the time that I notified my boss about the smell and the time that Dahmer was arrested, he killed Joseph Bradehoft who was reported missing on Friday July 19, 1991. Thus, Joseph Bradehoft became the last victim on Dahmer's death roll behind the closed door of #213 inside the Oxford Apartment.

At this point I consider *A Tribute to Dahmer's Victims*, which goes thus:

May their souls rest in peace. They are in heaven because their killer took away all their sins and they are at peace with God in heaven. They had the credit for the combined efforts of their ghosts in "Ghostworks" to push Dahmer to continue to murder until he was exposed and arrested. That was a mission that was accomplished by "Ghostworks". No serial killer stops himself and confesses to the murders until he is caught. This is the effect of "Ghostworks" on his mind once he starts to murder.

The effect of "Ghostworks" on the killer's mind even becomes more intense with the accumulation of victims. The ghosts tell the killer, "One more time" after each murder. That is why the killer continues until he is caught. Then the confessions follow; who was murdered, how they died and so forth.

I was not surprised that my boss was shaken like everyone else when the news about one of the apartment residents using the building as a slaughterhouse reached the public.

Residents using rental apartments for illegal activities caused such a widespread problem in the community that the government closed down any such property. Some properties found to be drug houses or prostitution parlors were closed down. These were lesser crimes than murder, so the Oxford Apartments was closed down.

Glenda's desire for the police to go back to check out Dahmer's apartment could have saved others who became victims after the young boy, if not the young boy himself. The appropriate time to have saved him would have been the moment Dahmer started speaking on the boy's behalf. The police officers didn't know either the boy or Jeffrey Dahmer and so in order to believe in their statements, their credibility should have been proven first. The officers should have run their names through the computer to establish whether they'd been in trouble before.

The record would show the officers how credible these two strangers had been in the community. Good police officers should always check on citizens with whom they come into contact to see if they have a warrant for an arrest, or they are committing some violation of the law, as was the case with Jeffrey Dahmer. The officers assumed that Jeffrey Dahmer was right, because he was white and they allowed him to speak on behalf of the boy.

Those police officers would have found that Jeffrey Dahmer was a convicted felon who was on probation. He was thus violating his probation when he had a minor as his homosexual lover. They didn't check the records because he was white and the boy was black or non-white race in the City of Milwaukee. They believed Dahmer over anything that anyone else had to say, even at the scene of the incident. Citizens at the scene who had called the 911 emergency phone line to help the boy were dismissed from the scene because in Milwaukee the rights of minorities are not respected. In the judgment of those police officers, Dahmer was superior to them and their opinions were of no value.

After Dahmer's arrest, it appeared as though those police officers helped the serial killer in taking the young boy's life. The police officers took Dahmer's skillfully worded statements and left the boy in his custody. No reports were filed regarding the 911 Emergency call of May

123

26, 1991 to help a young boy in danger. The police trusted Dahmer at first sight and didn't do their job properly. They say that looks deceive and in Jeffrey Dahmer's case, this proved to be true. Nobody would ever know from his appearance that Jeffrey Dahmer was a serial killer or even a criminal for that matter. Studies have shown that criminals do possess certain facial characteristics, but to the untrained eye, they may look like any other normal, law-abiding citizen. It is only when the criminal or serial killer is caught that a portrait becomes known, because then his face is exposed.

Sometimes people pretend to be bad as a way to psychologically fend off other bad guys. It is the secret bad guys like Jeffrey Dahmer who are the most dangerous, because they deceive people.

Had those police officers conducted checks, they would have found that Dahmer was on probation for an offence involving another boy. Had they searched Dahmer's apartment a little more thoroughly, they would have seen Tony Hughes' body lying in the bedroom. Inaccurate assumptions led to the bad decision the police officers made with Dahmer that night. Their best bet would have been to keep the boy in their custody for detoxification, because they knew that he was disoriented and was unable to stand erect. The best solution for the boy's apparent condition was detoxification.

Chapter 10

City in a Triangle of Conflicts

The story of Dahmer's arrest following the gruesome discoveries in his stinking one bedroomed apartment had spread through the world. The City of Milwaukee seemed to have been placed on the world map by most of the media channels in order to get the ratings for their stations. There was fierce competition for all the information relating to the story of the serial killer. In the city itself, there were serious conflicts throughout the various communities over the crimes that Jeffrey Dahmer committed. It was like a triangle of conflicts. Everything that was revealed after Dahmer was arrested opened up some long standing grievances over police insensitivity to the ethnic minorities in the City of Milwaukee.

The Triangle of Conflicts is illustrated in the diagram below. In the diagram, MPD means Milwaukee Police Department, MINO means Minority groups and GPUBLIC means General Public:

* MPD

MINO *   * GPUBLIC

In the Milwaukee Police Department, the union and its president were in an opposite stance against the Police Chief Philip Arreola. On the social scene, homosexuals tried to show opposition to the way they felt they were being treated, such as gay bashing by heterosexuals. And then across the entire city, black citizens and other minorities were totally outraged by the Dahmer murders that took away so many of their loved ones. They felt that the Justice System helped him, so they were against the Police Department. The blacks at that point in time were against the whites, because Dahmer was a white man and he had killed more black men than men in any other racial group. The police officers who ignored them during their intervention and gave away the little Laotian boy to Dahmer were white and the judge who gave Dahmer probation, instead of a hard prison term for the sexual assault of a child, was also white.

Before the sexual assault case, Dahmer had already murdered four people and never been apprehended, a fact the judge didn't know. Dahmer used every advantage that he had to continue to kill people. He understood how to handle each contact he had with the police. First he would admit he was wrong and then apologize. Next he made a promise to do better. He was outright manipulative and slipped through many close calls with the law.

Apparently, the black communities felt that this bad white guy had gotten away even with all the red flags of his criminal nature because he was white. The law enforcement officers and the judge were white and they treated Dahmer differently than others who were not white. In other words, the actions of the authorities had long standing racial overtones.

Back in 1981, Ernest Lacy, a young black man died in police custody. It was later found that he did not commit the crime and the black community was outraged. The uproar that resulted in that death set off protests and rallies in the City of Milwaukee which later settled the case out of court for $0.6 million to the Lacy Family. In June 1983, one police officer was dismissed and four others were suspended for their roles in the arrest of Ernest Lacy. Our great City of Milwaukee continued to be in a shock on the Jeffrey Dahmer murders.

In an attempt to hold his divided city together intact, the mayor, John Norquist, agreed with the true and popular claim that Dahmer would have been treated differently if he were a black man. He would have been locked up in prison long before now. Jeffrey Dahmer murdered more minority males in his murder spree because he was allowed to get out or get away each time he had a brush with the law.

Thus, all the commotion in the city started in 1991 as a consequence of what Jeffrey Dahmer did and how he did it. The murder and dismemberment of seventeen men, including two 14-year-olds, angered many people when it was disclosed that even after he had been in contact with the police officers who were at the scene, nothing was done to stop him. The fact that police officers had also been in Dahmer's apartment, but failed to do their job correctly to expose him, was like a bombshell on the minority communities who were most affected.

There was outrage from all sides and several allegations were made against opposing factions. The final blame ended up with the Justice System citing several incidents in the life of Jeffrey Dahmer when he could have been stopped. But that didn't happen because Dahmer was white, the accusers claimed. It showed that for the sake of race, black or minority people do not have equal protection under the law. This was the same feeling expressed by the Reverend Jesse Jackson when he said, "All that we want is equal protection under the law. The game should be played under one set of rules."

If the Laotian boy were a white boy under the circumstances and Jeffrey Dahmer were a black man when the police had the contact with them, there's no doubt that Dahmer would have been checked out on the records as the first duty in street policing.

Early in August of 1991, it was disclosed that the three police officers in contact with the little boy actually escorted him back to Dahmer's apartment from where he had escaped. The Milwaukee Police Chief Philip Areola suspended those officers John Balcerzak, Joe Gabrish and

Protubran immediately from duty with pay, pending an investigation.

From here, the public shifted the blame of the murders from Jeffrey Dahmer to the Milwaukee Police Department, which had a history of insensitivity to minority rights. The President of the Police Union, Bradley DeBraska, thought that such investigation should begin before the suspension of the officers, instead of the other way round. The president felt like the Chief had reached a guilty verdict before a trial. It is said that every man is innocent until proven guilty. He went on to organize the union members to cast a vote of no confidence in the Chief. It was not successful because of the public outrage over the poor work the police did on the 911 call for the Laotian boy. The president of the police union did not understand that it was a repetition. Police insensitivity involving minorities surfaced again, angering many people.

Good policing only happens when there is the cooperation of the people in the communities. That cooperation had been lacking because of how they felt about the police. During the early days of Dahmer's arrest, many neighborhood residents complained that either the police didn't want to act, or they couldn't act in the correct way with minority residents. If these communities did not have confidence in police protection, then they tended to do it themselves. This would create more problems that would divide the city even more. The government had done its best to make the laws to protect human rights, but the individual enforcement agents still enforce the law in a discriminatory fashion. That was why there came up the complaints about police insensitivity in handling minority problems.

Thus the Mayor intervened in what was going on in the Police Department to support his Police Chief based on the public outcry of police insensitivity to minority problems. What had been exposed of police conduct during

Dahmer's contact with them was indeed damaging. It was a time when the mayor was facing an election and it was critical for him to say something that could pull the people together rather than push them apart. The mayor went further to plead for calm along with other community leaders, primarily from the minority communities. He told everyone, "The greatest tragedy of all would be for the city to be torn apart."

The mayor understood the rage that existed, especially in the neighborhood most affected by the Jeffrey Dahmer murders. Like the mayor, everyone knew that this was the most traumatic time in the history of Milwaukee, so he called for a citywide "day of healing" on Sunday August 11, 1991 and buttressed it by an announcement of the availability of psychological counseling for the communities affected by the tragedy.

The Hispanic community expressed their outrage when the Police Chief Philip Areola was opposed by his police department, because he fired the three police officers who had left the intoxicated naked boy with the serial killer without checking on him. Had the police officers in that incident had done their job the way it was supposed to be done, Jeffrey Dahmer would have been arrested instantly, because he was already on probation for child molestation.

The Police Chief had popular support from his Hispanic community amongst others. Views and opinions over some issues in society might differ, but the views on what is morally right or wrong are very much in unison. If the police had followed procedure when they came into contact with this cool and calculated serial killer, a young boy would have been saved. The fact that they admitted being manipulated by Jeffrey Dahmer, demonstrated that they were negligent and allowed his color and appearance to take priority over following the correct procedure. That set off the turmoil that raged in the city through the entire period before the trial.

Quite often, unfavorable legal consequences make some people blind to the truth. Law suits and financial implications are sometimes the reason some people tend to shield themselves from the truth. It was time for someone to step up to the truth, hence Chief Philip Areola's action on those police officers. The chamber director Maria Monreal-Cameron of the Hispanic Chamber of Commerce pledged her support for the chief saying, "A vast majority of the Hispanic community is behind him. We think that he is doing a great job under the circumstances." The director also called for better relations between the police and the Hispanic community. She admitted that prejudice and racism in the Milwaukee Police Department could not be completely eradicated, but that they would make sure that the issues of race and prejudice were addressed whenever they came up incidentally.

The gay community was most adversely affected by Jeffrey Dahmer, although he was gay himself. The gay bars were some of his stalking grounds. He sought out gay activities like gay pride parades to locate and pick up his partners, who ended up losing their lives for his bizarre sexual fantasies and gratification. This one aspect of his demeanor raises the question, did he really enjoy being gay? If so, why would he exterminate his kind? If not, why did he not stop himself? It all stemmed from the confusion he had about his sexuality when he was a child.

When he finally confirmed male partners as his preference for sex, he hated his twisted gay orientation. He was gay, but he also had a mental complication driving him to fantasize about having sex with the dead. This mental complication called necrophilia, was one of his reasons for killing his sex partners. The other reason why he killed them was to prevent them from reporting him to the police.

He expressed the same confusion to his probation officer who advised him to contact the gay community in order to avoid problems that might arise from such a lifestyle. He later confirmed to her that he preferred men as sex partners. He didn't tell her about his desire to also have sex with them when they were dead. If Dahmer had admitted this desire, she would have known that he had a more serious problem. She didn't have the chance to find out, because even though the records showed that Dahmer was placed on maximum supervision, his probation officer didn't visit his home at all. Dahmer mostly told her lies, or deliberately withheld information that would have provided a more in-depth character analysis.

The black community was outraged by the way police handled the 911 Emergency call of May 26, 1991 to help a Laotian boy. As a result, he was free to continue slaying people in his apartment. Proper street policing required obtaining all the biographical information readily available through the police computer. It was something that had been done to me every time I was stopped by the police. After such a check, they would release me, because I am not wanted by them. Dahmer would have been immediately arrested during the Laotian boy incident, had they conducted the proper checks. Jeffrey Dahmer was too white, too calm and calculated to be distrusted. He looked too good to be a criminal, let alone a high profile criminal. His looks, eloquence and politeness in communicating made him so dangerous. Black people pointed out that if it were a black man in the position of Jeffrey Dahmer, police would have checked his records. In his outrage, the former Alderman Michael Mc Gee said, "In Milwaukee it's like this, if you're white, you're right."

Like a prince of the devil as one member of a victim's family put it, "He was probably using his psychic powers when speaking to the police officers in order to throw them off track." The next victim after Konerak Sinthasomphone was Matt Turner, a black man, aged 20-years-old whom Dahmer picked up in Chicago at the Gay Pride Parade. They rode on the Greyhound bus together back to

Milwaukee. Matt eventually became Dahmer's 6th victim inside the Oxford Apartments, the 9th victim in Wisconsin and the 10th in his murder history.

He made a hobby out of murdering and dismembering his victims and put a lot more of his time and effort into his macabre pastime than he gave to his job at the Ambrosia Chocolate Company.

As much as he hated people who were very rich, he also despised the people who were worse off and wanted to take from him. Dahmer, being a son from a high class American family, was a man with high expectations. He had intelligence, charisma and eloquence of speech. He had a high IQ, so he was someone expected to be successful in life. No one would ever have considered that his chosen profession would be one of murder.

Even though it was a time consuming process - from the time he contacted a victim to the moment he completed the mutilation or dismemberment - Dahmer continued to kill. He had to cut his time on his regular job to work on his fantasy shrine. As a result he lost his job, which he claimed was his only source of pride at the time he was insincerely pleading with the judge for leniency in sentencing on the child molestation case.

After the panicked residents moved out and resettled in various housing projects in the city of Milwaukee, an air of calm settled around the Oxford Apartment, but not in the city. Such newfound calmness inside the building was only going to last for a few months before the new owners issued the notice to all residents to vacate the premises. This notice came because of the turmoil that had erupted in the City of Milwaukee. There had been severe tension in the minority communities that were most affected by the deeds of the serial murderer. As the crimes of Jeffrey Dahmer and what transpired were revealed after his arrest, the people now turned the blame away from him and began pointing their fingers at the Justice System and the residents

132

of the Oxford Apartments.

Initially, John Batchelor, the resident of the apartment unit #212 who let the police officers into the building, was talking to the media. He had left his door ajar so that he could find out what was happening. The police officers who had to force themselves into Jeffrey Dahmer's apartment began an immediate search. John Batchelor was still listening in and he overheard one of the police officers. The officer opened the refrigerator and he was stunned with what he saw. They were the eyes of a severed head looking back at him. With a shock he hadn't experienced in his entire police career, the officer exclaimed, "This son of a bitch has a God damn head in here!" Batchelor heard him. His door still ajar, he listened more intently and heard the officers clicking the handcuffs on Jeffrey Dahmer and reporting back to the precinct what they had uncovered in an apartment of a suspect currently under arrest. Following that report and perhaps the request for backup, many more law enforcement agents and fire trucks were sent to the crime scene.

Several communities joined in rallies and candlelight vigils that were held in the City of Milwaukee following the revelations of the Jeffrey Dahmer murders. Many people made statements expressing how they felt about these murders committed by a white man who victimized so many black men.

It was hard for me to understand how a man who had a girlfriend and children could be gay too, as was the case with some of Dahmer's victims. They could play either a feminine or a masculine role during romance, commonly known as bisexuality. That way the bisexual person has a larger market in which to interact socially. Some of Dahmer's victims were like that socially. For example, David Thomas was one of Dahmer's victims and he also had a girlfriend Chandra Beanland and a daughter Courtia, who was only three-years-old when her father was murdered.

The City of Milwaukee had a long standing racial problem with minority citizens and when the Dahmer story hit the media, the people said, "Here we go again with another case of police insensitivity in the City of Milwaukee." The noble citizens who tried to prevent Dahmer from taking another life, but were dismissed by the police were black females. It really showed that Milwaukee's racism hadn't let up until now.

A black columnist with the Milwaukee Journal Sentinel newspaper, Mr Eugene Kane, published an article in the December 7, 2006 issue relating race and how everything else in life is influenced by it in Southeast Wisconsin, of which Milwaukee is an industrial urban center. The article was sensitive, but it was the result of a survey conducted by Jeff Browne, President of a think tank organization, the Public Policy Forum. Mr Jeff Browne said that the results of the survey revealed more distrust about race relations among blacks and Hispanics than among whites, but he also found more optimism about the future of race relations among all people. Some prominent leaders of the black community expressed themselves from their longest experience with racism in their communities in Milwaukee.

The founder and director of Career Youth Development in Milwaukee, the late Jeanetta Robinson, who was familiar with black experience of the civil rights' movement of the sixties, reacted to it. She organized people to hold a candlelight vigil in front of the Oxford Apartments in memory of Jeffrey Dahmer's murder victims during this period when the racial tension was at its peak in Milwaukee. Now, more than thirty years later from the civil rights' marches and rallies of the sixties, Jeanetta saw the same evils still existing in the world. She said, "When I was a little girl marching with Dr Martin Luther King Jr., I thought it would all be over in a while, but now I know that it is a never ending thing."

Queen Hyler, who was the founder and director of Stop the Violence organization in the City of Milwaukee, had known the negative effects of violence in the community. When she started the "Stop the Violence" organization, she thought that it was black people who were violent, but when the details of the Dahmer murders were revealed, she said, "Why should this terrible thing happen to us? How could anyone commit these hideous crimes against another human being?"

In her remarks, Queen said that Jeffrey Dahmer had dredged to the surface the long existing racial problems in the minority areas of Milwaukee. She felt her patience wearing thin over what had been a continuous discrimination of black and minority people by the law. She pointed out that it was easy to feel racism in the workplace, in the Police Department and everywhere. She had observed and had been part of the fight against racial injustice for too long. She said, "If any police officer puts on a uniform and vows to uphold the law, that is what I expect them to do, regardless of one's race or appearance." She indicated that she would remember the clean appearance of Jeffrey Dahmer in the court, his lack of remorse and she vowed that the death of Dahmer's victims would not be in vain. After all, "Good neighbors come in all colors" as was written on the T-Shirt of a woman in the crowd.

The Reverend Jesse Jackson who visited Milwaukee during this crisis went to preach at St. Luke's Emmanuel Baptist Church for the healing to start. The preacher also joined the candlelight vigil that was held at the Oxford Apartments. He also encouraged the people to support the Police Chief Phillip Arroela who was heading an embattled police department. The Reverend Jackson indicated that there was so much brokenness in the communities. He cited broken hearts, broken dreams, broken families, broken friendships and broken relationships as a result of the distrust among the people.

In the survey result from the Public Policy Forum, it was indicated, "Jobs go looking in Waukesha when there is high unemployment in the minority communities in Milwaukee." Maybe the jobs simply don't trust applicants in those communities. The Reverend Jackson said that the people in Milwaukee, black and white, rich and poor, homosexual and heterosexual, young and old, could live in harmony when they trusted one another. The Reverend therefore urged the people to have the will to pick up the pieces, turn to each other, rely on each other and thank God for what was left, so that no one would be so vulnerable in the future.

Mr Paul Henningson, an Alderman for the neighborhood where Dahmer committed the heinous murders, stated in his press conference, "We must pull together or Milwaukee and all of you will be another victim." In the rally at Juneau Park, people's emotions were raw and while rally participants lively showed their anger towards the police department, the Alderman pleaded for calm like all other community leaders. He said, "We cannot be enemies of the police; we cannot let our anger victimize us." Some rally participants didn't trust anything the leaders were saying, because they heard a guy in the crowd who yelled out, "The police are KKK members," as Milwaukee had been one of the most racially segregated cities in the United States.

The gay community was most outraged by all that transpired following the Dahmer murders. This was the hardest hit community, because all Dahmer's victims were gay. Gay people were bashed and harassed and called derogatory names such as "faggots," "fucking queers" etc. in the City of Milwaukee. It was just like any other kind of discrimination. They propositioned someone they admired in the same way as heterosexual people.

I remember us concluding our prayer with the line, "World without end, Amen." Now with the advent of gayocracy, the prayer line might change in the future to, "World with an end, Amen," if we are still here.

As a gay person, Jeffrey Dahmer's sexual orientation was distorted further by a mental disorder called necrophilia, which attacked him so frequently that he had to kill for that kind of sexual gratification. He could not stop himself until he was exposed. When he was finally arrested, he volunteered to make honest confessions regarding his victims. These confessions would help the law enforcement officers to solve the missing persons' cases for closure. He told detectives the missing persons that were his victims. He went on to tell the investigators the approximate dates and time of their deaths. He didn't remember their names, except that of his first victim, Steven Hicks of Ohio.

Chapter 11

The Panic Exodus

The management's rent reduction incentive didn't stop the panicking residents from moving out of the Oxford Apartments. The Red Cross and The Housing Authority of the City of Milwaukee started to make coordinated efforts to relocate all the residents. Approximately 90% of the residents moved out. As soon as arrangements were completed, the moving out began.

In addition to the residual energies remaining from the atrocities that had occurred in the building, the public harassment and threats directed at the residents made it even more unbearable to remain. Some members of the public who felt the pain of the residents did do something to help. A private donor through the management moved the residents temporarily into the Hilton Hotel for a couple of days, waiting for the day of moving.

I remember that during the couple of days' reprieve when the residents were at the Hilton Hotel, the Oxford Apartments was robbed of two air conditioners. The opportunists were taking advantage of the tragedy and the consequent chaos that followed, since the security guards were not yet in place.

As soon as arrangements were completed for relocation, the Housing Authority of the City of Milwaukee gave the green light for the Oxford Apartments residents to move. The rush to move out kept everybody busy with parking, loading and moving. During the mass exodus, an alarming discovery was made in one of the storage lockers in the basement. These storage lockers were located in the part of the basement where residents seldom went. In other words, it was not in the high traffic area of the basement, such as the laundry room. The mass move out had given everyone the excuse to look into the nooks and crannies of the common areas, including all the lockers in the storage area. In one locker belonging to a vacant apartment unit, we found a plastic zip lock bag in which there was a decayed hand visibly showing the bones of the fingers. We then called the authorities to take it away. I don't know what was done with it from there.

The Housing Authority in collaboration with the Red Cross moved the residents into public housing projects located in two places. Berryland and Westlawn housing projects are both located next to each other on Sherman Boulevard at the northwest side of the City of Milwaukee. These projects are subsidized by government. Most of the residents were moved into these two projects over a period of three days, a move which helped to heal their anxiety.

The mass move, which I called the Exodus, was like a clean out of all the illegal or illicit activities that made the Oxford Apartments a valley of death. Such activities often lead to conflicts among street gangs and often resulted in death from gun battles. For the rest of us, about five families who remained behind, there was peace and quiet, security and trust. All these values were lacking before the mass move out. It was so quiet inside the Oxford Apartments that we could hear every little noise very clearly at any time. Some familiar noises, such as when a building is settling, or when a key is dropped from a distance were clearly heard.

During my first year at the Oxford Apartments, I had been through some experiences that words can't describe. My boss, Mr Don Gregory, was happy for the way I conducted myself on the job and stayed safe. Of course, it was neither achieved by my power nor my might. The credit goes to God Almighty. My boss knew that I had been a good employee, but the tragedy in the building meant that the job had to be terminated. Whether fortunate or not, Mr Gregory offered to give me a two week vacation with pay. At that time, I was very homesick and wanted to visit my family at home, but two weeks was not enough for a trip like that.

I knew that my job was over when most of the residents moved out. In effect, I was a live victim for losing my job as a result of Jeffrey Dahmer's heinous crimes. I knew that I might find it difficult to get another job in a similar position because of the stigma from the last job. My boss understood my desire to avoid the vacation, so I continued to work for another eighteen months before the building was demolished.

The management could not shut down the building immediately and therefore it had to provide security, both for the building and the few residents who remained. Thus, the management employed the services of BMW Security who protected the building for one year, prior to its demolition. It was a time when the management started losing money because the operating expenses were much higher than the revenues collected from the remaining residents, who were paying reduced rents as the incentive to remain there.

The five residents, including myself, had to work closely with the security officers to deal with the human traffic of treasure hunters, gawkers and curiosity seekers on the outside of the building. All these people were trying to get the story of the sex serial killer. They were making every effort to enter the building just to look at Dahmer's infamous apartment #213.

Some people saw Jeffrey Dahmer's arrest as an opportunity to acquire souvenirs and, bizarrely, any piece of the property became a souvenir. I remember a couple who came all the way from Hartford, Wisconsin who gave me $2 for two bricks that they took from the cobblestone alley of the Oxford Apartments. The same couple had wanted to get the entrance door of the apartment #213. I told them to bring a replica of the door to replace it so that nobody could notice that the original door had been removed as souvenir. The couple were unlucky. The new owners of the building changed the lock on the apartment to prevent the access I used to have into the serial killer's unit. When the couple later returned to get the door, I was unable to open it. I didn't know how much value those treasure hunters placed on the tragedy that had taken place there.

At least once, the gawkers pulled apart the rear exit door nearest to apartment #213, because they were curious to see what Dahmer's apartment looked like. They imagined that the unit must be different from the other units in the building, but it was not the apartment unit that enhanced the killer's activity, but its location inside the building. Someone even ripped off the building directory that listed current residents, including Jeffrey Dahmer. It could be a great souvenir.

Blaming the residents for what Jeffrey Dahmer did was rather hypocritical, because not many people know exactly what their neighbors are doing in the privacy of their own homes. Many people do not care about what anyone does anywhere unless it affects them directly. They simply turn their heads, plug their ears and ignore a crime, even if they knew that they could have intervened to prevent it. This was the mood of the neighborhood. The people simply didn't want to be involved with the police because of the lack of trust between police and their minority communities. Many of them had a record with the police for previous offenses and so they wanted to avoid anything that brought them into contact with the police.

Jeffrey Dahmer was no stranger in this Avenues West neighborhood. He took advantage of the cold mood of the neighborhood when he moved in. I remember how I felt when I saw the bones on the green grassy slope behind the building when I first started the job. I didn't know what type of bones they were at the time, but it was certainly unusual in a metropolitan setting like that.

An air of loneliness filled the Oxford Apartments after most of the residents moved out. Strangers from the outside weren't to be trusted. There were 45 vacant units in the Oxford Apartments, so I had to make a special effort to fill them. The prank calls flowed in on a daily basis soon, but I had to try and screen the calls and kept working as usual and hoping for the best. It wouldn't be easy this time, as the building had become infamous. We continued to keep our guards up and watched out. Meanwhile, the traffic to the building continued. People drove by looking at the building with surprise and sometimes pointing at it. They were making some remarks and comments we didn't hear, but I believe they related to horror of what had occurred in a good looking building like that.

The atmosphere inside the building was eerie. Sometimes when walking down the hallway, I felt the push of the air around me when nobody was around. On several occasion, while walking down the hallway, I heard some footsteps behind me, but when I turned around to look, again there was no one there. One day, I even heard the sound of a knock on the door of an apartment across from mine. I looked through the pinhole to see who was there, but saw nobody. One night, I dreamed that I saw the entire Oxford Apartment in red. This was a dream I had just before the Dahmer trial started and I told my boss about it. I didn't know what it all meant, but what I didn't know about this tragedy would not hurt me drastically.

Exactly one year from the day that Jeffrey Dahmer was arrested, a community based organization, CYD (Career Youth Development), came to the Oxford Apartments with an organized candlelight vigil to commemorate the anniversary of Jeffrey Dahmer's victims. The victims' families came to pay their respects to their fallen loved ones. They assembled themselves right on the steps in front of the Oxford Apartments. They were accompanied by about fifteen hundred vigil attendants holding lighted candles. Security was provided by two policemen and an unknown number of detectives in plain clothes. A few notable dignitaries from the surrounding communities as well as those from out of State were present at this historic gathering. Among them were the Evangelist Gene Champion Jr., The Reverend Jesse Jackson, State Representative Jeanetta Robinson, County Supervisor Terence Pitts and State Representative Gwen Moore to name a few. An opening prayer lead by the Evangelist started the vigil and several speakers gave their speeches regarding the tragedy. The candlelight vigil was completed with a closing prayer by the Reverend Jackson.

At that time, it was indicated that this ritual would take place every year in memorial to remember the dead victims of Jeffrey Dahmer. It was a good idea to do so. What the organizers of the vigil didn't know was that the Oxford Apartments would not be standing for another year. The management sold the property to a buyer for possible tax incentives. Even though the building was structurally sound to operate in the rental business, the infamous stigma from the aftermath of the Dahmer serial murders inside it made the general public favor its demolition.

This was a double jeopardy for me. Firstly, I would have to find another job, but secondly the stigma attached to the last job may cause potential employers to be reluctant to employ me. Although I was totally unaware of what Dahmer or any others in the building were doing in their own apartments, the stigma remained. Many questions had been answered regarding the murders, but potential employers were not satisfied and were indeed wary, so I never had another chance to find employment in a similar position.

I am not excited by the same kind of job because of the flashbacks that constantly fill my mental picture on that job. In fact, I had gained the experience in property

144

management that I needed. I was no longer interested in being a resident manager of a building that I did not own. It has not been easy to forget the horrible memories I have about that job. Instead, I decided to provide realtor services with Ameriland II Realty to pursue a career in investments and marketing real estate.

During the panic exodus, the management company allowed each resident to keep the appliances in their own apartments. Thus thirty-six each of name brand refrigerators, gas stoves and air conditioners were moved with the residents. This was in addition to the losses that the company had already suffered since Dahmer was arrested.

The plot of land is currently owned by Andrzei Sitarski who bought building, tore it down and left the site vacant from 1993 to date. Nobody has been interested in that plot of land because of the stigma attached to it and the multiple murders that Jeffrey Dahmer committed on that site. There are some people who are still angry about that tragedy and I believe that they would raise the objections about it if an investor ever considers building on it.

The members of the public expected the residents to answer some awkward questions, to which they had no answer. Whilst in custody and during his trial, Dahmer gave the answers in as much details as to satisfy their curiosity.

Chapter 12

Earthly Judgment Day

This was the day that Jeffrey Dahmer's Serial murder case #F912542 was taken to court for trial. As it was stated in an all important but dead Latin language, "Vox populi vox dei," meaning in English, "Voice of the people is the voice of God". Jeffrey Dahmer had to face the people for his twisted crimes. Christians talk about the judgment day after death, which is the judgment by God to decide on whether one ends up in heaven or hell. Hence, I called this the "Earthly Judgment Day," because it is the people who decided the fate of the accused.

The preparation for this trial (The State of Wisconsin, Plaintiff, versus Jeffrey L. Dahmer, Defendant) had taken about six months from the day of Jeffrey Dahmer's arrest. During this period, both the defense and the prosecution assembled their teams of experts. Everyone was in serious preparation for the trial and the mood of the city had been tense since Dahmer's arrest. The defense lineup consisted of a team of highly trained and experienced professionals, including Gerald Boyle, the lead defense attorney, his assistants Wendy Patrickus and Ellen Ryan, who sat at the defense table, Dr Frederick S. Berlin, a psychiatrist from California and the lead defense psychiatrist and expert on sexual disorders and Judith Becker, a clinical psychologist from Tucson, Arizona and a professor at the University of Arizona. Ms Becker strongly believed in her opinion dissenting from a commission's finding that a link exists between pornography and violence. She gave an interesting testimony. Finally, on the defense lineup and the last expert witness to take the stand, was Dr Carl Wahlstrom, a psychiatrist from Chicago, Illinois.

On the prosecution team was E Michael McCann, Milwaukee's District Attorney and lead prosecutor. He assembled in his team Carol White, Assistant District Attorney, Dr George Palermo, a court-appointed psychiatrist from Milwaukee, Wisconsin, Dr Frederick Fosdal, a psychiatrist from Madison, Wisconsin and Dr Park Elliot Dietz, a psychiatrist and the prosecution's star witness.

Following Dahmer's arrest and all the gruesome discoveries of body parts in his apartment, the most difficult job was the arduous task of identifying the victims. The identification process utilized DNA procedures, dental procedures, photos and a lot of Dahmer's own recollections. Jeffrey Dahmer helped to identify some victims from the photos of missing person files. Meanwhile, as the medical examiner came up with more identified victims, E Michael McCann, the District Attorney and lead prosecutor without prejudice or hesitation, moved on to file criminal complaints on behalf of each victim. For the full details of the criminal complaints, please see Appendix B at the end of the book.

As the head count of victims increased, the bail money on Jeffrey Dahmer also increased accordingly. Initially, with eleven bodies positively identified, Dahmer's bail money was set at $1,000,000. But as the task of identification continued, four more bodies were added, making a total of fifteen. Bail money was increased to $5,000,000.

The tension over the tragedy in the City of Milwaukee was very high as the public was swayed with the bits and pieces of information that trickled out from the media regarding the murders. As the trial drew near, the ranks of reporters from around the world converged on Milwaukee and we could feel the frenzy, especially around the crime scene and of course downtown, one of Jeffrey Dahmer's stalking grounds. With these reporters were some sophisticated cameras that could film the minutest detail of an object at a distance.

Curious reporters visiting the Oxford Apartments were asking to talk to me for the story about the serial killer. I personally spoke with Noreen Taylor and Brendan Monk of the Globe magazine of London, England. All that I told them was how happy I was to be saved by the Grace during each attempt that Jeffrey Dahmer made to get me as his prime target. Brendan then asked to take my photo while I stood next to Dahmer's apartment door. He and Noreen also wanted an interview with me, which I declined. I recall another reporter, Arnaud Levy from the tabloid France-Soir in Paris, France, who also spoke with me, but no interview. I was still the manager of the building, so I had to have the permission of my employers to speak to the media. I didn't ask for such permission and I didn't give any interviews at that time.

Marilyn Fletcher and Ken Fink of ABC Television News in New York came with their satellite set up in the back of the building for an interview with me inside the Oxford Apartments. They were going to transmit the interview to their local stations, but I believed it was not the right thing to do at that time, because I was still employed to manage the building.

There were two pre-trial conferences. The first was on January 13, 1992, when Jeffrey Dahmer changed his plea. The second conference was on January 27, 1992. These conferences were important for both the prosecution and defense parties, because of the opportunity and the mutual acceptance to examine evidence with the help of professional psychologists and psychiatrists who would become expert witnesses during the trial.

For a midsize city like the City of Milwaukee ,with a population of a little over 600,000, this trial was like "The Trial of the Century". The courtroom was full each time Jeffrey Dahmer appeared and it felt more like a celebrity movie premiere. News Reporters came curiously from far and wide. The testimonies were quite sensational and emotions poured out from victims' families as Dahmer's confessions to the murders were revealed. Security was tight and the courtroom was heavily fortified with bullet proof glass shields for the protection of all who were present at the trial. Metal detectors were used to scan everyone for weapons and a dog was available to sniff everyone for possible explosives before entering into the courtroom. People from all walks of life were showing up to the trial.

Seating was arranged to further enhance the security of the defendant and the witnesses. The first row of seats went to the reporters, the second row to the victims' families and two seats were permanently reserved for Jeffrey Dahmer's parents. Jeffrey Dahmer's father Lionel and his stepmother Shari were present at the trial. His mother Joyce was unable to come to the trial because she was too distraught by what had happened.

I was a witness for the prosecution at the trial and I went into the courtroom only at the time of my testimony around February 11, 1991. As manager of the Oxford Apartments, Dahmer's last residence, the prosecution would ask me some questions to help the court in the decision process. I did just that in court, but I also had more to say out of court.

The motions, the plea and the verdict of this world acclaimed trial of an infamous, dangerous serial killer would be presented as precisely as possible. In the court of public opinion, Jeffrey Dahmer was guilty even before the trial started, because he had already confessed to these murders. However, the trial was necessary as part of his human right to be tried and convicted before that guilty verdict. The presumption of innocence of a suspect until proven guilty made the trial to be necessary. Also, the victims' families wanted to know how exactly their loved ones had died. Jeffrey Dahmer had included in his confessions many of these gruesome details to the detectives while he was in their custody. For example, he told them where he had met each of his victims. Dahmer picked up most of his victims at the gay bars, others at the mall and others at bus stops and adult entertainment news' stands.

The truth about money being the root of all evil was proven in Dahmer's case. He explained how he lured his victims with an offer of money to pose nude for a photo in his apartment. When they got to the apartment he provided videos and/ or fish in the aquarium to watch and one thing led to another. Next, he served something like a coffee or beer to drink. Then, as the guest became relaxed, comfortable and unsuspecting, he slipped the drug into their drink. Within a short time the drug knocked them out and then he strangled them.

The strangling stage in his murder process was when the most noise was made. Each victim's struggle to avoid being suffocated made a lot of noise. The resident of apartment #113, which was directly below Dahmer's apartment told reporters about the thumping noises on the floor above. The resident, Mr Aaron Whitehead, said that it was like the heavy noise you hear when two people are in a wrestling match. The struggle obviously taking place between Dahmer and his victim was so serious that sometimes the resident living in the apartment below thought that the bedroom ceiling would collapse on him. This showed that at least some of the victims may have been more conscious than Dahmer believed and put up some resistance when he started to strangle them.

Another time when a great deal of noise was made was during the dismemberment of the body. He used power tools such as an electric chain saw and a power drill, which helped him to handle the bones better. He could cut or drill through bones faster. Despite all the noise, nobody within the building suspected anything. He obtained a further kick from looking at the inside of the body and masturbating and sometimes eating parts of it.

Jeffrey Dahmer picked up his victims at random not for any negative emotion like hate. He dismembered his victims, took Polaroid photos of the body parts and had sex with the corpse. He kept the skulls for trophies, or disposed of the entire body. His attorney testified to that during the trial, but it was also reported that Jeffrey Dahmer threw racial insults at black servicemen when he was in the military while serving in Germany.

In his confessions Dahmer gave police the approximate date of death of each of his victims. These dates were confirmed by the medical examiner who conducted the autopsy on the body parts retrieved from Dahmer's apartment. Jeffrey Dahmer's good memory is why I believe he was rated to have a high IQ, even though he did not remember the names of all of his victims. He remembered only the name of his first victim, Steven Hicks, whom he killed in his boyhood home back in Ohio in 1978, a few months after graduating from high school.

One of the professionals hired to examine him while in custody testified to his IQ during the trial, while trying to prove his sanity. Dr Fosdal indicated in his testimony that Dahmer was intelligent and was normal-looking. Anyone could easily be conned by his smooth talking. He spoke clearly, giving answers that were coherent during his examination by the psychiatric and psychological experts.

Jeffrey Dahmer pleaded "not guilty" by reason of insanity during his first court appearance in September of 1991. Here, the defense would present an argument claiming Dahmer had a mental disease such as paraphilia, a type of a sexual disorder. The insanity plea was not feasible because in the State of Wisconsin this was the first time that this type of disorder would be presented in the courts as the excuse for murder. Paraphelia had not been known to make someone insane, nor to cause anyone to commit murder. Thus, on January 13, 1992, in his next court

152

appearance, Jeffrey Dahmer changed his plea to "guilty". Therefore, the trial proceedings would not be about whether or not he committed these crimes, but about whether he was consciously responsible for committing them. Here, the defense has the burden of proof that Dahmer was not legally responsible for the murders as charged.

The defense must prove with evidence both physically and otherwise that Dahmer did not know what he was doing when he committed the crimes. In short, it must be proven beyond all reasonable doubt that Jeffrey Dahmer didn't have the mental capacity to know when he committed these murders.

The defense position was weak with all the gory discoveries in the defendant's apartment. Even more damaging indeed were in his words. Jeffrey Dahmer personally confessed to these murders while in detective custody, yet the defense still had to go through with the trial. It was done for the humanitarian reasons, including what the public might learn from it.

On January 29, 1992, in the courtroom of Judge Laurence Gram Jr, Jeffrey Dahmer's defense attorney Gerald Boyle made his opening statement, claiming that his client had a mental disease and that Jeffrey Dahmer was obsessed with possessing a body. He said that Dahmer in his younger years had sexual fantasies about little boys. He continued by saying that at fifteen Dahmer even thought of killing for sex a jogger who often passed by his home in Ohio, but the jogger stopped coming that way before he could act on his fantasy.

Dahmer picked up his first victim, Steven Hicks of Bath Township, Ohio, when Hicks was hitchhiking on the Cleveland-Ohio interstate. Dahmer took him home and had a party and then, when Steven wanted to leave, Dahmer recalled his memory of abandonment by his parents and vowed never to let anybody abandon him again, so he killed his guest. It was a fist fight in which Jeffrey Dahmer hit Steven with a barbell. This first incident of murder couldn't have been intentional on the part of the young Dahmer. At the time of the fight, Dahmer probably didn't mean to kill the guest, but the blow from the barbell became fatal and Steven died. Dahmer was very scared at this point. After the act, Dahmer now had the burden of disposing of the body, something he did not think about at the beginning. He was confused and first decided to bury the body in a shallow grave. Later, he dug it up, dismembered it and packed the flesh in garbage bags. Then he broke the bones with sledgehammer and disposed of the bone fragments by throwing them around the property. He threw them far out in a circular direction so that the bone fragments were scattered at random points across the land.

Gerald Boyle presented his client as so unique that he captioned him "the Jeffrey Dahmer human being" to the jury. In his opening statement, Boyle warned potential jurors about how gruesome the evidence to be presented in court might be. He hinted human carnage, cannibalism, mutilation, sex with dead bodies and other unimaginable acts. He also relieved them with an apology and an assurance that it would get no worse than that. Indeed it didn't get any worse. The defense attorney continued his testimony with authenticity and vigor when explaining what had happened in the life of his client. Sometimes, with a low intonation in his voice, he drew the complete attention of the jury to connect with him. He referred to Dahmer's interest in dead animals at the age of about 14-years-old. He said Dahmer once brought home the head of a fetal pig, which he worked on in a biology class. He removed the skin and kept the skull, like he did with some of his human victims in adulthood.

Nobody in his family was aware of his sexual preference. Dahmer himself was unsure who he was when it came to sexual orientation. He discussed it once with his probation officer who advised him to seek counseling from the gay community.

Gerald Boyle revealed in his testimony that his client even desired to keep the victims alive without their memory, effectively in a zombie state, but his experiments failed in all of his attempts. Although Dahmer was not charged with cannibalism, the defense attorney explained that his client ate some of his victims' flesh to bring them alive in him.

Following his testimony, the lead defense attorney Gerald Boyle called upon his first expert witness, Dr Frederick S Berlin, to take the stand. Dr Berlin, the lead psychiatrist expert witness for the defense, testified for two days on the stand claiming that Dahmer had a mental disease called necrophilia and that it had made the defendant commit the murders. Dr Berlin mentioned necrophilia characterized by obsessive fascination with death and corpses and sex with corpses, a subject covered under Paraphilia, which was the focus of the defense's argument. Dr Berlin continued his testimony, touching on every related psychiatric string, which made it so boring to most of the people in court, including the jurors and also the laymen. The people in court hardly understood very much of what had been presented. Some of them actually went to sleep in their seats.

In his determination, Dr Berlin concluded, "Dahmer had fantasies and urges about having an initial sexual contact with someone alive. He then fantasized and imagined continuing sexual acts and intimate relationships in a transition state that's between life and death; a zombie-like state." The psychiatrist continued, "Dahmer acted on the fantasy, continuing to 'relate to the body of the person' after they are dead." Dr Berlin went on to say that Dahmer's feelings were involuntary because nobody would ever decide to have that kind of affliction. He said Mr Dahmer discovered he was afflicted with these recurrent, erotic fantasies of the sickest kind.

So, in Dr Berlin's medical opinion, "Mr Dahmer was out of control and becoming progressively more out of control and it was not going to be he who would stop it; it was going to have to be stopped by some outside force, which is exactly what happened." All who were affected by the boring testimony became alert and were again interested in what these expert witnesses had to say when the prosecuting district attorney, E Michael McCann intervened to cross examine Dr Berlin.

To Dr Berlin, McCann said, "Doctor, you spent far less time than any of the other experts with Dahmer, didn't you?" Dr Berlin said that it's not the amount of time, but the quality of time spent with the defendant to have unbiased view of the case. The prosecutor expected Dr Berlin to have spoken to Dahmer in order to present a defense statement, not from hearsay as information from police reports, or what was said by neighbors or what attorneys wrote. The district attorney felt that it was crucial to speak with somebody for a reasonable amount of time in order to know them. The prosecutor was not convinced that the doctor understood his client.

A little drama was observed when Dr Berlin felt that his integrity was questioned or challenged by the prosecutor's cross-examination. Of course, that was not the case, because Dr Berlin was an expert on sexual disorders at John Hopkins Hospital in Baltimore, Maryland. He was also picked to be the lead expert psychiatrist for the defense because of his experience in the subject.

The next expert witness from the defense, Dr Judith Becker, took the stand. She testified to her client's desire to have a shrine or a temple of skulls. She tried to describe what Jeffrey Dahmer gave to her in a sketch. The temple would feature the remains. These would be the skulls and skeletons of his victims. He wished to have a black table on which he would place ten skulls across, with incense burning at both ends of the line of skulls. Jeffrey Dahmer was very much a devil worshiper. In addition, a whole skeleton would be placed at either end of the table. There would be a black seat and lighting would include blue globe lights with blue curtains as the background. It would be a place for devil worship.

Dahmer had a strong belief in Satan and sometimes felt like the devil himself. Dr Becker also revealed Dahmer's expectations from having the shrine. He thought he would have social and financial benefits. Dahmer had this fantasy before he was imprisoned in 1989 for child molestation. As soon as he was released, he continued his quest for more skulls for the shrine. It was why he had about eleven skulls in his apartment at the time of his arrest. She said "He was going to be getting some kind of power that would help him socially and financially."

She went on to say that Dahmer was so consumed by his mental disease that he could not control his urge to kill, because he was obsessed with the dead. She concluded that Dahmer knew right from wrong, but he was so obsessed with necrophilia that he had insubstantial capacity to conform his conduct to the requirements of the law. Perhaps because Dahmer confided in Dr Becker, he revealed more of himself to her than he did to the police.

When he was only four-years-old, Dahmer experienced a serious pain from hernia around his groin area. He thought his genitals had been cut off. It must have had a psychological effect on him.

Dr Becker cited several other occasions where various incidents affected him in different ways. For example, she mentioned an incident when he had given tadpoles to his teacher, who he considered to be a good person, but she subsequently gave them to one of his classmates. It is claimed that he experienced rejection as a result. Apparently, he went to where those tadpoles were kept and poured motor oil into the container to kill them. On another occasion, Dahmer had asked another student to put his hand into a wasps' nest, which the boy did and was stung. Here, Dahmer was indifferent about his friend's suffering. He offered no help to the friend in any way. He enjoyed watching someone suffer as a result of something that he had perpetrated.

Dr Becker also cited the effect of an incident when Jeffrey Dahmer's father showed him how to cut open the fish in order to clean it. Dahmer remembered that the egg sac caught his eyes. It was the bright orange color of the eggs that attracted him. She said Jeffrey, for the most part in relating material, was pretty monotone and flat. "When he talked about cutting the fish open and seeing the inside of the fish, he became somewhat more animated, more alive in a sense.

Here he had the fascination with the colors of the insides of the fish, which related to his future fascination with the colors of the insides of his victims and explained why he cut open the stomachs of all of them. Dr Becker cited Jeffrey Dahmer's motivation for cannibalism. Dahmer had talked to her about why he ate some of his victims' remains. Dr Becker said that he bought a meat tenderizer for the heart. He tried tasting the flesh and the heart, from which he derived a sexual thrill. He felt that the man was a part of him and he internalized him. He reported having an erection while eating it.

Dr Becker also revealed that Dahmer performed sexual acts on every victim after death. He also derived sexual gratification from keeping the skulls of some of his victims. She quoted him as saying, "The head represented the essence of the person."

Referring to his fascination with body parts, Dahmer said, "Maybe I was born too late, maybe I was an Aztec." The Aztecs preserved the dead. At the end of her testimony, the prosecutor's assistant Carol White did not cross-examine Dr Becker's testimony.

The last expert witness on the defense team to testify

was Dr Carl M Wahlstrom, the psychiatrist from Chicago who said Jeffrey Dahmer was cunning, trying to hide his crimes by dismembering the bodies and that he was also capable of going for long periods without killing. He said that Dahmer didn't like killing and wanted to keep the victims alive in a zombie state. To overcome the repulsion, Dahmer would drink. A bizarre, grandiose delusion in him made him feel that he could actually perform a crude brain operation that would make the victims forget their memory and identity. In other reports, Jeffrey Dahmer described his procedure. From a syringe, he injected some doses of muriatic acid into the brain of his victims through a hole he drilled into their skulls.

Finally, after Dr Wahlstrom's testimony, he was not cross-examined by the prosecution, so it was there that the defense rested its case.

The prosecution sought the help of several witnesses and with the physical evidence retrieved from the suspect's apartment and the confessions from Jeffrey Dahmer's own words, the prosecution easily proved that Jeffrey Dahmer was not insane, just evil. He carefully planned and executed each murder.

E. Michael McCann the prosecutor and district attorney called upon Dr George Palermo, the psychiatrist appointed by the court. In his testimony, the doctor said that Jeffrey Dahmer suffered from a serious personality disorder, but he was neither insane nor psychotic; it was treatable. According to Dr Palermo, "He is an organized, nonsocial lust murderer who killed in a methodical and shrewd manner, driven by obsessive fantasies of power over others." He said he was shocked to see Dahmer as a likable person because he was expecting to meet someone crazy. The doctor said, "Whatever he has done, he's still a human being." He added that Dahmer spoke clearly and gave coherent answers. He even said that Dahmer was intelligent.

Thus, Dahmer had lied for years and was still lying. Dr Palermo neither believed that Dahmer planned to build a temple from the bones of his dead victims, nor the claim that he ate the flesh of any of his victims. The doctor testified that Dahmer embellished the facts. He also doubted that Dahmer drilled holes in the head of any of the victims while they were alive. Dr Palermo's testimony truly came as a rebuttal to Dr Becker's testimony, because Dr Palermo mentioned all the claims that Dr Becker mentioned; the first being sex with corpse, then the plan of a temple of skulls and skeletons and the cannibalism.

The prosecution sent a subpoena to people from all walks of life who ever had any contact with Jeffrey L. Dahmer. The testimony from these witnesses would support the prosecution's case that Dahmer knew all along what he was doing whilst he was habitually committing these crimes. The prosecutor E. Michael McCann called the carpet cleaner who had worked for Dahmer. The carpet cleaner explained that there was a stubborn dark stain about ten or so square feet on the bedroom carpeting, which he thought was a blood or wine stain. However, Dahmer told him that it was chocolate.

Jeffrey Dahmer rarely took a taxi cab directly to his residence. He was usually dropped off at about a block or half from his home, walking the rest of the distance. I remember Dahmer refusing to accept the offer of free carpet cleaning by the building's management company as an incentive for the renewal of his rental lease. At that time he told me that he was going to do it himself. He showed me the cleaning equipment he had rented from a grocery store to assure me that he had done it. He thought that this would not give the manager any excuse to come to the apartment when he was away. Of course, in August 1990, Dahmer had also installed a security alarm system.

The employee of a hardware store who sold Jeffrey Dahmer some muriatic acid was also called to testify. The acid was supposed to have been used by Dahmer for his crude lobotomy experiments in his effort to keep his victims alive, but without their memory or identity. He wanted them to stay with him while he commanded total control over them. He wanted them to be like zombies walking around in confinement and at his disposal. They would keep him company, thereby fulfilling his desire for companionship. It hadn't been easy for him socially, so he chose murder as his only solution.

Another witness called to testify was Ronald Flowers, along with Dahmer's co-workers at the Ambrosia Chocolate Company. Since his arrest, some of Dahmer's regular co-workers had expressed their surprise that the man they knew was actually a serial killer. Some told of sharing his food during break periods. They gave him credit for the good taste, but he told them that they would be surprised if they knew what he had cooked. From the time he confessed to cannibalism, those who ate his food were shocked to realize that they might have tasted human meat.

For the trial, Dahmer's supervisor testified that he had no problem with Jeffrey Dahmer and also said that he was polite. The plant superintendent Mr Heaney recalled what Dahmer had told him when he was arrested for a sexual assault of a boy in 1988. What Dahmer told him was a lie. Dahmer told him that he had propositioned a young lady that he believed was of age and later discovered that she was a minor. Here, Dahmer had sense enough to hide the truth. If he were insane, he would not realize that he had done anything wrong and would not have tried to hide the truth.

A very significant witness, the brother of one of Dahmer's victims who was sexually assaulted by Dahmer in 1988, was called to testify. Dahmer was imprisoned in 1989 for that crime, receiving five years for sexual assault and three years for enticing a minor for immoral purposes. At his sentencing, Jeffrey Dahmer displayed his characteristic skill and cunning. He pleaded with Judge Gardner for leniency. Dahmer said that the experience of being arrested and charged had been a living nightmare for him and that the shock was enough to make him to mend his ways. He admitted being an alcoholic and a homosexual and said that he was terribly sorry to have picked up a young boy, but that he was now ready to turn his life around, working hard to become a productive member of society. The judge placed him on five years' probation and one year in jail on a work-release program. This program enabled the prisoner to go to work and return to the prison after work.

Jeffrey Connor, a friend of Anthony Sears, who became Dahmer's fifth victim, also took the stand in the trial. Mr Connor testified that he gave a ride to both Sears and Dahmer from a gay bar to Dahmer's grandmother's house in March of 1989. Mr Connor said that he hadn't seen his friend since then. He had thought of Dahmer as a nice and kind person in that brief contact. Mr Connor remembered dropping them off at the intersection of South Fifty Seventh Street on West Lincoln Avenue in the City of West Allis, but didn't know which house they entered.

As a defense strategy, the lead defense attorney Gerald Boyle asked each witness the length of time they spent with Jeffrey Dahmer in order to show that their contact with him was too brief for them to get to know him well. However, prosecution witnesses who testified later had longer periods of contact with him. For instance, I had more to say both in and out of court about Jeffrey Dahmer. The interesting episodes not told in court form the main story in this book.

Another interesting witness the prosecution called was the police officer who previously arrested Jeffrey Dahmer at the Ambrosia Chocolate Company on a sexual assault complaint in 1988. Police Lt Scott Schaefer testified that Dahmer was very nervous and concerned about his employer not knowing why he was taken into custody.

Another witness, the manager of the Unicorn Bathhouse in Chicago, testified that Dahmer had been there at least ten times without incident between April of 1990 and February of 1991. Previously, Dahmer had been involved in incidents in that bathhouse and had been warned to behave himself.

Perhaps the most significant prosecution witnesses were the two police officers who responded to a 911 emergency phone call regarding a Laotian boy found naked and disoriented on a street on May 27, 1991. John Balcerzak and Joe Gabrish who were already fired from the Milwaukee Police Department for the way they handled the call, explained how they were deceived by Dahmer to leave the boy after Dahmer told them that he was his house guest and homosexual lover. The Police officers characterized Jeffrey Dahmer as a master manipulator who thoroughly convinced them that Konerak, the Laotian, was his friend. Dahmer showed them a Polaroid photo of the man posing nude or in leotard and told them his name. Dahmer gave the name of Jim Hmong. Konerak was killed immediately after those police officers left Dahmer's apartment.

I was called to testify about the complaints that residents had made about the smell in the building. I recalled how I confronted Dahmer regarding the complaints, but that when I inspected Dahmer's apartment following each complaint, the apartment was cleaner than most I had seen in the building. I testified that following the last inspection, I had warned Dahmer that I would call the police if the smell came back a third time. This was only about one month before he was arrested following the escape of Tracy Edwards, his next intended victim.

The Prosecution's star expert witness, Dr Park Elliot Dietz, spent two days on the stand. Dr Dietz had examined Jeffrey Dahmer through several hours and videotaped the interview. Dahmer told him how frightened he was when his crime was nearly exposed by a police officer who had kicked down a neighbor's door to see what was causing the smelling in the building. The neighbors who called the police thought that someone might have died. They found nobody dead in that apartment concerned. For Dahmer, this was a close call because at that time he had a corpse in his bathtub awaiting dismemberment. He subsequently hurried to complete the job. Again here, Dahmer showed that he was clearly aware that what he was doing was wrong and therefore feared exposure of his crime.

Dr Dietz went on to quote Dahmer as saying, "It's a strange situation to be in. I mean, I was so intent on having a great deal of control and shaping my own destiny and now it's all out of my hands. You can't keep running from the truth forever. Eventually you have to face the consequences. It may take years, but eventually you do. "

Dahmer was always conscious of his wrongdoing. There was plenty of evidence that he acted rationally and with the pursuit of self-interest. As an example, Dahmer always used condom when engaging in sex with a corpse as testified by the doctor. Dr Dietz felt that Dahmer's sexual attraction to the interior of the body went back to his years in high school when he started masturbating and at the same time was involved with dissecting animals in class. He had thoughts about animal parts while masturbating. "Then it becomes sexualized," Dr Dietz said. "If it enters his mind enough times while he masturbates, it becomes a sexy thought."

It was very confusing when all the evidence relating to Dahmer's sexual and murderous activities were presented for the public [the jury] to decide on. It is still believed that there is no connection between sex and violence [murder].

In his closing argument, the lead prosecutor E Michael McCann held up each victim's photo, calling each name and telling the jury, "Don't forget them." Following that, the prosecutor asked the piercing question, "Is that a kindly act or a cowardly act to drug them before he killed them?"

He said, "That was no favor." The D A and prosecutor continued, and speaking as if it were Dahmer's victims speaking, he said, "Don't kill me by drugging me; come at me with a knife and a gun. Let him have his knife and I'll confront him with my bare hands!

This statement exposed the raw emotions of the victims' families and made them cry. The jury was touched by his closing exclamation.

The lead defense attorney, Gerald Boyle, presented his closing argument with the diagram of a hub, with the spokes representing personality or characteristics existing within the same person, in this case Jeffrey Dahmer.

The hub was what the attorney referred to as the "Jeffrey Dahmer human being," from which all the other deviant characteristics radiated. In a fast and quite audible tone, the attorney read what all the spokes of the hub were, including skulls in locker, cannibalism, sexual urges, drilling, making zombies, disorder necrophilia, paraphilia, watching videos, getting excited about fish eggs, drinking alcohol all of the time, trying to create a shrine, showering with corpses, calling taxidermists, going to graveyards, going to funeral homes and so on. "This is Jeffrey Dahmer," the attorney said with a low tone in his voice. "There isn't a positive thing on this."

Mr Boyle called Dahmer "a runaway train on a track of madness, picking up steam all the time, on and on and on. And it was only going to stop when he hit a concrete barrier or another train. And he hit it, thanks be to God, when Tracy Edwards got the hell out of that room."

Here, McCann came up with a strong counter argument saying, "He wasn't a runaway train; he was the engineer!" McCann emphasized that this case was about sexual urges and that we all have them and must control them, but Dahmer chose not to.

By the end of the trial, most people had become confused on the issue of mental disease from the evidence and all the testimonies presented in total. The Honorable Judge Lawrence Gram clarified mental disease in his instructions to the jury for deliberation as follows:

"You are not bound by medical labels, definitions, or conclusions as to what is or is not a mental disease. You should not find that a person is suffering from a mental disease merely because he may have committed a criminal act or because of the unnaturalness or enormity of such act or because a motive for such act may be lacking.

"Temporary passion or frenzy prompted by revenge, hatred, jealousy, envy, or the like does not constitute a mental disease.

"An abnormality manifested only by repeated criminal or otherwise antisocial conduct does not constitute a mental disease.

"A voluntary state of intoxication by drugs or alcohol or both does not constitute a mental disease.

"A temporary mental state, which is brought into existence by the voluntary taking of drugs or alcohol, does not constitute a mental disease."

With the above instructions, the jury went into deliberation on February 14, 1992, returning with a verdict within five hours.

The court was quiet and tense as Judge Gram read the verdict. On Count 1, asking whether Jeffrey Dahmer suffered from a mental disease, the answer was, "No." The judge repeated the same question fifteen times for the fifteen victims. Each time, the answer was, "No."

The bereaved families sobbed and hugged each other.

A verdict of "guilty" and "sane" was delivered on all fifteen counts. Jeffrey Dahmer then prepared his statement of apology before his sentencing. At his sentencing he read his statement of apology, which ran to four typewritten pages. Part of the apology read as follows:

"Your Honor, It is now over. This has never been a case of trying to get free. I didn't ever want freedom.

Frankly, I wanted death for myself. This was a case to tell the world that I did what I did not for reasons of hate. I hated no one. I knew I was sick or evil or both. Now I believe I was sick. The doctors have told me about my sickness and now I have some peace.

I know how much harm I have caused. I tried to do the best I could after the arrest to make amends, but no matter what I did, I could not undo the terrible harm I have caused. I feel so bad for what I did to those poor families, and I understand their rightful hate.

I decided to go through this trial for a number of reasons. One of the reasons was to let the world know these were not hate crimes. I wanted the world and Milwaukee, which I deeply hurt, to know the truth of what I did. I didn't want unanswered questions. All the questions have now been answered. I wanted to find out just what it was that caused me to be so bad and evil. But most of all, Mr Boyle and I decided that maybe there was a way for us to tell the world that if there are people out there with these disorders, maybe they can get some help before they end up being hurt or hurting someone. I think the trial did that." Dahmer concluded his speech by saying, "Thank God there will be no more harm that I can do. I believe that only the Lord Jesus Christ can save me from my sins...I ask for no consideration."

Jeffrey Dahmer was sentenced to fifteen consecutive life terms, totaling 957 years in prison.

By the time the trial was over, the cost to the State topped $120,000, because in addition to the cost of the security shield for $15,000, all the witnesses, all the jurors, the security officers and the Medical Examiner had to be paid. It was a costly lesson for the public to realize the good that came out of this case. The prosecutor himself emphasized the need for people to recognize the ultimate danger of fantasy and that thinking about anything is a sure precursor to actually doing it.

The defense attorney himself felt that the trial revealed to anyone with serious problems that help exists. However, the actual reason or reasons why Jeffrey Dahmer carried out his crimes in the way he did still remains a mystery. The study of his mind while in prison was stopped when Dahmer was killed by another inmate shortly after his imprisonment. Surely, one thing on Dahmer's mind was not returning to prison. Perhaps he would not have killed his victims if he could have been guaranteed that they would not report him to the police after the effects of the drug had worn off. Nevertheless, his necrophilia and fascination for the inside of his victims' bodies may have been the main reason behind his desire to kill.

According to Dr Judith Becker, Dahmer did not have an erection when his victim was awake, so he had to first render the person unconscious before engaging in any sexual acts. He even told police that he liked the warmth from the inside of the victims after he had cut them open. Being a veteran medic, he felt that he could do a little extra work on people this way. With past experience of how chemicals like formaldehyde preserved dead insects, how soilex when boiled in water and a skull cleaned it out and how acid melted the flesh of animals into sludge, he was confident enough to carry out the experiments he had in mind.

Chapter 13

Exodus II, an Involuntary Moveout

It was no longer business as usual to operate the Oxford Apartments, because of the high number of vacancies, the added cost of security services and the related stigma from the murders that Jeffrey Dahmer committed there. After the sale of the building to another real estate company, a new manager was brought in to give eviction notices. When the news about plans to demolish the building hit the streets, I knew that Exodus II was about to begin. The old residents that remained in the building had been settled here. They were used to living there, despite the tragedy and these people did so because it was affordable, regardless of the stigma attached to the building.

All residents were given the disappointing 30 days' eviction notice to vacate the leased premises no later than November 2, 1992. At the service of such notices, the Oxford Apartments would experience unspeakable acts of vandalism, mostly by the current residents who were angry to be forced out of the building. The reason was that everyone wanted to keep a piece of history from the Dahmer Murder case. I had observed some residents who took pieces of carpeting that they cut out of the carpeting in their living room. Some took a few pieces of the ceramic tiles in their bathroom floor. Later I found that someone had taken away Jeffrey Dahmer's mailbox. Someone also removed the residents' directory of the Oxford Apartments.

Exodus II also heralded the opportunity for Treasure Hunters to come to the building and take anything they could as souvenirs. Some visitors would brag about actually having a photo of Dahmer's apartment door, his autograph, or anything that had any connection to him. As the building drew so many crowds day after day, the public wished to put it to rest by tearing it down; another of Dahmer's victims.

The new owners had little knowledge of the current residents. I had called Ken, the manager, but he was not there to take the call, so I left a message for him. I had wanted to tell him a little bit about the residents so that he would be able to work with them. While he didn't return my call, the new owners came to the building and started moving things out to prepare for the demolition of the building. Even when he met me in person, the new manager was too arrogant to speak to me. In the process, they moved some personal property belonging to some residents, which greatly angered those concerned.

When the caretaker investors failed to follow proper procedures to take occupancy, a chaotic environment developed inside the Oxford Apartments. The hunt for souvenirs, treasures or memorabilia intensified in and around the building. The result was an invasion of the building by total strangers. I remember some other apartment building owners who came to look for bargains on appliances, because they thought that the new owners might have a sale of these refrigerators, gas stoves and air conditioners. Instead, it was the vacating residents who were making deals on the side over these appliances. At one point the building was like no man's land and everything seemed out of control. Consequently, the new owners lost more appliances than they anticipated. This is what I called an "Open Season" inside the Oxford. It was like the deer hunting season when the hunters go for any deer that they can find.

Once the relocation began, some residents took with them ceramic tiles from the bathroom, some pieces of floor carpeting from the living room and anything they could grab on their way out. The building had come to the end of its demise and had to be demolished. All residents were evicted on notice and were given some assistance to move.

I was the last to move after coordinating the entire exodus.

Now I would need the services of placement agencies or personnel departments to find another job. But with the stigma attached to my previous role, I faced a rough road ahead.

The new owners of the building probably thought that they owned everything in the building once they bought it. That was not the case, because personal property belonging to the current residents in the building was not part of the sale of the real estate. Therefore, they didn't own the personal property that belonged to the residents of the building before they took ownership, but still "stole" some of it from the building. When the residents discovered this mistake, they demanded the return of such items. The new owners couldn't return any of the personal property, because they had immediately sold it. I lost all my tools, which I was using to work on my property at 1807 W. State Street. These included plumbing and electrical tools. Along with the tools were some faucets, plumbing and electrical fixtures that were removed and not returned to me. I was disappointed with the new owners for the loss of my tools and despite complaining to the new owners, they were never returned to me, nor was I compensated for the loss.

Although the residents were not happy about moving out, they were given some incentives to enhance their move. Moving expenses in the form of free transportation was provided for most of the residents to their various locations in the city of Milwaukee.

The new owners had stored all the refrigerators, gas stoves and air conditioners in two apartments. The residents who were angry about moving intruded into the two apartments and removed an undetermined number of kitchen appliances and air conditioners as they moved out of the building. The stolen appliances were the beginning losses that the new building owners began to sustain in this time of extended tension.

Finally, the building stood alone awaiting its demise as another victim of the serial killer. Although he was then sentenced to 957 years in prison, I did harbor some concern that he might escape from prison. Jeffrey Dahmer had an intelligence quotient equivalent to that of a genius and he could by chance possibly manipulate himself out of there unnoticed. So concerned was I about his possible escape from prison, that I had a dream about it while I was taking a nap in the afternoon on April 17, 1994. This was two years into his sentence. Almost a year later, in March 1995, I had an interview with an official of the German Public Television for a Documentary on Jeffrey Dahmer. At that time I expressed my concern to Mr Gero Von Boehm regarding Dahmer's possible escape from prison. I was very concerned by my dream, but Dahmer was murdered by another inmate before I ever had the chance to find out whether or not this would eventually have happened.

Chapter 14

The Dream of Dahmer's Prison Escape

"Presidents Live In Seclusion"

After testifying in court during the trial on February 11, 1992, I received one anonymous telephone call from a man who told me that my testimony was too incriminating. I was surprised this man was willing to protect a murderer like Jeffrey Dahmer, even after all the evidence that had been uncovered in his apartment and Dahmer's own confessions. I could only assume that this man must have been a member of the gang enhancing Dahmer's criminal activities in the building. I had to ask him if I should be in jail before Jeffrey Dahmer the criminal. He said good question and at this point he realized that I was not as dumb as he was and hanged up the phone. Although the caller didn't say who he was the voice sounded like one who used to live in the building in an official position.

This was an indication that Jeffrey Dahmer belonged to a street gang while he lived at the Oxford Apartments. The gang was going to protect him, except that this time it couldn't because too much crime had already been exposed to the public. This was the gang that I thought might assist him in a possible prison escape. As smart as he was, you never knew what he might do then; possibly the same old crimes of murder in series so that the families of the city would start to report on their missing loved ones.

My concern about his possible prison escape was so real that I had the dream about it. It was on April 17, 1994 at about 3.00pm when I went to bed for a short nap before going to work on a third shift job. While I was still asleep, I had this peculiar dream about Jeffrey Dahmer. In March of the previous year, I had expressed my concern about

Dahmer escaping to Mr Gero Von Boehm of the German Public Television when he interviewed me for an hour a documentary on Dahmer. I reflected on how he had skillfully manipulated his contacts with the authorities and I was not sure of what he might do next when he was in prison. With this concern always on my mind, I had this dream. In the dream I saw Jeffrey Dahmer living in luxury at the campus of a big university like that of one of the "Big Ten" American universities. He was secluded in a little shack, having only one room in a corner at the perimeter of the campus. The shack had only one dusty window on which someone had finger written in the dust, "Presidents live in seclusion." Under his bed was a unique pair of shoes made of leather. The shoes had solid high heels designed to let another shoe slide out. These shoes could be used together or separately. A large leather trunk box with sturdy belts and locks in shinny gold was also sitting under his bed. Wherever he was, he seemed to be enjoying his newfound freedom.

Occasionally, Dahmer left his room at will while watching out to make sure that no one knew of his presence there. He also relaxed among some shrubbery, which flanked the immediate vicinity of his room. I saw and recognized what looked like Jeffrey Dahmer's face at a distance. I was then curious about what I saw and at the same time on that campus I saw two young freshmen playing outdoor tennis that evening. I approached them and asked them for a favor to satisfy my curiosity. I sent the two young freshmen to get close enough to his shack to observe who it might be. The young freshmen would confirm then whether it was actually Jeffrey Dahmer himself or not. They went over and pretended to be playing around, so as not to alarm him in any way or arouse his suspicion. From there, the young men could observe closely.

The two spy kids returned to confirm that it was

Jeffrey Dahmer. Then we sat around for some time and discussed at length what a risk Dahmer had taken, because we knew that he had made deadly enemies from the mass murders he had committed. Now he was living in a place where someone could notice his presence. We were not those who would seek to hurt him for the murders he committed, but we thought that there might be others who would want to kill him for those crimes if they happened to spot him. We also discussed how much of a luxury he seemed to be enjoying there. We continued discussing the topic and expressed our concern for his safety.

Then I woke up and wondered what the dream meant. I was unsure of his prison security at this point and thought that he might escape one day and target more victims.

Shortly after this dream, Dahmer was killed in prison by another inmate, Christopher Scarver, who was serving a life term himself. Scarver attacked and killed both Jeffrey Dahmer and another inmate Jesse Anderson, claiming that he was inspired by God. Jesse Anderson was also in prison for murder, so I drew the analogy to the statement, "Those who kill by the sword die by the sword."

From the breaking news of his arrest, most of the information people had about Dahmer was the bloody murders, alcoholism, homosexual sex orientation and abandonment etc., but there were also the other things in his life that were positive that he just couldn't accomplish because of his nature.

After his sentencing and imprisonment Dahmer was on a "hit list" at the Portage Maximum Security Prison in the State of Wisconsin. At the Columbia Correctional Institution, inmates maintained a hit list of prisoners who had been marked for death. The names of Jeffrey L. Dahmer and Jesse Anderson were two among seven on that list, according to a letter that was sent to Dahmer's civil attorney Stephen Eisenberg by a transvestite inmate Derrick Hendricks.

An inmate had attempted to attack Dahmer previously with a razor blade, but failed to hurt him as other inmates intervened to prevent it. The prisoners were in devotion at the time and it must have been the presence of others that saved him from that attack. It appeared as though Jeffrey Dahmer was unwelcome there. The majority of his victims had been black males and there were black male inmates in the Columbia Correctional Institution. The inmates called Jeffrey Dahmer the "chop, chop man."

Another inmate on the hit list, Jesse Anderson, had stabbed his wife to death and falsely blamed two black men for the crime. Investigations connected him to the crime and he was convicted in 1992 to serve a life sentence in the same prison facility as Dahmer. While on a janitorial work detail in the prison one Friday, Jeffrey Dahmer and Jesse Anderson were both bludgeoned to death by Christopher Scarver, who was also serving a life sentence for murder. Christopher Scarver had racial sentiments because he believed that blacks were victimized by the justice system, while white people were favored and not to be trusted.

The Milwaukee Sentinel of Saturday December 3, 1994, reported that after a thorough investigation it was concluded that the incident was not racially motivated. The investigators did not settle on a single motive for the murder of the two prominent inmates. The then State Corrections Secretary, Michael J. Sullivan, concluded that the attack did not fit "within the stereotypical motivation of race-affiliated issues." It was neither group related, such as gangs, nor conspiracy related, such as a paid hit man.

The dream, "Presidents Live in Seclusion," was about my dream of Dahmer's prison escape in which he escaped from the prison and lived in seclusion at one corner of a big university campus. He lived in a shack with only one room and a window. "Presidents Live in Seclusion," had been written on the dusty window pane with the tip of a finger.

Jeffrey Dahmer had a political affiliation with the

Democratic Party, owned a membership certificate and belonged to a task force working to elect a president in 1992. He was arrested in the middle of all these activities.

Chapter 15

A Distraught Mother's Nightmare

While the furor of Dahmer's arrest were raging, it was even worse for his parents. His mother, Joyce Flint, was in hiding because she felt so distraught after hearing what had happened to her darling son. She stayed in touch with him while he was in prison. She felt that it was better to belong to the family of a victim than it was to be part of the murderer's family. It was too hard for her to believe that her son, to whom she had spoken less than three months' previously, was a serial sex killer. She finally decided to come out of hiding to tell the world her own side of the Dahmer story. She said, "There's nothing I look back on that gives any indication of anything abnormal. If there was, I'd want it known." She had gone over everything that she could remember. Some people blamed the broken home for Dahmer's deeds.

Joyce "Rocky" Flint contends that there were other children in a similar family situation who didn't become murderers. The statistics show that half of all marriages in the United States result in separation or divorce, which indicates that a large number of children experience their parents' break up, yet the majority of them do not become murderers. She remembered her son's religious education at about two and a half years of age. He memorized a bedtime prayer as follows, "Now I lay me down to sleep. I pray the Lord my soul to keep. God bless everyone. Make Jeffy a good boy. Amen."

"Jeff was a gentle boy," she said, because she observed him play with his pet turtle in quite a gentle manner. He loved his younger brother David as they were both growing amidst turmoil between their parents. They were heading for a divorce and when it was over she had asked Jeffrey and David to come along with her to Chippewa Falls,

Wisconsin, her original hometown, but Jeffrey refused to follow them. Consequently, she had to leave him in the house, even though he was an adult who could fend for himself. Jeffrey Dahmer's father, Lionel, had already moved out of the house, so Jeffrey Dahmer knew that he could take advantage of the privacy to start enjoying his depraved activities.

Most of the initial reports that came out about Jeffrey Dahmer's mother were very negative. For example, initial reports indicated that she had abandoned her son Jeffrey Dahmer, but now her own side of the story showed that she actually asked her son to come with her, but that he refused to do so. Because his father had also left the house previously, the reports made it sound like abandonment. In fact Joyce was a fine lady with a Master's degree in counseling from the University of Wisconsin. She was also an extremely likable, charming and articulate person, but unfortunately and understandably became emotionally troubled mother following the news of her son's arrest for mass murder.

At the time of Dahmer's arrest, Joyce turned down a request for an interview in return for approximately $10,000. Nevertheless, the tabloid still went on to shoot a few photos of her and filled up "three pages of lies," as she put it. The tabloid portrayed a horrific image of her, as though she was a monster-maker. She was consumed by her thoughts and had so much feeling for the victims of her son and their families. Dahmer's mother also felt so much guilt that maybe somehow, somewhere, sometime, she had done something that caused her son to do these horrific things. She understood grief and helped others in grief as a professional counselor, but at this time she was grieving herself. She was under tremendous stress, which was exacerbated by her unemployment at that time.

Joyce Flint was there for her son, rather than checking into a hospital for her own cancer treatment. She stayed in

touch with him until he was beaten to death in prison.
While she talked to her son in prison she observed that his
voice changed and he appeared to have another personality.
He told her that he was not afraid of anything in there,
because the implication was that he was so awful, but what
could they do to him in there?

He figured that she must have hated him. She didn't,
but nothing of what she told him, or what she said here, or
what other people said would in any way condone what he
did. It would, and never will, lessen the horror and anguish
and sorrow to the families of her son's victims.

Joyce explained that her son was suicidal when he was
first sentenced to life in prison and he tried to hide part of a
razor blade to use in suicide. He said that when the attempt
failed, he no longer felt suicidal. He said that he felt he
really needed to be punished for those crimes, and that to
take his own life would have been the easy way out. He
said that in order to receive the punishment he deserved, he
needed to live.

Furthermore, his mother said that he hated himself and
he thought that being gay was a sin. He was very glad that
he was in prison. She said her son still had those thoughts;
the thoughts he told the psychiatrists that drove him to
murdering, dismembering bodies and keeping them in his
apartment. She said her son didn't know if he could be
trusted in the prison community. She wished him to
continue to live, accept his punishment and help
psychiatrists to discover the reasons that were buried in the
darkness that he called his life. He kept changing his mind
between committing suicide and living on.

The birth of a baby is often a welcome blessing in a
family. So it was for the Dahmer family where the birth of
Jeffrey Dahmer brought happiness. At that time, his parents
made an ominous observation from his birthday to the age
of four months. They were scared by correctional casts that
the baby had on his legs from birth, but these disappeared

after the age of four months. If this happened in a less scientific society, his parents would have questioned what the correctional casts at his birth meant from a superstitious perspective. It is still unknown whether those correctional casts at his birth had anything to do with how he lived his life and the murders that he committed in adulthood. The correctional casts, in my opinion, were indicators that he might have been incarcerated in a previous life for habitual crimes. The correctional casts appeared at his birth to provide a warning to the people who are related to him.

When Joyce Flint finally felt able to give the true side of her son's story, she began by displaying photos of the early years of the man who the media portrayed as a monster. Her nightmare was not that Jeffrey Dahmer was a monster, but that he was her son whom she loved. Joyce said that she knew that just mentioning Dahmer's name frightened some people, but that people had to understand that a monster didn't do those things; a human being did, her son. And that's what scared her. That was the nightmare that would never end.

She had ordinary intentions that resulted in extraordinary consequences. Joyce would not dare to explain to any victim's family that she still had a meaningful relationship with her son. They would never understand, because Jeff had caused them so much heartache and taken away their children. She said that it was unbelievable she could have such a relationship with Jeff when there was a time when he didn't even want her to know his whereabouts. He would write and call her and sometimes picked out gorgeous gifts, which he then sent to her. She said that she could not change it for anyone, whether for him, his victims or herself.

As typical in most American families, they keep a baby book from birth to record the "Baby's Firsts". Joyce Flint kept such a book on her son. The baby book showed the photo of his first birthday on May 21, 1961. She gave a party on his first birthday in their apartment at 1655 N. Van Buren Street Milwaukee, Wisconsin and decorations for the party included hats, balloons, flowers and streamers to celebrate. The baby book went on to record the other "baby's firsts," such as baby's first word and first phrase.

When he turned two years and three months old Dahmer family moved to Ames, in the State of Iowa, where Jeffrey's father attended the Iowa State University. Joyce remembered the Christmas of 1963 when Lionel played Santa. Little Jeff loved him! He touched his beard and his fat tummy…laughing happily and gave him a kiss and a hug.

The baby book showed that Jeff had a double hernia operation on March 19, 1964 at the age of four. Joyce spent every minute with him. Sometimes at night he would ask her to leave so that he could sleep. The baby book then showed that when Jeffrey was about five years and four months old and in Kindergarten, he had some difficulty adjusting. By year end he had improved and showed great interest in insects and animal life. On July 24, 1966 he was excited to hear from his parents that he was going to be a brother.

His mother said that one day out of the blue, Jeff thanked her for all the good things she did for him and for having that baby in her tummy. Every so often he would pat her on the tummy and say that it was so the baby knew it had a brother. Every time they lay and talked in the morning, or had a conversation during the day, Jeff would suggest that they talked about babies.

In October of 1966, the Dahmer family moved again, this time to Doylestown, Ohio where Jeffrey Dahmer was making gradual progress, although frequent moving had indeed taken its toll on him. He had a new puppy, which he called Frisky. He was very fond of her and they (Joyce and Lionel) hoped that Frisky would help him to adjust to their new home, school and friends. He was adamant that the new baby must be a boy so he could play with him.

David Lionel was born December 18, 1966. Jeff named him David. This meant more adjusting for Jeff, but he loved Davy and was good to him, although Frisky came first in his heart.

In 1967, The Dahmer family moved to Barberton, Ohio and again in 1968 to Bath, Ohio.

Joyce Flint described their beautiful ranch home in Ohio. In contrast, the newspaper reported on July 24, 1991:

"Families haunted by memories of missing loved ones showed photographs to neighbors of Jeffrey L. Dahmer, the suspect to the multiple murders, and flooded the Police Department with calls for information about the victims' identities.

A mother of the youngest of her six children indicated 'It's like he just vanished from the world.'"

Jeffrey Dahmer's mother introduced herself. Flint, 57, was born in Columbus, Wisconsin, one of seven children that grew up in Chippewa Falls and Milwaukee, Wisconsin. After she graduated from Juneau High School, she went to work for Wisconsin Telephone Company in Milwaukee.

She met Lionel through mutual friends while he was selling Encyclopedias that summer. She was 23 and everybody she knew was married. She said that she didn't love him and shouldn't have married him. She got pregnant right away and remembered Lionel didn't want children.

Consequently she was very unhappy. It was like she married one personality, but when he went back to being himself, he was very much a loner who had only a few friends. She met two of his friends more often during the first part of the marriage. These were the friends who were very much like him, academicians driven by their lofty ambition and loved their studies more than women. To them romance was only a secondary obligation, thus her marriage was unhealthy and unhappy. She was looking for answers to the situation. She believed in counseling and had a degree in

184

it.

After Jeffrey Dahmer admitted that he had murdered seventeen young males, there were many rumors about members of the family and his mother, none of which turned out to be true. Flint said she had seen counselors and had been hospitalized for depression, but had never been diagnosed as crazy and that the insensitive rumormongers had made her life miserable.

Misery had been the main ingredient of Joyce Flint's life since July 23, 1991 when her son was first arrested and the news started to unfold. He was providing graphic details about what he did to his victims. All this information was coming through the media and since her son was portrayed as a monster, by association, she was now like a monster-maker.

Flint explained that it was a horrible year for the kids. Returning home after a visit to her dying father, she became embroiled with obtaining a divorce. A couple of years before she had pleaded with Lionel for a divorce because she said she couldn't continue living that way. Her husband didn't smoke or drink, so why was she so unhappy?

Joyce and her husband were opposites; she an extrovert, he an introvert. She said that toward the end of their marriage, they fought constantly. Her husband didn't respect her, often referred to her in derogatory terms and was often uncommunicative.

She managed to get Lionel to agree to sit down with the boys one Saturday. "They went into the playroom and sat on the floor. There they touched and cried. They told the children that their father was going to leave the house. Lionel was very cooperative. They stayed there and hugged each other and they talked about what was going to happen. But they never expected what eventually did happen.

On July 24, 1991, the newspaper reported, The *place crawled with police, reporters and curious residents, some of whom hoisted babies and small children above the crowd, which was four rows deep by afternoon. The circus-like atmosphere deteriorated into a mob scene at 4.30pm after police removed the yellow tape blocking access to the building. About seventy-five to a hundred people climbed up the building's fire escape and wandered up and down the halls, looking for a view. They saw nothing while viewing in curiosity.*

Flint denied any knowledge of her son's homosexual tendencies while he was in high school. The only change that she could look back on was that Jeff was caught drinking. They weren't drinkers and didn't have it in the house. She then recalled that from Kindergarten through High School, Jeff was never happy in school, although she had no indication that Jeff was gay. He never told her he was gay. However, being gay is not a reason for what he did, or else a percentage of our population would be wandering around murdering innocent victims.

Flint said that the only thing she noticed about Jeff was that he was introverted, like his father. Nevertheless, many people are introverts, but they don't commit unspeakable crimes. Jeffrey Dahmer's mother asked the same question that every one of us had asked, except that she had asked it a million times since her son was arrested for mass murder in his own apartment; Why did this all happen? Why did this happen to her darling child? She didn't understand.

His father wanted him to go to college, which he did, but he drank himself into a stupor.

When the parents split up, Flint took Jeffrey's brother David and asked Jeffrey to come with them, but he refused. She remembered begging Jeff to come with her, but he refused. He had just graduated from high school and wanted to stay alone in the big ranch home.

He then began his first wanderings. He murdered a hitchhiker. Far from the innocence of his younger years, a decade after the baby book ended, Jeff Dahmer's tumultuous and murderous secret life had begun.

186

When he was in the service, he sent his mother a set of dishes from Germany. He sent all these wonderful presents. He wrote about sunlight and blue skies and drew David a picture of some military hardware such as tanks. Then, suddenly, he stopped writing letters. She couldn't find him for many years, so he was always missing from her life.

After those missing five or six years, they had exactly the same conversation when she finally reach him by phone. He would say the usual, 'Hi Mom, I love you, I miss you.' He would then say he was sorry for not having written to her. He promised to write and didn't and she'd start calling again. She remembered writing to express that she didn't care what was wrong in his life, whether he was gay or an ex- murderer, but she wished that he could write or call.

Among the things that Jeffrey Dahmer's mother remembered about her son were the letters he had written to her in the past. From her sun drenched California porch, she pulled out one of these letters that expressed his thoughts and worries about her in recent times

He would indicate how late the time it was, say 3:00am 4:00am, as he wrote the letter. It showed just one of the nights when he couldn't sleep. It hurt him to know that she was sick and in pain. It was not that he didn't want to hear how she really felt, because he did. He just wished that things were better for her. He wished with everything in him that he could have given her happiness instead of pain. He expressed that he never meant to bring her pain.

He just wanted to let her know that he loved her very much and often thought of her.

He explained how strange it was that the season changed so fast from summer to Fall and how he liked to see the color of the leaves. He said he wished he had quit his job at the Ambrosia Chocolate Company years ago in order to be near to her in California.

He never liked the job because he fell into a rut at work, but the money was alright. He doubted he could have found a job that paid that much if he had moved to California, but he thought he should have just taken the chance hoping that things could have been different. He hoped and prayed that the cancer and pain would leave her so that the years ahead would bring hope and joy. He really wished that he could somehow make that happen for her. He pledged to love her always, telling her to take care.

Joyce Flint knew this Jeff well, had known him all of his life, but had been forced to come to know the other person, the Jeffrey that the public heard about, the serial killer and cannibal. She wondered whether there was any Jeff left, or whether there was a difference between Jeff and a Jeffrey. She shook her head in despair and began crying again.

When he stopped calling or writing she would track him down and was almost sure the last phone call she had from him before his arrest was just one or two months before Mother's Day. He had promised to call on Mother's Day, but failed to do so and now she was worried about him and the AIDS' disease.

Indeed, there was inadequate attention towards her son in his youthful days and now that he was an adult and away from her, she understood less about his secret life. She didn't know that he was gay for the five years they had been apart. She was in total shock when he was arrested and the details of all his planned methods of killing were revealed.

Chapter 16

Not Just a Serial Killer

A conversation with Jeffrey Dahmer's probation agent, Ms Donna Chester, revealed even more about the most twisted sex serial killer. Donna was able to observe the changes in his moods, but could not figure out what it was all about before his arrest.

On July 24, 1991, the newspaper reported: "Perhaps the most unusual feature of the apartment was a bolt lock on the outside of the bedroom door, which made it possible to lock someone behind it."

Jeffrey Dahmer had political aspirations. This might be a surprise to a lot of people. He might have kept this a secret too, or else he had concentrated all his efforts into his passion for murder. Jeffrey Dahmer was part of a Presidential Task Force preparing their candidate for the 1992 Presidential Election.

Dahmer's political party of choice was the Democratic Party. His reason for this choice might have been a reflection of the harsh experience of his childhood. He probably made this choice in opposition to his own father's political party, which I suspect was the Republican Party. It dated back to the youthful years of his life when, like most adolescents, he started to emulate somebody he admired in politics.

Jeffrey Dahmer was not just a serial killer; he was also an aspiring politician. While in college, I took a course in philosophy. During one of the classes the professor said that politics is about people and that it is the highest science. To support his statement, the professor explained that people are the most unpredictable in this world, so the politicians always had to risk more resources to have the people on their side. The money, the time, the speeches, the interviews, the phone calls and everything else that goes into a campaign for an election can drain the candidates, mentally, physically and financially. The goal of the politicians for risking all those resources is to win an election. When they achieve their goal, they gain all the control that Dahmer sought after. Jeffrey Dahmer was politically active when he was in high school and continued to be a democrat until the night he was arrested.

A certificate of his political activity is the evidence of his aspirations. The certificate is authentic with the signature of the chairman, the late Ron Brown. As was discovered during the trial, Jeffrey Dahmer liked power and control over people. He admired the politicians for the power and control that they had over others. He wanted to be in a position of power and control one day and he considered politics as a way of achieving that.

Even though he was raised in the Protestant Faith, he had planned to worship Satan in a shrine that he was going to build in his apartment. He had set a goal of collecting as many skulls as possible to build his fantasy shrine.

Was this a change in passion, or strategy? Jeffrey Dahmer turned to Satan for his passion of power and control. He thought of being a revered person in order to acquire the attention that he felt he never had. All his actions were deliberate and routine, as he had planned them. He enticed his victims with money, because he recalled, "money is the root of all evil" and as much as he felt evil himself, he just did it.

When in such a position of power among his followers, he would have control over them and continue in devil worship in his apartment. This was the reason why he could not use the insanity defense during his trial. As the defense attorney tried mental disease as a defense, the prosecutor exclaimed that Jeffrey Dahmer was not sick, just evil.

Imagine what publicity Dahmer was aiming to create. He knew that he would be caught one day, but he continued and even accelerated his pace in committing murder just to collect enough skulls for his fantasy shrine.

Whatever way one looks at it, Jeffrey Dahmer was aiming at something that would shock the world; something that would remind his former classmates in grade school of "that weird kid," the same thing that would remind his high school buddies of "that funny jester" and would also remind his former bunkmates in the military of "that alcoholic serviceman."

The news' coverage on Jeffrey Dahmer was colossal. All of a sudden he had become more famous for the crimes he had committed. He was almost like a celebrity. No matter how well he had done in his life in any other area, he never gained any notoriety. As a result, he felt inadequate. Jeffrey Dahmer was a smart man. He wanted to do something that would put him center stage, for people to recognize him for what he did, no matter how bad or weird it might be.

The members of the National Honor Society who blacked out his face from their photo when he was in high school would now see his face in more grandiose images on the tabloids, on television screens, on front page headlines of all newspapers and, of course, in low budget movies limited to videos. Here in Milwaukee any movie about Jeffrey Dahmer was not allowed to be shown on the big screen.

Dahmer felt that the military rejected him when it discharged him, no matter how well he had done during the Medic training courses. In fact, he performed extremely well in terms of reading up and retaining in his memory the contents of piles of material within a time limit. I believe that many of his course mates realized the degree of challenge they experienced in those courses for them to think that Jeffrey Dahmer had a high intelligence quotient. He was given an IQ of about 145, which indicated that he was a genius. He was a man who loved publicity and he often manipulated his way to acquire it. When he was in

191

high school and took part in a field trip to Washington DC, he made sure that the participants of the trip saw or met an important politician. Dahmer made the necessary phone calls and made a connection with the then Vice President Walter Mondale. The trip participants had this exciting experience of meeting the Vice President of the United States of America, because Jeffrey Dahmer pulled it for them.

They were all very impressed with Jeffrey Dahmer, which made him happy. Dahmer was motivated by the politicians and working for his party. He was offered membership in the Democratic National Committee and was part of the 1992 Presidential Task Force. Jeffrey Dahmer was committed to aspire to what is expected of a son from a high class American family like his. Maybe if he were able to stop himself after his first murder and followed a successful career, nobody would have known about it. In that case, the missing person who became his first murder victim would never have been found and the case would never have been solved or closed.

In High School he was involved with the school's only newspaper, The Lantern. He aspired to be among the smart students in the National Honor Society, even though he didn't make the grade to belong there. He managed to get into their honor roll photo by slipping into position just at the click of the camera shot. The NHS members were furious. They didn't think about taking another shot without Dahmer. Instead, they blacked out his face from the picture. Dahmer didn't like that. He thought of it as rejection and again it reminded him of abandonment and of being at home alone when he was younger. He was feeling more negative about life and could not interact with people to establish any lasting friendships. He therefore became a loner.

His political aspirations started to dwindle to the point when he developed an interest in occultism and satanic worship and he strongly believed in the power of the devil. He had a statue of the griffin, which is symbolic of the devil and Dahmer admitted feeling like it to Dr Judy Becker, who evaluated him and was an expert witness on his defense team during his trial.

Suddenly, his passion changed from political interests to the dark side of our human existence. It accelerated when he resumed killing again more than ten years after his first murder in 1978. From here on, his mind was twisted with the evil desires that led him to choose murder as his mission in life.

Jeffrey Dahmer had no friends and no dates because of his secret life style in which he habitually murdered them all. When he was finally exposed and arrested, his world came crashing down and there seemed to be no other solution for him but just to accept it and pay the price.

While in custody, he confessed to all the murders he had committed. Maybe he didn't confess to everything. He was able to remember seventeen victims. He denied anything to do with the missing persons where he had lived before, namely Florida in the United States and Baumholder in Germany. There was an unsolved murder in apartment #308 two months prior to his arrest, which appeared to be a Dahmer style murder. However, Dahmer denied anything to do with Dean Vaughn's unsolved murder.

Jeffrey Dahmer was not just a serial killer; he was also an infant biochemist. Being the son of a father that had a PhD in Chemistry, Jeffrey Dahmer had the gift of a chemistry kit from his father early in life. As a child he started to experiment with insects and small animals, like squirrels and rabbits. He preserved the dead creatures in formaldehyde, removed the skin and flesh from small animals and really observed how acid reacted to their flesh and bones.

As a child, Jeffrey Dahmer's interest in the Life

Sciences began to take root in his mind. As an adolescent, Jeffrey Dahmer started to imagine what the same chemicals could do to larger animals like dogs and cats, road kills like deer etc. At this time of his life, his family was falling apart. His father and his mother were preoccupied with an impending divorce, which deprived him of the benefits of good parenting and, most of all, the attention he so craved.

After his parents' separation and his mother's move away from the house, Dahmer increased his consumption of alcohol and started to become involved in occultism. These developments hampered his academic success, even though he was clearly very intelligent.

His loneliness resulted in Steven Hicks becoming Dahmer's first victim. He hid the body and went on to college. After just one quarter semester he dropped out and joined the military for the next two years as a Medic. What he learned about the anatomy of the human body during his training as a Medic inspired him to be curious about chemicals and the human body. This curiosity would motivate him to kill his second victim ten years after his first.

After Dahmer was discharged from the military, his sexuality problems started. He'd been with females both while he was in the military and before he killed his second victim, but he was not sexually attracted to females. He had social problems connecting with females as well as males. He thereby felt inadequate in himself and sought a way to have control over people. He thought about drugging them to have sex, but realized that that could pose a problem when the person regained consciousness. They might want to file a complaint with the police and he knew that he had not yet been apprehended for his first murder. He had also been convicted of child molestation and placed on probation after one year in the House of Correction. He hated his experience in prison and dreaded going back there. His probation required him to have treatment for alcoholism and other problems like depression.

He knew that he had the freedom to avoid treatment since he was not supervised closely by his probation agent. She helped him primarily with issues that he complained about, but he was hiding so much more from this probation agent.

Jeffrey Dahmer, the infant biochemist, was now an adult and retained his curiosity about the effect of chemicals on living creatures. This time, the closest living things to which he had access were human beings, so he sought out a suitable place to continue his experiments.

Dahmer's drug regiments included some prescription medicines for his depression, such as benzodiazepine and Lorazepam. The active ingredients in these drugs could render people unconscious when mixed with a substantial amount of alcohol. He also kept chloroform in his bedroom closet. Dahmer was experimenting with these drugs in the bathhouses to observe how effective they were on an unlucky patron. Other drugs found in the systems of Dahmer's victims included cocaine, halcion and marijuana, which he probably acquired on the streets.

He finally came up with a concoction that was as effective as the sleeping pill to drug the guests when they tried to leave his apartment.

Jeffrey Dahmer was an alcoholic. He started drinking from elementary school age, something very uncommon among children in that age bracket at that time. Alcohol was the single main factor that ignited the anger and hate that Dahmer felt inside. It was not easy to tolerate him when he was drunk, because he would become aggressive and abusive. He would fight, throw racial insults at black people and continue to drink until he passed out. When he sobered up, he was a nice guy who was shy and would behave well. He would fool people. They would never have guessed that he was a silent serial killer on the loose.

The excess alcohol Dahmer consumed reacted with his

medication for depression and exacerbated his mental condition. He abused alcohol to the point where he had to drink it when he planned to murder and to mutilate his victims. At best, the only times when Dahmer was not abusing alcohol were when he was asleep or at work. However, he was chronically absent from work so he could use that time to drink more alcohol and commit more homicides.

The reason he left the little Laotian boy in his apartment was so that he could go and buy some more beer from the tavern down the street. In a way he associated the use of alcohol with murder, so that anytime he drank alcohol heavily enough, his mind instantly transformed into that of a killing monster. He stocked up on alcohol to use each time he earmarked a victim for murder. It began socially at first, but then Dahmer would want to take it further, fantasizing about sex with the dead while drinking alcohol with the guest. The moment the opportunity arose, he slipped the pills into the drink of his guest. The alcohol reduced his control of self and thereby made him feel less accountable for any crimes he might commit.

He had to have the victim under his control so that he could have his way. It was very cowardly to drug his victims before sodomizing, killing and then stealing from them. Dahmer's drug regiments were like the culprit for his actions in crime. The combination of alcohol and drugs put Dahmer in a mood that had no room for pity or sympathy. The alcohol stole his social conscience so that he was only capable of ruthlessness in his mission to murder. No kidding! The alcohol in a drunken head created more fantasies that Dahmer strived to pursue as his realities.

He needed someone to stay with him and keep him company, but as soon as any of his guests showed the desire to leave him, the relationship became fatal. He wanted to control.

Dahmer was called the "BTK" killer (bind, torture, and

kill). I thought of him as the "DSSM" (drug, sex, strangle, and mutilate).

Strangling was Dahmer's second stage, but he told the custodian detectives that he stabbed one victim in the neck, because the effects of the drug had almost worn off and it would have been difficult to strangle him. I believe Dahmer must have stabbed the Laotian boy too, because the boy was almost conscious when the police officers left him with Dahmer. It was such a horrible death for that boy. He should have expressed his desire to leave when the police officers were still there. He probably thought that he had to do whatever a white man told him to do, because he saw that the officers had driven away the witnesses who called the 911 emergency. Those were the ones helping him, but when they were dismissed from the scene, he maybe assumed that everything was alright.

Jeffrey Dahmer derived some sort of gratification from each of the three stages he engaged in while committing murder. The first stage action which is the drugging gave him the opportunity to listen to the unconscious victim's heartbeat. Dahmer loved to hear the heartbeat. The thob, thob sound of the heartbeat of a living thing thrilled Dahmer and he would place his ear close to the heart on the victim's chest and continued to listen until the effect of the drug was about to wear off. He had another use for the heart when it stopped beating.

The next stage was strangling, which gave Dahmer a feeling of power and control over his victim. In reality, this was a false sense of power and control over the victim, because they were not conscious. However, during the strangulation process, they did react to the perpetrator and made some noise from the stumping of the feet and hands.

Depending on what his choice might be at the end of each stage, Dahmer would have sex before the next stage. In other words, he would have oral sex with the unconscious victim, sucking the penis and having anal sex.

The next stage was the mutilation and dismemberment of the victim's body. Mutilation was the stage during which Dahmer also decided which body parts of a victim he would retain as a trophy of his deeds. Dahmer told police that he derived some sexual gratification from each of the stages in which he was engaged with the victim. He had a special fondness for the victims whose body parts he retained. There were some victims whose body parts he totally disposed of, because he thought they were not his type. He wrapped them in plastic garbage bags and tossed them out into the dumpster behind the Oxford Apartments.

He would cook and eat some of the body parts that he chose to keep, such as the heart. Other body parts such as the head, Dahmer would clean and sometimes paint as a souvenir. When he was arrested, eleven skulls were discovered in his apartment.

Following Dahmer's arrest, four severed, uncleaned heads were found wrapped in garbage bags and placed in his freezer. Apart from the refrigerator that came with the apartment, Dahmer had his own upright freezer especially for storing body parts of his victims. When he had too many for the freezer, some parts were left out to begin decaying in the apartment. The smell from such decay drove Jeffrey Dahmer to buy the 57 gallon plastic barrel into which he put some acid to melt all other body parts he didn't need. Dahmer was not sure if the use of the barrel would solve the smell problem, but he tried it as an experiment. As an additional remedy for the bad smell, Dahmer gave me some liquid deodorant in a plastic bottle to give to the residents to eliminate the smell in their apartments.

Dahmer had no intention of buying any other sort of meat from the grocery store. Nobody at the Oxford Apartments ever saw Jeffrey Dahmer coming home with a bag of groceries. The only food items found in the apartment after his arrest were some potato chips, mustard, ketchup and mayonnaise.

Jeffrey Dahmer had an array of drug regiments.
When convenient, he had always experimented with them
trying to come up with a concoction that would do the job
most effectively. It was reported that in an incident at one
of Milwaukee's bathhouses, Dahmer had tested his
concoction on a patron who shared a stall with him. The
patron passed out in the stall and was taken to the hospital
for emergency detoxification. Other patrons who observed
Dahmer leaving the stall reported it to the owners of the
bathhouse and Dahmer was banned from coming there
anymore.

Sex of course was also a significant complement of
each action Dahmer engaged in while he murdered his
victims. He described to the police how he had oral sex
with the victims after he had drugged them, then anal sex
after he had strangled them and more sex with the open
parts of the body during the mutilation of each victim. He
always took Polaroid shots of the mutilation stage and kept
the photos as evidence of his accomplishments. That was
how one bereaved mother identified her son. Dahmer had a
photo of the face of the severed head of her son David
Thomas and she identified her son from viewing that photo.

Dahmer's alcoholism negatively affected his
performance and attendance on the job wherever he had
worked. It affected his studies while he was in college.
Excessive use of alcohol had cost him everything in life.
Alcohol cost Dahmer his job, his friends and family and,
worst of all, his freedom. He was not able to concentrate on
his studies at the University of Ohio, so he dropped out. He
only served for two years in the military because a soldier
with such an appetite for alcohol was not fit for the kind of
a teamwork that was required. All field or combat
personnel in the military depend on one another. The
military had to let him go because they felt that he could do
better in a civilian work environment where a mistake

could only hurt a few people. If someone like Dahmer were allowed to continue to serve in the military, he could possibly make it dangerous for the others around him because they could not depend on him while he continued to drink heavily. Under the influence of alcohol, Dahmer was like the weakest link in the chain of command on the frontline of duty. Thus he was discharged early from the military. He was truly offended by this termination from the military and once again he perceived this as rejection.

He was unable to stop drinking and he did not go for treatment available free of charge because he thought that it was a waste of money. The problem intensified after he returned home to Bath Township, Ohio from the military. There he openly violated the laws regulating the use of alcohol. Nothing was getting any better for him. He was cited by the police regarding the use of alcohol in a public domain and his new family in Ohio had knowledge of his alcohol problem for the first time. His father's new wife, his stepmother, had maintained a homely environment quite unlike what he was used to when his own mother was the lady of the house. He knew what those tumultuous years of his childhood had done to him. His present family did not know that he had committed a murder right in the house where they now lived.

Dahmer was also feeling the sexuality pressure. He started to engage in lewd behavior, such as indecent exposure. He was confused about his own sexuality and he was not making the big bucks from the type of work he obtained in Ohio. Dahmer now started to seek something that would make a positive difference in his life, so he chose to leave Ohio. His next best destination that he believed would give him a cover for his initial living expenses and the warmth of a family environment, was his paternal grandmother's house in West Allis, a little suburb of the City of Milwaukee in the State of Wisconsin where he was born.

Once he moved back to Wisconsin, he sought out his favorite spots to meet people. He found the location of gay bars, the mall and the streets where the most vulnerable people might be found.

Dahmer had not told anyone about his first murder and at least once while he was in the military, he attempted to talk about it, but he withheld it, putting all of his bunk mates in suspense. When he left the military, he did promise them that they would hear about him again. They didn't know what he meant until they received the news of his arrest in July 1991. The promise he made to his bunk mates and the way he cooperated in confessing after his arrest, were a show of his pride for the murders he committed.

Chapter 17

A Serial Killer Plus

A serial killer, plus his pride in successfully executing his acts of murder behind his closed doors, is reflected in the apology he rendered to all the people at the end of his trial. He was proud to confess to the murders and proudly apologized to the victims. In his apology, he mentioned the names of all the people he hurt. First he named the victims' families, the judge who gave him a suspended sentence for child molestation and then the three police officers whom he convinced to leave a disoriented Laotian boy with him whom he later killed. Next he mentioned his attorney, Gerald Boyle, who had always been on his defense. Apparently, he was proud to show how the justice system took care of him even after he had been in a brush with the law several times.

Jeffrey Dahmer was not just a serial killer; he was also a Pedophile, sexually molesting the children who he enticed with his Polaroid camera and money. He had already been charged with one incident of sexual exploitation of a child and a second-degree sexual assault. He was found guilty of this offense and charged for the first time in 1989. At his sentencing, he spoke to the judge Gardner in his own defense saying, "I don't know how much weight you put on what I have to say. I am an alcoholic. Not the sort that has to have a drink every single day. But when I do drink, I go overboard; and I imagine that labels me as being an alcoholic."

The judge then told him how the abuse of alcohol eventually leads to criminal behavior, because it impairs the ability of a person to control their behavior. The judge explained that people generally have the natural pressure to have a socially responsible behavior, but that alcohol abuse could lessen that pressure to act responsibly, thereby making someone a criminal and that was where Dahmer was.

Dahmer continued to speak in his own defense, attempting to salvage his freedom. "I've been a fairly regular drinker ever since I was in the army for three years to serve in Germany. The prosecution has raised very serious charges against me, and I can understand why. What I've done is very serious. I never meant to give anyone the impression that I thought otherwise. I've never been in this position before, nothing this awful. This is a nightmare come true for me. If anything would shock me out of my past behavior patterns, it's this.

"The one thing I have in my mind that is stable and that gives me some source of pride is my job. I've come very close to losing it because of my actions, which I take full responsibility for. I'm the one to blame for all of this. What I've done has cut both ways. It's hurt the victim, and it's hurt me. It's a no-win situation.

"All I can do is beg you, please spare my job. Please give me a chance to show that I can, that I can tread the straight and narrow and not get involved in any situation like this ever again. I would not only ask, I beg you, please don't destroy my life. I know I deserve a great deal of punishment. I'm not trying to elicit your sympathy, but I would ask you please don't wipe me out completely."

Nobody knew that as of this sentencing appearance for that case, Jeffrey Dahmer had already wiped out the lives of four male victims in a more serious crime; murder. He lied about not being a person that drinks every single day. His plea for leniency was not sincere; he conned the judge who thought he was handling the case of a pedophile rather than that of a serial killer. Dahmer admitted being a homosexual. The judge asked him whether he had relationships with adult males and Dahmer answered, "I have had in the past, not recently." He continued as the judge listened, "This enticing a child was the climax of my idiocy. It's just, it's going to destroy me, I'm afraid, this one incident. I don't know what in the world I was thinking when I did it. I know I was under the influence.

"I do want help. I want to turn my life around despite what the prosecution has told you. She doesn't know me like I know myself. This one incident has jolted me like nothing else."

Dahmer was only testing to see the effectiveness of his skill with words. The judge was more convinced by Dahmer's penitent statements and the defense attorney's arguments against a long prison sentence. The judge truly admitted that the sentencing was difficult for him, saying "I'm really concerned that unless there is some type of substantial change in yourself, that you are going to repeat, because it's a drive. It's almost a biological urge that you have. You've got to learn to control. It may never go away, but your conduct has to change."

After the judge's warning and demand Jeffrey Dahmer responded, "I can't stress it enough that I desperately want to change my conduct for the rest of my life. I imagine you may think I'm saying that just because I'm sitting here facing prison. I mean that sincerely that I do want to change."

The judge knew that there was no alcohol treatment program in the prison and Dahmer would become worse if he was sent there. The prosecution believed that treatment in the community would not work for Dahmer, because his criminal track record showed that he would repeat his crime. Despite all these red flags on the record against him, the judge sent Dahmer into the community. Dahmer's sentence of five years on the second-degree sexual assault charge was stayed so that he was put on probation for five years. The judge also stayed a three year prison sentence on the charge of enticing a child for immoral purposes and put Dahmer on probation for three years, which was to run concurrently with the five years he was given on the second-degree sexual assault.

The judge ordered Dahmer to spend one year in the Milwaukee County House of Correction under a work release program in order to keep his job. The judge cannot be criticized here for trying to give someone a second chance to become a better person. He just didn't know that he was looking at a murderer as Dahmer defended himself in the courtroom.

Dahmer was only buying time to do more crime. He was eloquent in speech and polite in communication. He was a charming disciplined officer of the United States Army. So Dahmer conned the judge with his sweet talking and headed out for his next victim immediately he left the courthouse. Shielded, he had an opportunity to commit more crime. The shield consisted of a combination of his wits, his color and the mask of a polite demeanor. He was neat in appearance and looked like any other ordinary human being. I had no reason to suspect that he was a serial killer living among us and committing such atrocities in his own apartment. Jeffrey Dahmer realized the advantages of being white in Milwaukee. The judge didn't know that he had just helped a murderer who would celebrate this ruling with Anthony Sears as his next victim.

Now loose on the streets as usual and silently operating a mass murder factory in his own apartment, Dahmer started stalking the new building manager whom he considered to be a threat to his secret life. Jeffrey Dahmer believed that the new manager was a security risk to his secret operations. Dahmer gathered the steam that would power his engines to go like a runaway train. I didn't know that he was constantly stalking me. As mentioned in earlier chapters, Jeffrey Dahmer made three desperate attempts to eliminate me, but failed. Thank God.

My next door neighbor, Dean Vaughn in the apartment unit #308, was not so lucky. He was murdered by an unknown killer. Dahmer denied being responsible for it even after his arrest two months later.

Dean was found dead in his own unit in May of 1991 just two months before Jeffrey Dahmer was arrested for mass murder in his own apartment inside the Oxford Apartments. Although Dahmer at that time denied having anything to do with Dean's death, the method of the killing was very similar to the method Dahmer had confessed to using on his victims. Dean's throat was crushed and he was also sodomized.

The investigation into the death of Dean Vaughn was a close call for Dahmer, because there were already many body parts in his apartment at that time. The officers who were investigating the case were standing just outside the door and in the hallway while asking the residents some questions for the investigation. If the investigating officers had taken the time to enter and sit down in each apartment with the resident to talk, they would have found much more than the case in hand. They would have discovered mass murder right there in Dahmer's apartment when they questioned him about Dean's death. If they had exposed him at that time, the lives of six men would have been saved. Dahmer kept slipping through the valves of the justice system.

Miraculously, I was lucky enough to be out of the huge apartment building the same night that Dahmer himself was arrested. The discoveries made in his apartment included body parts, cleaned skulls, uncleaned skulls, painted skulls, unpainted skulls, a heart in a freezer, hands, penis and bones in the closet and torsos soaking in vats of acid contained in a huge blue plastic barrel. It was giving off an awful smell in the apartment, because Dahmer had not been able to empty it. It was a new problem he did not anticipate when he decided to melt the flesh in acid as a means of disposing of the victims' bodies. The smell was poisoning the air he breathed, which was not healthy for him and he knew it. The barrel was a 57 gallon, 40" high container and with its contents was too heavy for one man to lift. Dahmer wouldn't attempt to haul it out of his apartment. He could not even do it in piece meals because it was too messy. The only way to remove it was to haul the barrel away with a dolly. This was a task that was impossible for him. His worries about being exposed were mounting. The huge barrel was hauled away by the authorities after Dahmer's arrest. John Batchelor remembered my warning to Dahmer for the plastic blue barrel in his apartment. "That must go," I warned him during the second inspection of his apartment following complaints about the stench in the building.

Jeffrey Dahmer was a cannibal. He did not just kill for the thrill of it and leave the body of the victims alone. He found some other uses for the body parts. He feasted on the flesh of his victims. He liked the meat so much that he could not stop killing and actually lost track of how much meat he could handle safely. After his arrest he confessed to eating the bicep muscle of one of his victims. Jeffrey Dahmer also told police that the heart they found in the freezer section of his refrigerator was to be eaten later. Dr Park Elliot Dietz, who was in Dahmer's apartment, confirmed the evidence of cannibalism. I realized then that the bones on the green slopes of the Oxford Apartments which I discovered when I started the job were human.

Jeffrey Dahmer was so busy killing and chopping that he forgot where in his apartment he had stashed away all the body parts. For example, a big kettle found on the bottom shelf of his bedroom closet contained decaying body parts. He stumbled over the head of a victim that was already decomposing on the floor of his bedroom closet in the apartment and later put it in the refrigerator next to an open box of baking soda to soak up the stench. I don't know how he did it, but there was no smell in his apartment on the two occasions that I went to inspect his apartment. He was overwhelmed by all the meat he gathered in a short time, so had to discard some by simply wrapping it in garbage bags and tossing in the dumpster behind the building. If the garbage was not picked up within the week by the City's Sanitation Department, the decaying meat started to foul the air in and around the building. The stench was so bad that people could smell it from a three miles radius.

It was bad news for the structurally sound and beautiful Oxford Apartments, because rental apartment shoppers were repelled by the odor of rotten body parts, although of course, nobody realized what the source of the smell was. Our rental traffic logs showed a sharp decline in new move-ins, while notices to move out increased.

As manager, I was supposed to have access to all the units with a master key, but I did not wish to abuse such a privilege and I did not. Dahmer was so concerned by my presence and the risk of exposure that he installed an alarm system in his apartment so that he would know when someone gained entry to it. A 400 square foot, one bedroomed apartment would not take a great deal of time to search through. In reality, an intruder could easily have gone through the entire apartment before Dahmer would have had time to reach the apartment if the alarm went off.

Even though he confessed to it, Dahmer was not charged with cannibalism. He didn't get all the charges he deserved. He was only charged with the serious crimes like mass murder that were levied against him. He was neither charged for not reporting a death in the case of Steven Tuomi, whom Dahmer said was dead when he woke up in a hotel room that both of them shared. There was not enough evidence to prosecute Dahmer on this case, because they only had Dahmer's testimony and nobody else had anything to say about it.

Jeffrey Dahmer was also a thief, because he stole from his victims. Where did their money go after they were dead in his apartment? It is inconceivable that he threw away the little money that his victims had in their pockets when they visited him. He didn't throw their money away like he did some of their body parts. Jeffrey Dahmer told the world in his confessions how he promised to give his victims some money if they went home with him, but he did not reveal what happened to the money after he killed them. He stole the money. Some of these poor victims might have had a little money on them when he first met them. If Dahmer ever gave the victims the money, he promised it as a lure.

When he was in college at the University in Columbus, Ohio, there was the complaint about missing items and money in the student dormitory where he lived. Someone contacted the police who came to question Dahmer as a suspect of theft in that incident. No report was filed, but Dahmer dropped out of the college soon after that incident.

Dahmer complained to his probation officer that he was burgled in the Oxford Apartments, but there was no police report on the incident. Was he telling a lie to the probation officer or was he avoiding the police himself? The latter would be the obvious reason for him not reporting it. He tried to remain elusive. Dahmer knew that the police might find more than what they were looking for, so he avoided the police altogether and accepted his loss. He would take vengeance in a different way. He would go on to rob victims of their lives.

Ronald D. Flowers of Zion, Illinois, whom Jeffrey Dahmer took to his grandmother's house in the City of West Allis back in 1988, but elected not to kill, made a complaint. Mr Flowers had filed a complaint with West Allis police claiming that Dahmer drugged him and stole his wallet and a gold bracelet. An investigation uncovered no significant evidence on which to press charges. Dahmer was a smart man. A good clean up of a crime scene would leave no evidence for any charges to be brought. Ronald was lucky to be alive because of his body weight. Dahmer didn't want to deal with the burden of disposing of Mr Flowers' 250 lb body.

Dahmer's main goal was to create a shrine of human skulls. Unnatural and macabre as this may sound, there are some people who dabble in the trade of human remains. For example, an artist who went to check out some mannequins for sale at a Bucktown apartment found a skull in a pot of boiling water on a stove. The artist was shocked, but the owner of the store assured him that it was nothing unusual to see human skull and bones as items of trade on the internet. The sale of a human skull was a new addition to all other items of trade in this particular apartment. The artist, Jojo Baby, remembered a friend who was an anthropologist and told him what he saw in that store in the hope that he might find something interesting to buy. Ron Shaw, the anthropologist, was shocked to hear the story that sounded like a Hollywood horror movie and advised his artist friend to call the police. The artist was not willing at first, but the anthropologist persuaded him saying that if there was nothing nefarious about the skulls, then the owner of the store, Brian Sloan, would not be in trouble.

Both the artist and the anthropologist were equally curious about the source of the skulls, so the artist finally called the police about the owner of the store. The police arrived unexpectedly and Sloan was obliged to answer all of their questions. Sloan, who was also a Penn State Dickinson Law School graduate, explained that the skulls were trade items and that they were in demand by people interested in the study of human anatomy. He indicated that these items had been actively traded online.

Further investigations traced the skulls to China. This story with the headline, "4 skulls plus 1 pot add up to hot water," appeared in the Chicago Tribune newspaper on Thursday, May 3, 2007. It must have been expensive to obtain these skulls on trade in the market, so some people like Jeffrey Dahmer, decided to obtain his skulls firsthand.

Jeffrey Dahmer was a Collector. Perhaps one of the most important reasons for not leaving his victims after he killed them was his urge to collect their skulls as souvenirs. As was disclosed after the discovery of body parts in his little apartment, two skulls were found in a big kettle that he had on the top shelf of his bedroom closet. Further searches revealed three skulls in the upper drawer of a filing cabinet and two skulls Dahmer had stored in a computer box. He cleaned out the fresh heads by using the kettle and then painted them gray to give the impression that they were replicas sculpted from clay. He had seen similar replicas made of rubber or plastic in stores during the Halloween season. It is a season of eerie displays all around the porches and front lawns of homes that line the streets throughout the city. Creepy objects like artificial skeletons and skulls and carved, lit pumpkins are displayed all around and people dress up in spooky costumes and gory masks to emulate evil characters.

The aim of Dahmer's fantasy shrine was to attempt to conjure up the spirits of his victims to gain power and control over his potential victims. This was a psychic belief associated with devil worship, which Jeffrey Dahmer had embraced. He had renewed confidence in himself once he rented from the Oxford Apartments, which he believed was an ideal location for the continuation of his crimes. This shrine of skulls was Dahmer's main goal according to the clinical Psychologist Dr Judith Becker of Tucson, Arizona who testified for the defense at the trial. She presented a sketch of the shrine that Dahmer himself drew. She said that Dahmer had elaborate plans to build a temple or shrine that featured his victims' remains in hopes of quote, "receiving special powers and energies."

He expected to acquire the kind of powers that would help him socially as well as financially. In other words, Dahmer did believe in the power of the devil to do these things for him. He believed that it would need a sacred place of worship, which he would build in his apartment.

Dahmer was deeply involved in satanic worship,

something he started from high school. His prom date in the high school, Ms Geiger, was invited to a party at the Dahmer home in Bath, Ohio. What happened as she saw it was symbolic of devil worship. There were a few other people in that party who had the same beliefs as Dahmer, because they followed his rituals during that party. She had to leave the party immediately. She observed that Dahmer had developed a persona that switched to the devil in a moment's notice. He had the statue of a mythical animal called the griffin, which has the head and wings of an eagle and the hind legs of a lion. This was part of Dahmer's collection. He told Becker that he felt like the griffin, which represented the devil. This was why he was obsessed with movies as The Exorcist II, Return of the Jedi and Silence of the Lambs.

Dahmer was not the only Wisconsin serial killer. Long before Jeffrey Dahmer, there was a white man by the name of Edward Gein of Plainfield, Wisconsin, whose memories started to return as the news about Jeffrey Dahmer hit the television screens. Back in 1957, Gein was discovered to have killed two innocent women and mutilated their bodies and he had robbed the graves of loved ones that had been laid to rest. Edward Gein even made clothes such as belts, vests and masks from the skin of his victims. It sounded so bizarre to know that Gein even had his furniture covered in human skin. Like Dahmer, Ed Gein believed in the power of Satan and at times invoked the spirit of his dead mother to bring luck in his endeavor while he wore those clothes he made from the body of his victims.

Both Dahmer and Gein were more than serial killers for having some other things to do with the corpse of their victims. They committed these crimes with hideous cruelty; striking at will and without notice. Dahmer was America's most twisted sex serial killer as told by the authors of "Milwaukee Massacre," Dvorchak and Holewa. It was unknown how this rating was established, but it was accepted. Jeffrey Dahmer's motivations for killing were compared to those of other serial murderers. Dahmer had a twist to each comparable motivation, thereby showing how he was similar in some ways, but different in others. A case in point was that of Dennis Nilsen, an English serial killer who, like Dahmer, was killing his guests for company, yet unlike Dahmer, Nilsen did not eat their flesh although he mutilated their bodies for easier disposal.

There was another white man by the name of Michael Herrington who was called the first of Milwaukee's serial killers, because he had killed a woman and a ten-year-old girl and missed the slaying of another young girl.

Jeffrey Dahmer was also a Con Man. He lured his victims to their death by promising them money in return for posing for photos and offering them drink. He would then add his concoction to the victim's drink to render him unconscious.

He took pictures at all stages of the murder. Some pictures showed the victims when they were alive, after he had strangled them and then of the dissected body parts while he mutilated them. With each stage of the process, Jeffrey Dahmer reward himself with sexual gratification. He would then store their remains in the freezer and in the refrigerator for later uses. These actions fulfilled his fantasies as he told detectives during his first sixteen days in custody. Psychiatric patients often exhibit behavior that is perceptible to the general public, but Jeffrey Dahmer displayed no such tell tale signs. He was clean shaven, spoke with confidence and offered money to anyone willing to take it. This is why Jeffrey Dahmer's psychiatric case was considered to be on the borderline. He was dangerous because it was not easy to know that he had a psychiatric problem just by looking at him.

Jeffrey Dahmer continued to con his guests with the luring offers of money, videos and sex. In the words of the district attorney and prosecutor of the Dahmer trial, E.

Michael McCann as he addressed the jurors, "Don't let him con you."

The records show that Jeffrey Dahmer conned Judge Gardner, who handled Dahmer's charges on sexual molestation of a child against him back in 1988. Before this sexual molestation charge, Dahmer had already killed four victims without being apprehended in a period of almost thirteen years. He conned the police officers who responded to the emergency call for a distressed young Laotian boy, whose skull was found among others in Dahmer's apartment after his death.

Chapter 18

Fatal Sex Orientation

Jeffrey Dahmer's homosexual sex orientation was a fatal one to others because there was a twist to it. The mental disease called necrophilia made his homosexuality deadly for all those who he enticed back to his apartment. He wanted to experience sex at a higher realm of life with a dead partner. This was not easy for Dahmer, because he had to do it with a different and new partner each time. He must get rid of the last partner's body, a task that is cumbersome, yet he was committed to do it. It was obviously a task that he had to do alone, for obvious reasons. An average body weight of between 100lb and 175lb is too heavy for one person to haul for disposal. There was the risk of exposure when hauling whole bodies. To avoid the consequences of exposure, the artful dodger thought of other ways in which to dispose of his victims.

However, he discovered that there were no easier ways of disposing of the bodies, because many other problems would arise no matter what method he used. He realized, just before his arrest, that he shouldn't have attempted to melt the body parts in the vats of acid contained in the 57 gallon blue plastic barrel. He thought at first that this was a more effective way of disposing of the body parts, but he actually regretted it because he could not empty it and it was giving off the awful and nauseating smell.

He decided to mutilate or dismember each victim, because it would be easier to dispose of smaller body parts. This option required cutting though back bones, neck bones, thighbones etc. It was also a messy option, because Dahmer had to deal with the blood, the body fluids, the waste and the flesh from each victim. However, he thought he would be able to do it, so he went and bought the appropriate tools for dismemberment such as an electric chain saw, an electric drill, a sharp butcher knife and a strap that he used to strangle his victims. He effectively reduced the bodies to pieces so that he could haul them in garbage bags. This new method of disposing of the bodies of his victims was alright until his killing spree accelerated and he had more bodies than he could actually handle at any one time.

Body parts, or even whole bodies, remained in the little one bedroomed apartment. The decomposing bodies posed a brand new problem for him. It was unhealthy and unpleasant, both for himself and the other residents of the building. Dahmer was also afraid that the stench might lead to his exposure, since the residents had continually complained about it. On two occasions between August, 1990 and July 1991, the smell of rotting meat engulfed the building.

The smell of the decaying body parts in his apartment was a serious concern to Dahmer. He knew that there was the possibility that the management might conduct an all out search into every apartment, in which case he might be caught. He therefore had to devise a way to eliminate the stench. It was simply beyond his control. He had wanted to lock it in his apartment, but that was impossible so he just let it be. However he knew that under this condition his risk for exposure had increased so he handed to me the clear liquid deodorant called "Odor Away " for the residents to use in their apartments. Dahmer said to me that a few drops of the liquid on a glass surface would quickly eliminate the odor in each apartment. I gave the deodorant to a few residents who used it to help clear the smell. I told them that he said he was so sorry for the inconvenience that the smell had caused them and that he was offering this liquid deodorant to help with eliminating the smell. He said he was so sorry and that he was taking care of clearing the smell. Nobody even thought of suspecting Dahmer of such heinous crimes.

I had told Dahmer that if the smell came back I was going to call the police. I had also told some of the other residents that I would call the police the next time. Luckily, Tracy Edwards escaped from Dahmer's apartment before that next time came.

Everything that Dahmer did as a mass murderer according to the revelations in his confessions made people ask "Why?" Seeking the answer to this question, many professional psychiatrists, psychologists and numerous other interested parties were keen to study Dahmer as a subject. However, they never had the opportunity to delve into his mind because he was murdered by another inmate two years into his sentence.

Although we may never truly know what was in Dahmer's mind, it is apparent that his motivation for killing changed from his first to his last victim. In his first murder his motivation was anger, presumably the result of how badly he felt about himself for the way people often treated him and the rejection that he had felt throughout his young life. He had experienced emotional hardship as a child and he wanted to prevent it from happening again. He didn't want people to leave him once they were with him. He therefore chose to keep them dead or alive.

To Dahmer, a dishonorable discharge from the military was rejection when he was an adult. He felt that nobody paid him any attention so he started to do what brought him the attention he wanted. Nevertheless, there are many neglected children in this world, yet they don't all grow up to become serial killers. Dahmer's sinister choice for attracting attention was to commit murders.

He finally realized that he preferred male partners for sex, even though he did not feel comfortable with his sexual orientation. He was reluctant to discuss it with his probation officer who advised him to seek counseling from the gay community in order to prevent problems that might arise from such a lifestyle.

Dahmer may have experienced self-loathing as a result of his homosexuality, which could explain his inability to have sex with a conscious partner, or maybe he was projecting his self hate onto his victims. His necrophilia surely triggered Dahmer to kill over and over again. They term this as "homosexual overkill" in the gay community. Although he knew that it was wrong to kill, he could not stop himself.

Alcohol and drugs appeared to fuel Dahmer's evil behavior. When under the influence, he needed to satisfy the craving to have sex with a corpse, even though he knew that it was wrong.

Jeffrey Dahmer had multiple ailments and each ailment was influencing his personality. This was evident to his defense attorney, Gerald Boyle, who presented to the jury what he referred to as "the Jeffrey Dahmer human being," With a diagram of the wheel of a bicycle as a hub in which each spoke represented Dahmer in a different personality and the things he did as a human, the attorney made his closing statement in defense of his client. After listing all the spokes, he said, "This is Jeffrey Dahmer. There isn't a positive thing on this."

There is a fitting slogan by the United Negro College Fund that goes, "A mind is a terrible thing to waste." Dahmer's did not only waste his mind, he was destroying it. He allowed his afflictions to control his behavior and desires. He then took a walk on the dark side of our human existence and began hurting others, before eventually destroying himself. His body became the devil's workshop.

Appendix A

Life and Death Chronology

Following Dahmer's arrest on Monday 22, July 1991, the investigations into the murders, Dahmer's own confessions and the building manager's time slots in contacts with Dahmer revealed the following chronology of events:

May 21, 1960.
Jeffrey Dahmer was born to Mr Lionel Dahmer and Mrs Joyce Dahmer at the Diconness Hospital in Milwaukee, Wisconsin.

May 17, 1974.
The Dahmer family moved to Ohio, residing at 4480 West Bath Road, Bath Township, Ohio. There Jeffrey Dahmer started grade school education and continued through high school.

June 04, 1978.
The young Dahmer graduated from Revere High School.

June 18, 1978.
The young Dahmer picked up Steven Hicks hitchhiking on the Cleveland- Bath Interstate. Jeffrey Dahmer accidentally killed Steven who wanted to leave after the party. Dahmer hid the body and later disposed of on the family property.

July 24, 1978
Jeffrey Dahmer's parents Lionel and Joyce Dahmer were finally granted a divorce.

August 1978.
Jeffrey Dahmer's mother Joyce Dahmer took his younger brother David with her and moved to Chippewa Falls, Wisconsin, while his father Lionel Dahmer had already moved out and was living in a motel.

September 1978.
Jeffrey Dahmer enrolled at Ohio State University in Columbus, Ohio. He dropped out after only completing a quarter semester.

December, 1978.
Jeffrey Dahmer's father Lionel Dahmer remarried to Shari Shinn Jordan.

December 29, 1978.
Jeffrey Dahmer joined the army and reported for duty on January 12, 1979.

July 13, 1979.
After his training as a Medical Specialist, Dahmer was deployed in Baumholder, Germany for a tour of three years.

March 26, 1981.
After early discharge from the military in Baumholder, Germany for an excessive consumption of alcohol, Dahmer lived in Miami, Florida for six months, then went home to Ohio.

October 07, 1981.
Dahmer was cited for disorderly conduct while drinking in a public place by the Bath, Ohio Police.

January 1982.
Dahmer moved to West Allis, Wisconsin, with paternal grandma Catherine Dahmer.

August 08, 1982.
Dahmer was cited for indecent exposure by the Wisconsin
State Fair Park Police. He lowered his pants in the crowd.

January 14, 1985.
Dahmer employed as a laborer with the Ambrosia
Chocolate Company, located at the north east corner of 6th
Street & Highland Blvd, Milwaukee, Wisconsin.

September 08, 1986.
Dahmer was cited for urinating in public by Milwaukee
Police, but the citation was later reduced to disorderly
conduct. Two young boys claimed that they observed him
masturbating, but he said that he was urinating in the
woods.

September 15, 1987.
Steven Tuomi, Dahmer's first murder victim in Wisconsin,
was missing for over a year before Dahmer admitted that he
had woken up one morning at the Ambassador Hotel on the
West side of Milwaukee and discovered Tuomi laying
dead. He claims he did not know how he died because they
had both been drunk the night before.

January 16, 1988.
Dahmer picked up James Doxtator, a Native American or
an American Indian, only 14-years-old, took him to his
grandma's house where he lived in West Allis, Wisconsin
and killed him.

March 24, 1988.
Dahmer enticed Richard Guerrero from a gay bar, took him
to his grandma's house in West Allis, killed him and
disposed of the entire body.

April, 1988.
Ronald Flowers claimed Dahmer drugged him and stole his wallet and a bracelet so he filed a complaint. Investigations were carried out, but no evidence was found on which to press charges.

June 1988.
Dahmer moved from his grandma's house to an apartment at 808 N. 24th Street. There he was arrested for molesting a minor male.

September 25, 1988.
Dahmer was charged with second-degree sexual assault and enticing a child for immoral purposes after he offered a child fifty dollars to pose before his camera. Dahmer reportedly drugged the coffee with sleeping pills before fondling the boy.

January 30, 1989.
Dahmer was convicted of second-degree sexual assault and enticing a child for immoral purposes.

March 25, 1989.
Dahmer met Anthony Sears at the La Cage gay bar and enticed him with the promise of money and sex. Dahmer celebrated his verdict from the sexual molestation case when he took Sears home to grandma's house in West Allis and killed him.

May 23, 1989.
Dahmer was convicted for second-degree sexual assault and enticing a child for immoral purposes. He had five and three years concurrently and was put on probation in a work release program at the House of Correction for one year.

March 02, 1990.
Dahmer was released from confinement on five years' probation.

May 13, 1990.
Dahmer signed a lease for apartment unit #213 inside the Oxford Apartments located at 924 N. 25th Street. Milwaukee, Wisconsin. This was in the same neighborhood as the apartment building in which he lived and committed the child molestation offense.

May 28, 1990.
Dahmer murdered Raymond Lamont Smith, his first victim at the Oxford Apartments.

June 14, 1990.
Edward Smith became Dahmer's next victim in apartment #213 at the Oxford Apartments.

July 10, 1990.
Sopa Princewill became the new Resident Manager of the Oxford Apartments. Dahmer showed his concern. He was clearly worried about whether the new manager had been employed to expose him.

July 25, 1990.
Dahmer requested the new manager to put a lock on his mailbox.

August 10, 1990.
The first nauseating smell was noticed in the building. A neighbor thought the smell was coming from Dahmer's apartment #213.

August 12, 1990.
Dahmer's apartment was first inspected for the nauseating

smell. The manager, Sopa Princewill, didn't smell anything inside the apartment during the inspection, although Dahmer told him that his freezer had broken and the smell was probably due to rotting food.

August 15, 1990.
Dahmer installed a Security Alarm System so that he would be warned if anyone entered his apartment. This was the first evidence of his concern for the change of manager and the fact that he could have access to the apartment at any time.

September 02, 1990.
Dahmer brought his next victim, Ernest Miller, to his apartment where he killed him and kept his remains.

September 24, 1990.
David Thomas became Dahmer's fourth victim inside the Oxford Apartments. David Thomas was a bisexual with a girlfriend and a daughter.

December 27, 1990.
Jeffrey Dahmer attempted to lure the new manager, Sopa Princewill, with some beer, but failed in his attempt because Princewill had a friend with him at the time. This was Dahmer's first attempt to eliminate the new manager of the Oxford Apartments.

February 18, 1991.
Dahmer brought Curtis Straughter to his apartment where he killed him and kept his skull.

March 25, 1991.
Dahmer told his probation officer, Donna Chester, that he had received a call from his mother for the first time in five years. He was satisfied to know from the conversation that

his mother accepted him for his homosexuality.

April 07, 1991.
Dahmer brought his next victim, Errol Lindsey, to his apartment where he killed him and kept the victim's skull.

April 25, 1991.
First homicide occurred in apartment #308 inside the Oxford Apartments. Every resident was aware of this. Investigations continued, but the murder remained unsolved. Dahmer himself denied being responsible for it at the time and continued denying responsibility following his arrest for the other murders inside the building.

May 24, 1991.
Dahmer brought deaf and mute Anthony Hughes from a gay bar to his apartment and murdered him. Tony had known Dahmer for a while.

May 26, 1991.
While his previous victim's body was still lying in his bedroom, Jeffrey Dahmer brought Konerak Sinthasomphone to his apartment. This 14-year-old Laotian boy tried to escape after Dahmer had drugged him. The police were called in by neighbors who felt that the boy was in danger because they found him naked and disoriented on the street. Dahmer convinced the police officers to leave the boy with him, claiming that they had just had a lover's quarrel. The boy's skull was found in Dahmer's apartment two months later.

May 27, 1991.
The Oxford Apartments' rear exit door was seen smeared with blood. Nobody realized until after Dahmer was arrested that the blood was from the boy who tried to escape from Dahmer's apartment.

June 30, 1991.
Dahmer brought back Matt Turner whom he picked up from a Gay Pride Parade in Chicago. They both rode the Greyhound bus together back to Milwaukee. Then Dahmer killed him as his ninth victim in his apartment inside the Oxford Apartments.

July 04, 1991.
Dahmer cooked out on Independence Day, July 4, 1991. The type of meat he cooked on his grill was not known. Following his arrest, one could only assume that it had been human flesh.

July 05, 1991.
In Chicago, Dahmer spotted Jeremiah Weinberger at a bar, from where they rode the Greyhound bus together back to Milwaukee. Both took a city veteran taxi cab to Dahmer's apartment and there Dahmer performed his standard murder ritual.

July 10, 1991.
The nauseating smell returned for a second time. Princewill went to inspect Dahmer's apartment for a second time. Dahmer invited Princewill to inspect the vat of acid, but Princewill didn't inhale the vapor as Dahmer was hoping. A friend of Princewill's also accompanied him during the visit. Hence Dahmer's plan to add Princewill to his list of victims failed for a second time.

July 15, 1991.
Dahmer lost the job he had held for six years at the Ambrosia Chocolate Company. He brought Oliver Lacy to his apartment as his eleventh victim inside the Oxford Apartments.

July 19, 1991.
Joseph Bradehoft was at a bus stop when Dahmer lured him to his apartment and killed him

July 22, 1991.
Dahmer's third attempt to get his prime target, Sopa Princewill, once again failed. Princewill left the building that night to stay at his own house for the first time in a year, a decision that probably saved his life. Dahmer went out immediately to bring Tracy Edwards to his apartment with intent to murder him in the same way as his other victims. Tracy escaped and Dahmer was arrested. No one knew where Princewill was and many assumed that he must have become another of Dahmer's victims.

July 23, 1991.
The Oxford Apartments' building was thrown into the spotlight and the city of Milwaukee was in a state of shock. There were serious tensions between racial factions, sexual factions and political factions and the majority of the residents of the Oxford Apartments demanded to move out.

July 24, 1991.
The Good Samaritan 911 callers Glenda Cleveland, her daughter Sandra Smith and her niece Nicole Childress revealed that they had told police on the night Konerak Sinthasomphone was murdered that he was not an adult. Their attempt to save the boy was totally neglected by the police officers in Dahmer's favor.

July 25, 1991.
On the basis of four identified victims, Dahmer was charged with four counts of first-degree intentional homicide and his bail amount was set at $1,000,000, making thus Dahmer the "million dollar" serial killer.

July 26, 1991.
Three police officers involved in the response to the 911 call of May 27, 1991 concerning Konerak Sinthasomphone were suspended with pay by the Police Chief Philip Arreola, pending an investigation.

August 04, 1991.
Following Dahmer's confession to his first murder victim Seven Hicks, the authorities went and found bone fragments in the backyard of Dahmer's boyhood home in Bath, Ohio.

August 06, 1991.
As a result of eight more identified victims, Dahmer was charged with first-degree intentional homicide and his bail amount increased to $5,000,000. Nobody advanced this money of course, because under tight security, Dahmer was going nowhere.

August 07, 1991.
The Milwaukee Police Association cast the vote of No Confidence in the Police Chief Phillip Arreola, but authorities disregarded it in order to concentrate their efforts on the peoples' business.

August 10, 1991.
The most tragic of Dahmer's victims, 14-year-old Konerak Sinthasomphone, was cremated after a traditional Buddhist ceremony

August 13, 1991.
The residents were traumatized by the morbid discoveries of human carnage in Dahmer's apartment. They were also subject to bomb threats from the public who blamed them for what Dahmer did in his own apartment. The public believed that they must have known what was going on and

should have been able to stop Dahmer. The media were constantly harassing the residents for a story about the serial killer, even though they knew nothing. The building also became the centre of attraction for curiosity seekers, some of whom had traveled hundreds of miles just to visit site of such a macabre crime. A private donor subsequently arranged to temporarily re-house the frightened residents of the Oxford Apartments at the Hilton Hotel for a two day reprieve before the relocation move.

August 15, 1991.
The Exodus of terrified Oxford residents began.

August 17, 1991.
Following the mass move out by most of the residents, the manager, Sopa Princewill struggled to rent out ten more apartments in one year. The renters were slow in coming because of the Dahmer tragedy.

August 22, 1991.
Following the identification of three more victims, Dahmer was charged with murder for a total of fifteen counts in Wisconsin. Prosecutors had no remains as evidence to prosecute on two out of seventeen murders to which Dahmer had confessed.

January 27, 1992.
The trial of Jeffrey Lionel Dahmer (defendant) vs. The State of Wisconsin (plaintiff) commenced.

February 11, 1992.
Sopa Princewill testified in court as one who had had several contacts with Dahmer during his stay in the building.

February 14, 1992.
Dahmer was found guilty of murder on all fifteen counts
and was sentenced to fifteen consecutive life terms for a
total of 957 years in prison without parole.

November 02, 1992.
Exodus II began. This was an involuntary move out of the
current residents of the Oxford Apartments prior to
demolition of the building.

June 30, 1993.
The Oxford Apartments were demolished.

Appendix B

The Criminal Complaints Against Jeffrey Dahmer

The following is a transcript of the criminal complaints filed by The State of Wisconsin against Jeffrey Dahmer on August 21, 1991 in connection with the murders he committed in the City of Milwaukee and the City of West Allis in the State of Wisconsin.

CIRCUIT COURT
STATE OF WISCONSIN CRIMINAL DIVISION
MILWAUKEE COUNTY

STATE OF WISCONSIN, Plaintiff	AMENDED CRIMINAL COMPLAINT
VS	CRIME(S): See charging section
Jeffrey L. Dahmer 05/21/60	STATUTE(S) VIOLATED See charging section
924 N. 25Th St. Milwaukee, WI	COMPLAINING WITNESS: Donald Domagalski
Defendant	CASE NUMBER: F912542

THE ABOVE NAMED COMPLAINING WITNESS
BEING DULY SWORN SAYS THAT THE ABOVE
NAMED DEFENDANT IN THE COUNTY OF
MILWAUKEE, STATE OF WISCONSIN

COUNT 01: FIRST DEGREE MURDER
In January of 1988, at 2357 South 57th Street, City of West
Allis, County of Milwaukee, did cause the death of another
human being, James E. Doxtator, with intent to kill that
person contrary to Wisconsin Statutes section 940.01.

COUNT 02: FIRST DEGREE MURDER
In March of 1988, at 2357 South 57th Street, City of West
Allis, County of Milwaukee, did cause the death of another
human being, Richard Guerrero, with intent to kill that
person contrary to Wisconsin Statutes section 940.01.

COUNT 03: FIRST DEGREE INTENTIONAL
HOMICIDE
On or about March 26, 1989, at 2357 South 57th Street,
City of West Allis, County of Milwaukee did cause the
death of another human being, Anthony Sears, with intent
to kill that person contrary to Wisconsin Statutes section
940.01(1).

COUNT 04: FIRST DEGREE INTENTIONAL
HOMICIDE
During the spring or early summer of 1990, at 924 North
25th street, City and County of Milwaukee, did cause the
death of another human being, Raymond Smith a/k/a Ricky
Beeks, with intent to kill that person contrary to Wisconsin
Statutes section 940.01(1).

COUNT 05: FIRST DEGREE INTENTIONAL
HOMICIDE
During the summer of 1990, at 924 North 25th Street, City

and County of Milwaukee did cause the death of another human being, Edward W. Smith, with intent to kill that person contrary to Wisconsin Statutes section 940.01(1).

COUNT 06: FIRST DEGREE INTENTIONAL HOMICIDE
On or about September 3, 1990, at 924 North 25th Street, City and County of Milwaukee did cause the death of another human being, Ernest Miller, with intent to kill that person contrary to Wisconsin Statutes section 940.01(1).

COUNT 07: FIRST DEGREE INTENTIONAL HOMICIDE
On or about September 24, 1990, at 924 North 25th Street, City and County of Milwaukee did cause the death of another human being, David Thomas, with intent to kill that person contrary to Wisconsin Statutes section 940.01(1).

COUNT 08: FIRST DEGREE INTENTIONAL HOMICIDE
On or about February 18, 1991, at 924 North 25th Street, City and County of Milwaukee did cause the death of another human being, Curtis Straughter, with intent to kill that person contrary to Wisconsin Statutes section 940.01(1).

COUNT 09: FIRST DEGREE INTENTIONAL HOMICIDE
On or about April 7, 1991, at 924 North 25th Street, City and County of Milwaukee did cause the death of another human being, Errol Lindsey, with intent to kill that person contrary to Wisconsin Statutes section 940.01(1).

COUNT 10: FIRST DEGREE INTENTIONAL HOMICIDE
On or about May 24, 1991, at 924 North 25th Street, City

and County of Milwaukee did cause the death of another human being, Tony Anthony Hughes, with intent to kill that person contrary to Wisconsin Statutes section 940.01(1).

COUNT 11: FIRST DEGREE INTENTIONAL HOMICIDE
On or about May 27, 1991, at 924 North 25th Street, City and County of Milwaukee did cause the death of another human being, Konerak Sinthasomphone with intent to kill that person contrary to Wisconsin Statutes section 940.01(1).

COUNT 12: FIRST DEGREE INTENTIONAL HOMICIDE
On or about June 30, 1991, at 924 North 25th Street, City and County of Milwaukee did cause the death of another human being, Matt Turner, with intent to kill that person contrary to Wisconsin Statutes section 940.01(1).

COUNT 13: FIRST DEGREE INTENTIONAL HOMICIDE
On or about July 7, 1991, at 924 North 25th Street, City and County of Milwaukee did cause the death of another human being, Jeremiah Weinberger, with intent to kill that person contrary to Wisconsin Statutes section 940.01(1).

COUNT 14: FIRST DEGREE INTENTIONAL HOMICIDE
On or about July 15, 1991, at 924 North 25th Street, City and County of Milwaukee, did cause the death of another human being, Oliver Lacy, with intent to kill that person contrary to Wisconsin Statutes section 940.01(1).

COUNT 15: FIRST DEGREE INTENTIONAL HOMICIDE
On or about July 19, 1991, at 924 North 25th Street, City

and County of Milwaukee did cause the death of another human being, Joseph Bradehoft, with intent to kill that person contrary to Wisconsin Statutes section 940.01(1).

HABITUAL CRIMINALITY

On January 30, 1989, Jeffrey L. Dahmer was convicted in the Circuit Court of Milwaukee County in Circuit Court Case Number F-882515 of the felony offences of Second Degree Sexual Assault and Enticing a Child for Immoral Purposes in violation of 940.225(2)(e) and 944.12 of the Wisconsin Statutes, and that said convictions remain of record and unreversed and therefore defendant is a repeater pursuant to Wisconsin Statutes 939.62, and is subject to a total sentence of not more than ten (10) years on each count recited in addition to the mandatory life sentence for each count of First Degree Intentional Homicide and First Degree Murder. Upon conviction of each count of First Degree Intentional Homicide and count of First Degree Murder, Class A Felonies, the penalty is life imprisonment. Complainant states that he is a Captain of Police with City of Milwaukee Police Department and bases this complaint upon the following:

VICTIM JAMES DOXTATOR, DOB: 3/1/73

1) Upon the statement of the defendant, which statement is against (the defendant's) penal interest that in January of 1988, he met a young male he thought was Hispanic who was waiting for a bus in front of the 219 Club on South 2nd Street in the City and County of Milwaukee, State of Wisconsin; he (the defendant) approached him and asked him if he would like to make some money by posing in the nude, viewing videos and having a drink at the defendant's residence; at this time he (the defendant) lived at South 57th Street in the City of West Allis, County of Milwaukee, State of Wisconsin; the two of them went to that location by bus and they had sex and then he gave the young male a

237

drink with sleeping portion and after he passed out killed him by strangling him; he dismembered him and smashed the bones with a sledgehammer and disposed of them.

He did not keep any portion of this individual; further he remembers that the young male told him that he lived with his mother in the vicinity of 10th and National; he further recalls that the young male had two scars close to each of his (the young male's) nipples that were approximately the circumference of a cigarette. The defendant viewed a copy of a booking photo of James E. Doxtator, DOB 3/1/73 that had been taken on September 23, 1987 and indicated that he was 75% sure that this was the male that he met by the bus stop, although he remembered him as looking somewhat older and heavier.

2) Upon the statement of Debra Vega, an adult citizen, that she (Vega) in January of 1988 lived at 1010 East Pierce in the City and County of Milwaukee, State of Wisconsin, and that her son is James E. Doxtator, DOB 3/1/73; she reported her son missing on January 18, 1988 and has never seen him since or been contacted by him since. Further her son had two small scars in the area of his nipples that looked like cigarette burns; also that her home in 1988 at 1010 East Pierce was approximately one block from 10th and National; also that her son was a Native American.

VICTIM RICHARD GUERRERO, DOB: 12/12/65
1) Upon the further statement of the defendant, that in approximately March of 1988 he (the defendant) met a Hispanic male in the Phoenix Bar located on South 2nd Street near the 219 Club in the City and County of Milwaukee, State of Wisconsin; he (the defendant) asked this man to come to his residence, which at that time was his grandmother's house located at 2357 South 57th Street in the City of West Allis, County of Milwaukee, State of

Wisconsin; he invited him to come to look at videos and take photos or engage in sex and the man came with him; they had oral sex at the house and then he drugged the man; while the man was drugged he killed him and dismembered the body and disposed of it completely without keeping any parts; he recalls that he later saw in the personal section of a local newspaper a photo of this victim and a report that he was missing; further the defendant viewed a photograph from the January 7, 1989 Milwaukee Journal of Richard Guerrero, DOB: 12/12/65, and identified this as the person he killed in this incident.

2) Upon the statement of Pablo Guerrero, an adult citizen, that he (Guerrero) is the father of Richard Guerrero and that he had not seen his son since mid March, 1988; at that time he (Pablo Guerrero) reported his son as missing to the Milwaukee Police Department; further that advertisements with his son's picture were placed in local newspapers indicating that his son was missing.

VICTIM ANTHONY SEARS, D.O.B: 1/28/65
1) Upon the further statement of the defendant, that he met Anthony Sears (whom he identified in a photograph) at a club called La Cage; that a friend of Anthony Sears drove him (the defendant) and Anthony Sears to the area of his (the defendant's) grandmother's house in the City of West Allis, County of Milwaukee, State of Wisconsin; that his grandmother's house is 2357 South 57th Street, that after they arrived at that residence they had sex and he gave Anthony Sears a drink with sleeping pills in it and that he strangled him and dismembered the body; that he kept Anthony Sears head and boiled it to remove the skin: further, that he kept the skull and painted it.

2) Upon the statement of Jeffrey Connor, an adult citizen, that he (Connor) was with Anthony Sears on the evening of

239

March 25, 1989 and on that evening they were at a bar on 6th and National; they closed the bar and that Anthony Sears had met a white male named Jeff who said that he was here from Chicago and was visiting his grandmother who lived at 56th and Lincoln; that he (Connor) then gave Jeff and Anthony Sears a ride to the vicinity of 56th and Lincoln where they (Jeff and Sears) got out of the car and walked southbound.

3) Upon complainant's personal knowledge of addresses in Milwaukee County and that the intersection of 56th and Lincoln is north of and close proximity to the address 2357 South 57th Street in the City of West Allis.

4) Upon the statement of Dr Jeffrey Jentzen, Milwaukee County Medical Examiner, that during the early morning hours of July 23, 1991 he (Jentzen) with Milwaukee police officers and other members of the County of Milwaukee Medical Examiner's Office were present at 924 North 25th Street in the City and county of Milwaukee, State of Wisconsin in Apartment 213; that he was present at that location when seven human skulls (three of which were painted), four human heads, and numerous other body parts were recovered; that all the human remains were transported to the Milwaukee County Medical Examiner's Office.

5) Upon the statement of Dr L.T. Johnson, a Forensic Odontologist, that he (Johnson) made a comparison of the painted human skulls recovered from 924 North 25th Street in the City and County of Milwaukee, State of Wisconsin during the early morning hours of July 23, 1991 with known dental records of Anthony Sears and determined that one of the painted skulls is that of Anthony Sears.

VICTIM RAYMOND SMITH A/K/A RICKY BEEKS, D.O.B: 8/10/57

1) Upon the further statement of the defendant that approximately two months after he (the defendant) moved into Apartment 213 at 924 North 25th Street in the City and County of Milwaukee, State of Wisconsin he met a black male at the 219 Club and offered him money to be photographed and have a drink and watch videos; that the man agreed and came with him (the defendant) to 924 North 25th Street, Apartment 213; that at that location he (the defendant) gave the man a drink which was drugged and the man fell asleep; that he the defendant then strangled the man and removed the man's clothing and had oral sex with him; further that he dismembered the body but kept the skull and later painted it; further, that he (the defendant) identified photographs of Raymond Lamont Smith as being the photograph of the man to whom he had done this.

2) Upon the further statement of Dr L.T. Johnson, that he (Johnson) examined the painted skulls recovered at 924 North 25th Street in the City and County of Milwaukee, State of Wisconsin during the early morning hours of July 23, 1991 with known dental records of Raymond Lamont Smith and determined that one of the aforementioned skulls is that of Raymond Smith.

3) Upon your complainant's personal observation of a copy of the defendant's rental application for the living premises at 924 North 25th Street, Apartment 213; that the aforementioned rental agreement has an initial lease date of May 13, 1990.

VICTIM EDWARD SMITH, D.O.B: 8/2/62

1) Upon the further statement of the defendant, that during the summer of 1990, approximately in July, he met a person whom he identified through a photograph as Edward

W. Smith, D.O.B: 6-2-62, at the Phoenix Bar on South 2nd Street in Milwaukee and offered him money for sex and to pose for pictures. They took a cab to his (the defendant's) apartment at 924 North 25th Street in the City and County of Milwaukee, State of Wisconsin; they had oral sex and he gave Smith a drink that contained sleeping pills and then strangled him; he dismembered Smith and took four or five photos of him; he completely disposed of Edward Smith's body by placing it in garbage bags and at a later time he also got rid of the photos of Edward Smith; he further recalls that Smith wore a headband like an Arab.

3) Upon the statement of Carolyn Smith, an adult citizen, that she (Carolyn Smith) is the sister of Edward W. Smith and that she has had no contact with him since June 23, 1990; further that her brother was called "the Sheik" because he frequently wore a turban-like wrap on his head.

VICTIM ERNEST MILLER, D.O.B: 5/5/67
1) Upon the statement of Vivian Miller, an adult citizen, that she (Miller) is the aunt of Ernest Miller and that on September 1st, 1990 Ernest Miller came from his home in Chicago to Milwaukee to visit for the Labor Day weekend and that he left her home during the early morning hour of September 3, 1990 and she has not seen him or heard from him since.

2) Upon the further statement of the defendant that during the summer of 1991 he met a black man (whom he identified through a photograph of Ernest Miller as being Ernest Miller) in front of a book store in the 800 block of North 27th Street in the City and County of Milwaukee, State of Wisconsin and that he offered the man money to return to his (the defendant's) apartment at 924 North 25th Street in the City and County of Milwaukee, State of Wisconsin; that when they returned to his apartment they

had sex and then he (the defendant) drugged Ernest Miller and killed him by cutting his throat; further, that after taking photos of him, he dismembered the body and disposed of the flesh except for the biceps, which he kept in the freezer; he also kept the skull, which he painted after the skin was removed; he kept the skeleton which he bleached.

3) Upon the further statement of Dr L.T. Johnson that he (Johnson) has compared the painted skulls recovered on July 23, 1991 from the defendant's apartment at 924 North 25th Street in City and County of Milwaukee, State of Wisconsin with known dental records of Ernest Miller and determined that one of the aforementioned painted skulls is that of Ernest Miller.

VICTIM DAVID C. THOMAS, D.O.B: 12/21/67
1) Upon the further statement of the defendant that he in the Autumn of 1990 met a black male in the vicinity of 2nd and Wisconsin in the City and County of Milwaukee, State of Wisconsin and offered the man money to come to his apartment at 924 North 25th Street; when they got to his apartment they drank and talked but he had no sex with this man because the man wasn't his type. That he gave the man a drink with a sleeping portion in it and killed him even though he did not want to have sex with him. He thought the man would wake up and be angry; that he dismembered the body but did not keep any of the body parts because the man wasn't his type; further, that he photographed the man while he was in the process of dismembering him.

2) Upon the statement of Chandra Beanland, an adult citizen, that she (Beanland) is the girlfriend of David C. Thomas and that she reported him missing on September 24th, 1990 to the Milwaukee Police Department.

3) Upon the statement of Brian O'Keefe, a City of Milwaukee Police Detective, that he (O'Keefe) contacted the family of David C. Thomas in the course of this investigation and specifically spoke with Leslie Thomas who identified herself as David C. Thomas' sister and that he (O'Keefe) showed Leslie Thomas the facial portion of the photograph that the defendant identified as having been taken during the course of dismembering David C. Thomas; further, that the facial portion showed no injuries at the time it was shown to Leslie Thomas and that Leslie Thomas identified the person in the photograph as being her brother, David Thomas; that the Thomas family supplied a photograph of David Thomas sleeping which they had; further, that the face in this family photograph appeared to him (O'Keefe) to depict the same individual as in the photograph the defendant had taken while dismembering this victim.

VICTIM CURTIS STRAUGHTER, D.O.B: 4/16/73
1) Upon the statement of Katherine Straughter, an adult citizen, that she (Straughter) is the grandmother of Curtis Straughter and that she last saw her grandson on February 18th, 1991.

2) Upon the further statement of the defendant that in February of 1991 he observed Curtis Straughter (whom he identified through a photograph) waiting for a bus by Marquette University and offered him money to come back to his apartment at 924 North 25th Street in the City and County of Milwaukee, State of Wisconsin; that Straughter did accompany him back and at the apartment he (the defendant) gave Curtis Straughter a drugged drink and had oral sex with him; the defendant then strangled him with a strap and dismembered the body; he also took photos and kept the man's skull.

244

3) Upon the further statement of Dr L.T. Johnson that he (Johnson) compared the unpainted skulls recovered from the defendant's apartment with known dental records of Curtis Straughter and determined that one of the unpainted skulls was that of Curtis Straughter.

VICTIM ERROL LINDSEY, D.O.B: 3/3/72
1) Upon the statement of Yahuna Barkley, an adult citizen, that she (Barkley) is the sister of Errol Lindsey and that she last saw him on April 7, 1991 when he went to the store and that she has not seen him since that time.

2) Upon the further statement of the defendant that in the spring of 1991 he met Errol Lindsey (whom he identified by photograph) on the corner of 27th and Kilbourn in the City and County of Milwaukee, State of Wisconsin and that he offered Errol Lindsey money to return with him (the defendant) to his apartment at 924 North 25th Street, City and County of Milwaukee, State of Wisconsin; that after they returned to his apartment he gave Lindsey a drugged drink and after he fell asleep he strangled Lindsey and then had oral sex with him; he then dismembered the body and saved the skull.

3) Upon the further statement of Dr L.T. Johnson that he (Johnson) compared the unpainted skulls recovered from the defendant's apartment on July 23rd, 1991 with known dental records of Errol Lindsey and determined that one of the unpainted skulls is that of Errol Lindsey.

VICTIM TONY ANTHONY HUGHES, D.O.B: 8/26/59
1) Upon the further statement of the defendant that in May of 1991 he met Tony Anthony Hughes (whom he identified through a photograph) who was deaf and mute in front of the 219 Bar on South 2nd Street in the City and County of Milwaukee, State of Wisconsin; that he communicated with

245

Hughes by writing and it appeared that Hughes could read lips; that he offered Hughes $50.00 to come to his (the defendant's) apartment at 924 North 25th Street in the City and County of Milwaukee, State of Wisconsin to take photos and view videos; further, that he gave Hughes a drink with a sleeping potion and then killed him and dismembered his body and kept his skull.

2) Upon the further statement of Dr L.T. Johnson that he (Johnson) has compared the unpainted skulls found in the apartment of the defendant with known dental records of Tony Hughes and determined that one of the unpainted skulls is that of Tony Hughes.

3) Upon the statement of Shirley Hughes, an adult citizen, that she (Hughes) is the mother of Tony Hughes and that Tony Hughes came to Milwaukee from Madison during the late afternoon or evening of May 24, 1991 and that she has not seen him since and further that her son, Tony Hughes, is deaf and mute.

VICTIM KONERAK SINTHASOMPHONE, D.O.B: 12/2/76
1) Upon the statement of Sounthone Sinthasomphone, an adult resident that he is the father of Konerak Sinthasomphone who was 14 years of age and that during the afternoon of May 26, 1991 his son left home and did not return and he has not seen him since.

2) Upon the further statement of the defendant that he (the defendant) in late May of 1991 met a young Oriental male (whom he identified by photograph as Konerak Sinthasomphone) in front of Grand Avenue Mall in Milwaukee and that they went back to his [the defendant's] apartment at 924 North 25th Street in the City and County of Milwaukee, State of Wisconsin; that Sinthasomphone

246

posed for two photographs while he was alive and that he (the defendant) gave Sinthasomphone a drink laced with a sleeping potion, and that they then watched videos and while they were watching videos, Sinthasomphone passed out; then he (the defendant) went to a bar to get some beer because he had run out; that while he was walking back from the bar located on 27th just north of Kilbourn, he saw Sinthasomphone staggering down the street and he (the defendant) went up to Sinthasomphone and then the police stopped him; that he told the police that he was a friend of this individual and that the individual had gotten drunk and done this before; that the police escorted them back to his (the defendant's) apartment and he told the police he would take care of Sinthasomphone because he was his friend; that they went into the apartment and after the police left, he killed Sinthasomphone by strangling him and then had oral sex with him and then he took more photographs. Then he dismembered body and kept the skull.

3) Upon the further statement of Dr L.T. Johnson that he [Johnson] compared the unpainted skulls recovered from the apartment at 924 North 25th Street with known dental records of Konerak Sinthasomphone and determined that one of the skulls which was recovered from that location is that of Konerak Sinthasomphone.

VICTIM MATT TURNER A/K/A DONALD
MONTRELL, D.O.B: 7/3/70
1) Upon the further statement of the defendant that on June 30, 1991 after the Gay Pride Parade in Chicago, he met a black male at the Chicago Bus Station and offered him money to pose nude and also view videos at his apartment back in Milwaukee; he (the defendant), with this black male, returned to Milwaukee on a Greyhound and then took a City Vet cab to his [the defendant's] residence in Apartment 213 at 924 North 25th Street in the City and

247

County of Milwaukee, State of Wisconsin; he (the defendant) gave the black man something to drink, which had been drugged and the man passed out and he (the defendant) used a strap to strangle the man and then dismembered him and kept his head and put it in the freezer in his apartment and placed his body in a 57 gallon barrel that he had in his residence; further that he (the defendant) looked at a photograph supplied by the Chicago Police Department of Matt Turner a/k/a Donald Montrell and indicated that he thought this was the person that he had killed in this incident.

VICTIM   JEREMIAH WEINBERGER, D.O.B: 9/29/67
1) Upon the further statement of the defendant that on or about July 5, 1991 he met a Puerto Rican male at Carrol's Gay Bar on Wells Street in Chicago and that he offered the man money to come with him to Milwaukee to pose for him and to view videos; they took a Greyhound Bus from Chicago to Milwaukee and then took a cab to the defendant's apartment at 924 North 25th Street in the City and County of Milwaukee, State of Wisconsin; this man stayed with him for two days and on the first day they had oral sex and on the second day the man indicated that he wanted to leave and he (the defendant) didn't want the man to leave so he gave him a drink with a sleeping potion in it and strangled him manually and then took photos of him and dismembered the body. He then took more photos and kept the man's head in the freezer and body in the 57 gallon drum he (the defendant) looked at a photo supplied by the Chicago Police Department of Jeremiah Weinberger and indicated that this was the man that he had killed in this incident.

2) Upon the statement of Dr L.T. Johnson that he (Johnson) at the Milwaukee County Medical Examiner's Office compared one of the human heads recovered from the

248

freezer at 924 North 25th Street with known dental records
of Jeremiah Weinberger and determined that the severed
human head that he examined in comparison with those
records was the head of Jeremiah Weinberger.

VICTIM OLIVER LACY, D.O.B: 6/23/67

1) Upon the further statement of the defendant that on or
about July 15th, 1991 he met a black male on 27th Street
between State and Kilbourn in Milwaukee and that the man
stated that he was going to his cousin's house he invited the
man. He invited the man to his residence to pose, for photos
and the man agreed to come and model; when they got to
the residence at 924 North 25th Street in the City and
County of Milwaukee, State of Wisconsin, they removed
their clothes and did body rubs and he gave the man a drink
which had sleeping potion in it; when the man fell asleep,
he strangled him and then had anal sex with him after
death; he dismembered the body and placed the man's head
in the bottom of the refrigerator in a box and kept the man's
heart in the freezer to eat later; he also kept the man's body
in the freezer; he kept the man's identification which
identified the man as Oliver Lacy, date of birth 6/23/67.

VICTIM JOSEPH BRADEHOFT, D.O.B: 1/24/66

1) Upon the further statement of the defendant that on or
about July 19th, 1991 he met a white male on Wisconsin
Avenue near Marquette University; the man was waiting
for a bus and he had a six pack under his arm; he (the
defendant) got off a bus at that location and approached the
man and offered him to pose and view videos and the man
agreed; they returned to the defendant's residence at 924
North 25th Street in the City and County of Milwaukee,
State of Wisconsin; they had oral sex and then gave the
man a drink with a sleeping potion in it and then strangled
him with a strap while he slept; he dismembered this man
and put his head in the freezer and his body in the same

blue 57 gallon barrel where he has placed the bodies of the black male and the Puerto Rican male; he kept this man's identification card which identified him as Joseph Bradehoft, date of birth 1/24/66.

AS TO VICTIMS TURNER, LACY AND BRADEHOFT
1) Upon the statement of Dr Jeffrey Jentzen, Medical Examiner for Milwaukee County, that on July 23, 1991 he was called by the Milwaukee Police Department to Apartment 213 at 924 North 25th Street in the City and County of Milwaukee, State of Wisconsin and inside the apartment at that location, among other evidence, he observed a refrigerator with a freezer section; the refrigerator contained a human head and the freezer section contained human body parts. Also there was a floor standing freezer, which was found to contain three human heads and other body parts and there was a 57 gallon drum, which contained human body parts. Jentzen further stated that at the Milwaukee County Medical Examiner's Office these human body parts were examined and that fingerprints were lifted from hands that had been found at the scene and also efforts at dental identification were made; that Dr L.T. Johnson, whom he (Jentzen) knows to be a forensic odontologist, did the dental examination and that fingerprint lifts were submitted to the Milwaukee Police Department Bureau of Identification for analysis.

2) Upon the statement of Wayne Peterson, that he (Peterson) is a Bureau of Identification technician and supervisor employed by the City of Milwaukee Police Department and that he (Peterson) made comparisons of fingerprints lifted by the Milwaukee County Medical Examiner's Office from body parts recovered at 924 North 25th Street on July 23rd, 1991 with known prints of various persons and was able to identify the prints of Oliver Lacy, Joseph Bradehoft, and Matt Turner a/k/a Donald

Montrell as having been lifted from human body parts
discovered in that apartment.

AS TO HABITUAL CRIMINALITY
Complainant further states that he has viewed a certified
copy of Judgment of Conviction in Milwaukee County
Circuit Court Case No. F882515 and a copy of that
Judgment of Conviction is attached hereto and incorporated
herein and the aforementioned Judgment of Conviction
indicated that the defendant was convicted of felony
offences in Milwaukee County within five years of the
offences listed in this complaint and that he (the defendant)
is therefore a Habitual Criminal.

Appendix C

"In His Own Words"... A Verbatim Report

In his own words, Jeffrey Dahmer confessed to the homicides for which he was arrested during the first seventeen days of his arrest. This chapter narrates the interviews with Dahmer in custody conducted by investigating detectives and allows the reader to draw his or her own conclusions as to why this tragedy happened.

After the discovery of evidence of mass murder in his one bedroom apartment on Monday July 22, 1991, Jeffrey Dahmer was arrested, taken to the Squad 93 in handcuffs and driven down to the CIB.

At this time the police officer who rode along with Dahmer narrated the following interactions with Dahmer. These reports are as written and have not been edited, so any errors, grammatical or otherwise, are those of the report writers, not the author of this book.

"Once at the CIB, I advised Jeffrey L. Dahmer of his constitutional rights and he stated that he fully understood them and that he wished to freely make a statement regarding the incident. At this time Mr Dahmer states that he is 31 years of age, born in Milwaukee, WI.
He states he moved to Richfield, Ohio, when he was about 6-years-old and he was raised there and attended and graduated from Revere High School.

"He states he spent three years in the Army after graduation and moved back to Milwaukee when he was approximately 23 or so years-old. The subject states he has a father who lives in Pennsylvania and a mother who lives in California.

"He states he has one brother, 26, living in Cincinnati, and his grandmother on his father's side lives in Milwaukee.

"Subject states he was raised in the Protestant Faith as he was growing up, but he now considers himself to be an atheist. He admitted that he had been arrested in the past and states he is currently on probation for taking Polaroid pictures of a minor. Subject states that when he was 18 years of age and living in Richfield, Ohio, he picked up a hitchhiker whom he described as a white male about 19 years of age. He states he took him home and had homosexual sex with him and states they were drinking beer and got intoxicated.

"He states they got into a physical fight because the 19-year-old individual tried to leave and that during the fight, he states he struck the hitchhiker with a barbell. He states that the blow of the barbell caused the death of the hitchhiker, and at this time he took the body into a wooded area by his house and left it there to decompose for about two weeks. He states he returned with a sledgehammer at this time and used it to break the bones and then he scattered them about the woods.

"The subject states he moved to Milwaukee after a three-year tour in the Army and a one-year stay in Miami, Florida, where according to the subject, nothing of this nature occurred. Subject states he moved in with his grandmother at 2357 S. 57th St. when he returned to Milwaukee, and he states that he was about 25 years of age and living in Milwaukee, when he picked up a white male, approximately 25 years of age, at the 219 Tavern.

"He states they got a room at the Ambassador Hotel and they got very drunk and passed out. Subject states that when he woke up the guy was dead and had blood coming from his mouth. He states he went to the mall and bought a large suitcase and stuck the dead body into it. He states he called a cab and placed the suitcase in it and went back to 2357 S. 57th St. He states that he took the dead body down into his basement near a floor drain and used a knife to cut the flesh off the body and then dismembered the body, placed the various parts into plastic bags and then threw them into the trash. The subject feels this occurred in 1984, during the summer.

"He indicates that there had been many times that he has had sex with men where no violence was involved and states about two months after this incident, he met a Hispanic male, about 18 years of age, also at the 219 Tavern, at about 1.00am. They went back to his grandmother's place and the subject had sex with him, and put sleeping pills in his drink. He states when the guy fell asleep, he strangled him with his hands and took the body down to the basement by the drain and used a knife to dismember him and a sledgehammer to break up the bones, and then placed them in plastic bags and threw them in the trash.

"He goes on to state, about a month later, he met a black and white mixed male, about 20 years of age, at the La Cage, a tavern on National Avenue, and took him back to his grandmother's house where he had sex and used sleeping pills with him. He states when he was asleep, he strangled him and then dismembered his body and disposed of him in the same manner as before.

"The subject states a year went by and he met a Hispanic male, about 19 years of age, at the 219 club and returned with him to his grandmother's house where he again had sex, used sleeping pills and strangled him, and again dismembered and disposed of the body in the same way.

"Subject states he moved to 808 N. 24th St. and lived there for a year and was arrested one time for taking pictures of a minor. After one year of work release from the house of Correction, he moved back to his grandmother's house and lived there for approximately six months. At this time he moved to 924 N. 25th St., # 213. Subject states in the winter of 1989, he met a black male, about 24 years of age, in front of the bookstore on 27th St., and took him to his apartment where he took pictures of him in various sexual poses and had sex with him and put sleeping pills in a coffee and rum drink, which he gave to the black male. When the black male fell asleep, he stabbed him with a large hunting knife, which he described as having a 6" blade and a black handle. He stabbed him in the neck. After the guy was dead, he put him in the bathtub and dismembered him. He states he used the knife to dismember him. The subject states he used a plastic trash container or garbage can and put the bones in it with hydrochloric acid and let them sit for about three days until they turn to a mushy substance, and then he flushed them down the toilet. The flesh that he filleted from the body he put into trash bags and threw them out.

"The subject states he also, starting with his 3rd victim, boiled the head in a cleaning solution and kept the skulls. He kept the skulls in the closet. All identification and jewelry of the victims, he states he cut up and threw out in the garbage.

"The subject states about two months later, he met a black male, about 20 years of age, around Wisconsin and Water, and walked home with him and again had sex, used sleeping pills, which were placed in a coffee mixture, and strangled him. He then dismembered the body and disposed of him in the same manner as before. Subject states he began getting quicker at cutting up the bodies.

"The subject states about one month later, he met a tall black male, about 26 years of age at Ciest La Vie and they took a taxi home to his apartment and he repeated the same scenario with him, but he did not boil and keep his head. The subject states this was due to time constraints.

"Subject states about 6 months later, he met a black male, about 20 years of age while in Chicago, and rode back to Milwaukee by Greyhound bus. He states before this he met a Chinese male, about 15 years of age, at the Grand Avenue Mall; this was around May or early June. He states they took a bus back to his apartment. It was during the day or the afternoon. He states the Chinese posed for Polaroid photos and then he gave him sleeping pills in the coffee rum drink. After he passed out, he strangled him and dismembered and disposed of his body parts in the same way as before.

"The subject states that the body parts gave off an awful smell in the trash, but nobody ever did anything, so he just kept following his usual procedure of disposal. Regarding the black male from Chicago, he states that he repeated his usual action with him. Regarding the head in refrigerator, he states he met him, a black male, about 25 years of age, at 27th and Wisconsin, and took him home and repeated the same actions with him.

"He states about one month ago, he bought a 57 gallon industrial drum and began placing body parts in it. Subject states on about July 19, 1991, he met a white male, about 25 years of age near Marquette University and took him home, had sex with him, gave him sleeping pills in the coffee rum drink, strangled him, filleted him in the bathtub, dismembered him and placed the body parts in the industrial drum.

"Regarding the Chinese male, the subject states that after giving him sleeping pills, he fell asleep and he, the subject, went to a bar on 27th St. He states that as he left the bar, he saw the Chinese guy running down the street naked and the police saw him and stopped him, and he was not speaking any English so he (the subject) talked with police and said that he was a friend of his and that he was staying with him. At this time, he took the Chinese guy back to his apartment and gave him some more coffee and rum solution with the sleeping pills in it, and after he fell asleep again, he strangled him, dismembered him, and disposed of him in the usual way. He then boiled his head. He states it takes about an hour to boil a head.

"Regarding his last victim, he states that his ID can be

257

found in the bedroom of his apartment. Regarding 7-22-91, the subject says he met a black male, about 25 years of age, at the Mall on Wisconsin Avenue. He states he offered him $20 in cash to let him take some nude pictures of him. Once at his apartment, they drank rum, and he the subject, got intoxicated. Subject states that he tried to put handcuffs on the victim and the victim ran out and got the police. Subject states he is not sure what happened next because he was drunk. Regarding the handcuffs, he would ask his victims if they would allow him to take a bondage picture with the handcuffs on and that is how he would get them handcuffed. The subject states there is an ID from the male he met on 27th St. and Wisconsin in his wallet.

"The subject states that all his victims knew that homosexual activity was the idea, and possibly pictures.

"At this time, after the subject gave this statement verbally, I advised him that I would like to write it down verbatim on paper. However, before I did so, I had to ensure that he understood and wished to cooperate, and at this time, I went and got Detective Dennis Murphy who entered the room and, together, we reiterated his constitutional rights, which he stated he understood and that he wished to waive them in order to help us with this investigation. It was at this time that a 4-page confession was written out by myself, Detective Kennedy, and read back to the subject who also read it and then stated that it was accurate and true, and then he signed it, Jeffrey Dahmer. He also initialed each page of the 4-page confession.

"It should be noted that during the entire time that I spoke with the subject, Jeffrey Dahmer, he was given numerous cigarettes, 4-5 cups of coffee, two glasses of water, and two cans of coca-cola soda pop. He was also allowed to use the bathroom upon request. This entire interview and confession started at approximately 1.30am and finished at approximately 7.15am. After the confession was completely written out, read over, and signed by the subject, he was asked if there was anything that he would like to do or that if he was hungry. He stated that he was not hungry and probably would not be hungry for a long time. However, he wanted to just sit and talk about the offenses a little bit more.

The conversation that followed at this time has been recorded by Detective Dennis Murphy, and he will file a detailed supplementary regarding what was said during this interview."

Report per Detective Patrick KENNEDY, 7-23-91.

"On Tuesday 7-23-91, after obtaining the signed confession from the subject, Jeffrey L. DAHMER, W/M, DOB; 5-21-60, he requested that we just sit in the interview room (#411) and talk with him, so he could have a couple of cigarettes, some coffee and think as to what had occurred. We, Detectives Dennis Murphy and Patrick Kennedy, then talked with Jeffrey Dahmer regarding his family and he stated his mother and father are divorced. His mother, Joyce Flint, is presently living in Northern California somewhere and his father, Lionel Dahmer, is presently living in Pennsylvania and worked for the (blacked out). Further checks gave no clue and that phone number there is (blacked out) and a home number of (blacked out).

"Jeffrey stated he has not seen either parent for quite some time and he believes that the last time he saw his father was in 1979. He also stated he has a brother in Cincinnati, but he has not seen him for quite a while. We then questioned him regarding his address at the time that these homicides first occurred when he was 18-years-old and he stated that his hometown was Bath, Ohio, and that while he was there he picked up a hitchhiker in Bath, Ohio, across from the fire house and took him to his house at

4480 W. Bath Rd., in Bath, Ohio. He stated they had sex, got into an argument and he killed this individual by hitting him with a bar bell. He stated after this occurred, he cut him up, put him in garbage bags and threw the bags in the woods behind his house, to the west, and left him there for about two weeks. He stated after two weeks, he went to the woods with his sledgehammer and broke the bones up into little pieces and scattered them about the woods.

"He stated that after this he joined the Army, in 1979. He was subsequently discharged in March of 1981. He stated that after he was discharged, he lived in Miami, Florida, for approximately one year. He then moved back to Bath, Ohio, for four months. Then in about June or July of 1982, he moved in with his grandmother at (blacked out). He stated that from the first homicide through all this time, he was not involved in any other homicides.

"Regarding any activities as to why he has kept some body parts of the victims or whether or not he had consumed any of the body parts, he stated the only time he ever did consume any body parts, was one time and it was the biceps (he pointed to his right biceps) of the black male whom he had met on 27th and Wisconsin. He stated the reason he consumed this biceps was because it was big and he wanted to try it. He then stated he didn't want to talk about it anymore. He also stated he would masturbate in front of the body parts and skulls he had collected because it brought back memories of the victim. He stated he would put these body parts in formaldehyde and he would boil the skulls to get rid of the skin. He stated he also spray painted several of the skulls. This will be reflected on a separate supplementary report.

"He stated of all the victims he killed, which he believed to be in the vicinity of possibly 15, he did not keep three skulls. He stated one of the skulls was from the victim in Ohio and then there were two others of black males. He stated he put these two skulls in acid and got rid of them that way. He stated the total length of time that this occurred was about six years he believed. He stated the type of pills he used to put the victims to sleep prior to him strangling them, were sleeping pills which he had obtained from a Dr HONG. He stated the reason that he killed these homosexuals and he stated they were all homosexuals, was because he wanted to be with them. He stated he kept the skulls of the good looking ones because he didn't want to lose them.

"He also stated that he felt he could hang on to them if he would in fact kill them and keep their skulls. He stated the last three skulls that were in the refrigerator and not boiled, belonged to his last three victims. At this time, Mr DAHMER stated he was tired and he wished to get some rest. He was then taken to the City Jail."

Report per Detective Dennis MURPHY
DM/1h, 7-23-91.

"On Tuesday, 07-23-91, I, Detective KENNEDY, of squad 126, while investigating the above incident and filing reports down on the 4th fl., of the CIB, was given a message, by the head jailer in LUCAD, that the suspect in this offense, one Jeffrey DAHMER, had requested to speak with me again.

"At this time I proceeded to the 5th fl., LUCAD lock up, where I went to the cell, where DAHMER, the suspect was sitting. At this time I asked if he had in fact requested to see me again, and he stated, "Yes I did". At this time, myself and Detective Dennis MURPHY escorted DAHMER back down to the 4th floor, CIB, to an interview room, where we conducted the following investigation.

"At this time DAHMER stated that he wished to talk to us about an additional two homicides that he forgot to mention in the original interview. This information was given to Detective MURPHY and he will file a separate

261

detailed supplement regarding this.

"Also during this interview I asked DAHMER what substance was sprayed on some of the skulls, which were found in his apartment, as the Medical Examiner stated. There appeared to be a paint-like substance on three of the skulls. To this DAHMER stated he had gone to the Pallette Shop, which is an Art Store, located on South Water St. He states at the store he purchased some enamel spray paint, type of color being fake granite.

"When asked why he used this spray paint on the skulls, he stated he sprayed them in order to give them an artificial look; in case someone would see them, they would feel they were not real. Upon asking him which skulls he did spray, he stated the black male whom he met on 27th St., was one of the skulls, the mixed mulatto male whom he met at La Cage, on West National, was the second skull sprayed and a black male prostitute whom he picked up in front of 219 S. 2nd was the third skull he sprayed.

"At this time, I also questioned DAHMER, regarding the numerous boxes of Soilex, which is a cleaning powder that was found in his apartment. To this he stated that he used the Soilex, along with a water solution to boil the heads, which he had decapitated from his victims. He stated the Soilex would effectively boil off the skin and hair from the skulls, in about an hour's time. He also stated one of the torsos that he had taken from a victim he had also boiled in a large kettle, in which he kept the Soilex.

"At this time I also questioned DAHMER regarding the homicide investigation of Dean VAUGHN, who also resided at 924 N. 25th St., on the 3rd floor. To this DAHMER stated that he recalled several months ago, a detective coming to his apartment to question him regarding the Dean VAUGHN Homicide. He states, he in no way had anything to do with this. He states when the detective came to his door, he felt that he was sure he was going to be apprehended for the numerous homicides, which he has already admitted to. However, when the detective began speaking of a black male, by the name of Dean VAUGHN, he was relieved, as he knew he had nothing to do with that and he told the detective so. He states he had nothing to do with the VAUGHN Homicide and since he has already admitted to several other Homicides, he would not be afraid to admit if he had participated in that offense.

"At this time, there was one other question, which I asked DAHMER and that was pertaining to the fact that numerous types of ether were found in his apartment, and to this he stated that he has brought the ether in an attempt to use it on some of his victims, after he had drugged them, to attempt to keep them in a sleep like state longer. However, he stated that the ether did not work very well and only made them slightly intoxicated or high, and didn't put them to sleep. At this time my part of the interview of DAHMER was terminated."

Report dictated by: Detective Patrick KENNEDY
PK: hvs 07-23-91

"On Tue., 7-23-91 at 12.45 P.M, we Detectives Dennis MURPHY and Patrick KENNEDY, were requested by the suspect to come to the jail so he could give us additional information regarding our investigation. We proceeded to the location, where Mr Jeffrey DAHMER, was taken from the jail to the interview room at the CIB, where he stated that he had more information regarding other homicides. We advised Mr DAHMER of his Miranda rights, which he stated he understood. And he stated, "I've told you everything already. I have nothing to hide, so I might as well tell you about these ones I forgot."

"He stated there was one more Hispanic male that he met in Chicago about two weeks ago, just after the 4th of July and he stated this Hispanic male was about 25-years-old and he met him at Carol's, a gay bar on Wells St.

"He stated he and this Hispanic male then took a Greyhound back to Milwaukee and the Hispanic male stayed two days. He stated he does not recall his name; it may have been Tony, but he is not sure. He stated that after the first day, they had oral sex with each other and got along together.

"On the second day, the Hispanic male stated he was going to be leaving, at which time the defendant, Jeffrey, stated he did not want him to leave, so he gave him sleeping pills in the coffee in order to keep him there. He stated that after he passed out, he then strangled the Hispanic male and dismembered and put his head in the refrigerator. He stated he did not boil the head and when he would boil the head he would use "Soilex" to boil the heads. He stated he also purchased a 57 gallon drum, in which he put the torsos of three of his victims. He stated he even sprayed some of the skulls with spray paint so they looked artificial. Mr DAHMER stated he purchased the spray paint from an art shop on Water Street.

"I then questioned him regarding the torsos in the 57 gallon tank and he stated one was that of the Hispanic male from Carol's bar, one was from the black male on 27th St. and the third one was from the black male he met at the bus station in Chicago. I informed him there was a skeleton recovered in his apartment and he stated that was from the black male he met in front of the bookstore approximately one year ago.

"Mr DAHMER further stated he would cut off the penis and body parts, and put them in formaldehyde to preserve them and then look at them and masturbate for gratification. He further stated he had experimented with ether to put the people asleep, but it didn't work. Regarding the other six torsos that are apparently missing and that cannot be accounted for by the amount of heads that were discovered in the apartment, he stated that these torsos had been placed in acid and were eaten away and then flushed down the toilet when they became sludgy."

"Mr DAHMER then stated he remembers another victim, and this homicide occurred about five months ago, and this was a black male about 20-years-old and he met at 27th and Wisconsin. He stated he got this individual to pose for him, gave him a drink and then cut off his skin. He eventually put the skin in acid. He stated he skinned the entire body and then boiled the skull of this individual and subsequently disposed of the body in plastic bags after dismembering same. He stated that when he would strangle his victim; he used his hands and about four times he used a black strap, leather type that he had bought for that specific purpose.

"Regarding his activities upon joining the Army, he stated he joined in 1979, was discharged in March of 1981 stationed in Baumholder, Germany.

"He stated after that he went to Florida for a year, retuned to Bath, Ohio, in March of 1982, and stayed for four months. He then returned to the residence of his grandmother at 2357 South 57th St. He stated he had originally said the killings started in 1984. He was not sure of the exact time when it started, but to the best of his recollection, he believes these killings started in 1987.

"Mr DAHMER stated that this was all he could remember at this time and if he did recall any further information he would contact either me or Detective KENNEDY. He stated these are the only homicides he can recall being involved in at this time.

"While questioning Mr DAHMER regarding the sledgehammer he used to break up the bones of his victims while he was living at his grandmother's house, he stated the sledgehammer was kept in the garage and had a grey handle. I was subsequently informed by Detective FARMER that they recovered a sledgehammer in the garage and upon Detective FARMER returning to the CIB with the sledgehammer, it was shown to the defendant and upon viewing it, stated this is the sledgehammer he used to break up the bones of the victims at 2357 South 57th St. This sledgehammer will be placed on inventory by Detective FARMER."

Report per Detective Dennis MURPHY.
DM/1h   7-23-91

"On Wednesday, 7-24-91, I, Detective KENNEDY, Squad-126, along with Detective Dennis MURPHY, were requested at approximately 8.30am by the suspect in this offense, Jeffrey DAHMER, to speak with him. At this time I proceeded to the 5th floor, LUCAD, where I in fact asked the suspect, Jeffrey DAHMER, if he had requested to speak with me, at which time he stated he did. I took him with me from the 5th floor down to an interview room at the CIB, where we again began to speak of the offense.

"During this time, Jeffrey DAHMER stated that he wished to speak slightly regarding earlier years of his life in Ohio. At this time he states that he remembers his early family life as being one of extreme tension. He states the tension came from the relationship that existed at that time between his mother and his father. He stated although he was not physically or sexually abused and he did not witness any physical abuse from his parents, he stated that they were 'constantly at each other's throats' and arguing.

"He states that his mother appeared to have some psychiatric problems and had in fact suffered a nervous breakdown at one time during his early childhood. He states that she was on medication and had been seeing a doctor much of the time. He states that he was advised by relatives that his mother suffered severe Post-Partum Depression after he was born, and he took that as an indication that he was at least partially the problem for his parents' bad marital state. He states that he believes that his mother became depressed after his birth and never quite fully recovered, and thereby he states he felt a certain amount of guilt in regard to the bad marriage of his parents.

"He states that when he was approximately 18 years of age, a divorce occurred between his mother and his father and at this time his mother moved to Chippewa Falls, WI. His father had been court ordered to stay out of the house and had moved to a motel, which was several miles from the house. He states at this time his mother took his younger brother, who was approximately 6 years' younger than him when she moved out and that he was left all alone at the house in Richfield, Ohio. He states that it was at this time when he started to have strong feelings of being left all alone, and that it was at this time that he remembers having strong desires of not letting people go.

"He didn't want people to leave him. He stated it was also at this time that he began hating to sleep alone at night. He further indicates that it was around this time in his life that he became familiar with alcohol and that he immediately became a heavy drinker and abused alcohol on a regular basis. When he went into the Army, he indicates that his alcohol intake increased and that he was actually released 6 months early from the Army because of abuses of alcohol. He states that he was a Field Medic (blacked out).

"The suspect, Jeffrey DAHMER, states that he began having fantasies of killing people at the early age of 17 or 18. He states although these fantasies were fleeting, he feels that he had the fantasies to overcome the feelings he had of frustration and emptiness which he felt were in his life. He states that after he moved to Milwaukee in 1981, the fantasies of killing people began to excite him and became more frequent.

"Regarding his victims, he states that he received physical pleasure from being with the victims when they were alive and he would have preferred that the victims remained alive; however, he states that it was better to have them with him dead than to have them leave. He states that when he felt when they were about to leave, that is when he would decide to kill them.

"Regarding the fact that he had in fact eaten the parts of one of his victims, he states that he feels that by eating parts of the victim, this was his way of keeping them with him even longer and making his victim part of himself.

"At this time, Jeffrey DAHMER answered other questions put to him by Detective MURPHY and he will file a detailed supplementary regarding that part of this interview."

Report per: Detective Patrick KENNEDY
PK/slb   7-24-91

"On Wednesday, 7-24-91, at approximately 8.30 am., I along with Detective Patrick KENNEDY, were notified by the jail that the suspect in this offense, Jeffrey DAHMER, requested to speak to us regarding this investigation.

"We proceeded to the County Jail where he was taken from the cell and conveyed to Room #407 at the CIB, where he was re-interviewed by us. We informed Mr DAHMER of his "Miranda Rights" and he stated he knows his rights, but he just wanted to talk to us regarding this investigation.

"We then talked to him regarding his childhood and family status and a supplementary report will be called in reflecting his statements to these questions.

"We asked Jeffrey some additional questions regarding the first homicide that occurred in Bath, Ohio, and he stated that prior to that he had just started drinking when he was 17-years-old. He states that his friends were straight that he knew of. He states he had a friend named (blacked out) and they all smoked marijuana in high school. He states that he

268

did not know of any friends being gay, but that he himself had homosexual tendencies and had never gone out with a girl or had sex with any females.

"He states his first homicide which occurred, he believes, around October of 1978, was of a white male hitchhiker, whom he describes as 18 years of age, 5'10" tall, skinny build, maybe 150 lbs, having straight brown collar length hair, not wearing glasses, clean shaven and he believes he was not a homosexual.

"He states he didn't have sex with this individual; he just invited him in for a drink and when the individual wanted to leave that's when he hit him with a "barbell" and subsequently disposed of the body behind his residence. He states he did burn his clothes and identification.

"He again went through the various places that he lived and after joining the Army in 1979 and being discharged in March of 1981, where he was a Field Medic (blacked out) and left about October of 1981. He states that he then went back to Bath, Ohio and lived there until around December of 1981 or January of 1982.

"He states he then moved to Milwaukee with his grandmother from about December of 1981 or January of 1982 until 1988, when he moved to 808 N. 24th St. He states he remained there 6-months to a year, then moved to his present address of 924 N. 25th St.

"He again states that there were no homicides occurring until the one at the Ambassador Hotel, he believes in 1984, where the individual died and he subsequently took him to his grandmother's residence at 2357 S. 57th St., and there dismembered the body and disposed of the body parts.

"He goes on to relate that there were three other homicides at his grandmother's location and the rest were at his present address, 924 N. 25th St.

"He states the reason there were no homicides from 1978 to 1984 was because he was busy with what he was doing. He said he was busy in the Army and after work he'd go out drinking with the guys and then go to bed and get up and work. He states when he went to Florida he was too busy and when he arrived in Milwaukee he was too busy, until he discovered the gay bars. He further states that he did not have a homosexual relationship while he was in the Army or in Florida.

"He states the first experiences started after arriving in Milwaukee and going to the gay bars. He states that he would not maintain a relationship with the individuals with whom he had sex and most of them were one night stands. He states he enjoyed the company of these individuals, but did not like to see them go.

"After the murders started, he states that being with these other homosexuals gave him pleasure and he preferred them alive, but if they wanted to leave and he couldn't have them alive, then he would have them dead and that's why he would dismember them and save either their skulls or other body parts. He states that the victim, whose right bicep he had eaten, was one that he cared for and the individual had big biceps. He stated that he put Crisco on the bicep, softened it up with a meat tenderizer, and then fried it in a skillet. He states he also saved this individual's heart in the freezer and a portion of an arm from the black male that he had met at a bookstore about 1 year ago. He states he did intend to consume these parts.

"He also states that he had anal and oral sex with the victims after death, but not all of them. He states that when he was in high school he had fantasized about killing someone, but it did not take effect until 1978, the first time and then later in 1984, in Milwaukee.

"We asked him why he just didn't have oral or anal sex with the individuals while they were alive and let them go, and he stated because he didn't want to lose them and that the death and dismemberment led to the excitement and gratification.

"We then asked him if he had ever talked to a psychiatrist and he states that he talked to a Dr CROWLEY, who works for the Social Service, a couple of times, possibly 2 or 3 times, in the past month or so. He states that Dr CROWLEY had prescribed medication for him, but he states he didn't get any because he felt he didn't need it. He also states that he was fired from his job on July 7, 1991, and he had known the week prior that he was going to get fired and he feels this is the reason why the killings escalated because he was alone at night and did not want to be alone. He had no company and felt that these individuals would keep him company (next 4 lines blacked out).

"We then asked Mr DAHMER if he would be willing to view the photos that he had taken; namely, the Polaroids that were recovered in his apartment and to try to identify the victims for us, and he stated that he would, and he would look at any other photos we had available of any of the alleged victims and try to make identification for us. He also stated that he will try to remember any physical descriptions of the victims to help us discover their identity.

"We then informed Mr DAHMER of the Probable Cause Hearing, which would be taking effect this afternoon, and he stated that he would like to talk to us after that hearing."

Report per: Detective Dennis MURPHY.
DM/slb 7-24-91

"On Wednesday, 7-24-91, we took the suspect, Jeffrey DAHMER, from his cell and conveyed him to the CIB where he met with his attorney Gerald BOYLE and his assistant, Wendy PATRICKUS. At that time he signed a consent form to talk with us regarding this investigation on anything related to the Wisconsin Homicides.

"At approximately 4.20pm, we sat with Jeffrey in room

271

407 of the Detective Bureau and gave him cigarettes, coffee and soda and questioned him regarding the Polaroid photos that he had taken of the homicide victims in an attempt to make identification of these individuals and to establish an order of the homicides and what had actually occurred. Mr DAHMER stated that he would be glad to cooperate with us in any way.

"We started with the first homicide committed in Milwaukee and he stated that it occurred in either November of 1984 or November of 1985 to the best of his recollection. He stated that he met this victim and they went to the Ambassador Hotel. He described this individual as a white male, 25 years, 5'6", 10 lbs, slim build, blonde hair, shoulder length straight, maybe parted in the middle and clean shaven. He stated he was of fair complexion and had smooth skin and was possibly wearing jeans.

"He indicated that he went to the hotel with the individual; they were drinking and he gave him a drink, which contained sleeping pills. When he awoke the subject was dead next to him and blood was coming from his mouth. He stated that he then put the subject in a suitcase and took a cab to his grandmother's house at 2357 S. 57th Street where he drained the blood, cut the body up and used a sledgehammer to break the bones. He stated that he then disposed of the body in plastic garbage bags.

"He indicated that in January of 1985 or 1986 he met victim #2 in front of the 219 Club on South 2nd St. He stated that the victim was waiting for a bus, which was heading towards the south side. He described this individual as a Hispanic male, 16 to 18, 6'0, 150 lbs, slim build, dark straight short hair, clean shaven. This individual was possibly wearing a t-shirt and tennis shoes.

"He stated that when he met this individual and all of the victims, he would approach them and ask them if they would like to make money by posing for him in the nude, viewing videos and coming for a drink at his residence. He

272

related that he would offer various amounts of money to these individuals. He stated that each individual accepted his offer and would go with him to his residence. He indicated that the second victim went to his grandmother's house at 2357 S. 57th Street with him by taking the bus. There he gave him the sleeping potion, killed him by strangulation and then smashed the bones with the sledgehammer and disposed of the bones. He stated that he did not keep anything from this individual, nor did he keep anything from the first victim.

"The third victim he met about two months later, probably March of 1985 or 1986. He stated that he met another Hispanic male in the Phoenix Bar located on South 2nd Street near the 219 Club. He related that this individual was a Hispanic male, 19 to 21 years, 5'8", 130 lbs, slim build, light brown complexion, having straight short black hair, clean shaven, and smooth skin. He was wearing a long knee length brownish vinyl coat. He stated he asked this individual to come to his residence to look at videos, take photos or engage in sex. He stated that this victim did accompany him to his grandmother's house where he had oral sex with him. He then proceeded to drug this individual so he slept. He subsequently killed him, dismembered the body and disposed of it.

"He related that he did not keep any body parts from this victim. The fourth victim, whom he stated he met sometime in1987, but is not sure because it could have been when he was at his grandmother's house the second time in 1989. He was not sure of his dates, but he stated that he did meet this individual at La Cage at closing time. Upon viewing a photo of Anthony SEARS, DOB 01-28-65, he stated that this is the individual that he believes he met at La Cage. He described this victim as a black male, 21 to 22 years, 5'9", 150lbs, slim to medium build, light complexion, having short curly hair and a small ponytail in back with a rubber band. He stated that he was wearing jeans.

"He stated that he and this individual that he identified as Anthony SEARS through a photo of Anthony SEAR got into his friend's (friend of Sears) auto and his friend drove him to his grandmother's house. He described the auto as a large beat up older model, dark blue.

"He indicated that after arriving at the residence he used the same ploy to get the individual to come with him. He related that when they got there, they engaged in sex, he gave him the drink that put him to sleep and he subsequently killed him and dismembered the body. He indicated that this is the first one where he kept anything of the individual.

"He stated that he kept the victim's skull, which he boiled to remove all the skin; he kept the skull, the scalp with the small ponytail because he liked it and he kept the genitals of this person. He states that at the time of his arrest it was in the black metal cabinet. He also stated to preserve the skull and genitals he had called the hardware store and asked what would dry out a rabbit skin and they recommended acetone, which he used to dry out the scalp and genital area. He stated the reason he kept the scalp was because he liked it. He also stated that the skull he kept he painted.

"The fifth victim was two months after he moved into his apartment at 924 N. 25th Street, which he figures was in 1990. He stated that this individual was the first one he also took photos of. We showed him a photo album, which contained 15 photos of a black male in various positions and he identified this individual as the person he met in the 219 Club Area and offered him the same line as to come to be photographed, to have a drink and look at dirty videos. He indicated that this victim agreed and he took him to 924 N. 25th Street # 213 and there he drugged him and subsequently killed him by strangulation.

"After removing his clothes he saw the tattoo "Cash D"

on his chest with pitchforks going up above the name "Cash." The photographs in the album depict this openly. He described this individual as a black male, 22 years, 5'8" to 5'9", 140 lbs, curly black hair with a slight mustache. The photo also depicts this. He stated that after "Cash D" had died he had oral sex on him.

"The next individual, victim #6, was met at the Phoenix on South 2nd St. and he again approached this individual with the same line as to having to pose for photos and having to view videos and drink. He describes this individual as a black male, about 24, 6'2", 170 lbs, medium built, dark skin, prematurely bald, close cut hair, clean shaven, and he said he used to be with the Milwaukee Ballet. He states that he had oral sex with this individual and then killed him by the same procedure; drugging him until he slept, strangling him and then dismembering him. He states he did not keep anything from this individual.

"Upon viewing a photograph of a missing person, he identified victim #6 being SMITH, Edward Warren-M/B, B of I # 244654. He states that this photo does look like the individual he picked up and states he did not keep any body parts.

"Regarding victim #5, Cash D, he states he did keep this individual's skull and painted it after it had dried out. He then continued on with victim #7 who he stated he met in front of the bookstore in the 800 block of N. 27th St. He states this occurred in the summer of 1990 and he describes him as a black male, 24, 6', 160 lbs, medium build, medium complexion, chin whiskers, short black hair and states he approached him with the same line, had sex and then drugged him and killed him by cutting his throat. He states after taking photos of this individual, he dismembered him, disposed of the body parts except for his bicep, which he kept in the freezer and his skull, which he painted after the skin was removed and it had dried. Also states he kept the entire skeleton and bleached it.

"He states he met victim #8 at 2nd and Wisconsin by the bank about two months after victim #7. He states that this individual was a black male, about 20, 5'9", 150 lbs, slim build, medium to dark complexion, short black hair, and they walked to his residence up Wisconsin Ave. He states he approached him with the same line and when they got to his apartment they drank and talked but didn't have any sex because he wasn't his type. He states that he killed him because he had already given this individual the potion and after doing that he did not want sex with him and he thought this individual would wake up and be pissed off at him, so he killed him. He states he did not keep anything from this individual after he dismembered him because he wasn't his type.

"He continues on that he met victim #9 in February of 1991and the subject was waiting for a bus by Marquette. He states this occurred about four months after meeting victim #8. He describes this individual as a black male, 18, 6', 140 lbs, slim build. This individual was also with a medium complexion, with a 3" perm and a thin mustache. He states he approached him with the same offer and the guy agreed to accompany him to his apartment, subsequently gave the drinking potion, had oral sex and then killed him by strangulation. He stated that he used the strap to strangle him this time and that the subject was wearing an earring. He states he kept the skull of this individual, the hands and the genitals. Upon viewing a family photograph which was submitted by one of the relatives, this individual was identified as being Curtis STRAUGHTER- M/B, dob-4/16/73, B of I #231279.

"He continued on that he met victim #10 in March of 1991 on the corner of 27th and Kilbourn. He described him as a black male, 25, 5'9" to 5'10", 150 lbs, short black hair, medium built and medium complexion. He stated that he went through the same procedure in meeting this individual and the same offers and upon getting him to his residence, he subsequently drank the potion when he strangled him. He then had oral sex with the victim after his death. Mr DAHMER viewed the B of I photo # 220831 of an Errol LINDSEY M/B, dob-3/3/72 and states he believes is the same individual whom he identified as victim #10. He states he also saved this individual's skull.

"He then continued on and stated that he met victim #11 in front of 219 Bar on South 2nd St. around May of 1991and this individual was deaf and dumb. He states this individual's friends drove him to 23rd and Wells and they were a white female and a heavy set white male and they were also deaf mutes. He stated that he communicated with this individual by writing and that he felt this individual could read lips partially. He stated he offered this individual $50 to come over to take photos, to view videos, but it was not known if he had sex. He states that he gave this individual the drinking potion, passed out and when he woke up he was dead. He states he continued through the same procedure as to drain the body of blood, dismembered it and disposed of it and that he did keep this individual's skull.

"He then viewed a Wisconsin Driver's License with the photo of Tony A. HUGHES-M/B, dob 8/26/59, described as 6', 150 lbs, and lived at 1019 Coby St, Madison, WI, and upon viewing this photo, he states that is the deaf mute that he had met at the bar and took to his house and subsequently killed. He identified him as victim #11. Hughes' ID was found in the suspect's apartment.

"He stated he then met victim #12 in late May in front of the Grand Ave. Mall. He states that he went through the same procedure of offering money to have photos taken and he describes this individual as being an Oriental male, about 14, but whom he thought at first was 17 or 18, 5'5", 120 lbs, slim build, having dark hair. He states that he and this male took the bus back to his residence and this individual posed for two photos while he was alive and then he gave him the drink mixture which contained a sleeping potion. He states they were watching videos and this individual passed out. He states he then had oral sex with him and then went to the bar to get some beer because he ran out of beer. He states while he was walking back from the bar, which was located on 27th just north of Kilbourn, called the Gare Bear Bar, he saw the oriental male staggering down the street.

"He states he went up to him and the police stopped him. He states that when he told police that he was a friend of this individual and that he had gotten drunk and done it before, the police escorted them back to his apartment. And he stated he would take care of him because he is his friend. He states he then went into the apartment and subsequently killed this individual in the same way as he killed the others by strangulation and after this he had oral sex on the victim. He states he then took more photographs and dismembered the body, keeping the skull. He also states that he had anal sex with the victim after death. After viewing the photograph of the victim that he took, this was the same individual that had run down the street and was retrieved.

"Another individual was waiting for a bus and had a six pack in his arm. He states that he got off the bus and approached him with the same offer as he did the others and this individual agreed to go along with him. He states that they went to his residence where he had oral sex on this individual before killing him. He states he gave the potion and when the individual went to sleep he strangled him with the strap. He states he subsequently put his head in the freezer and his body in the same blue 57 gallon barrel in his residence. He states that these are the only homicides he had committed and that the only other one was the one that we knew about in 1978, which was the one in Bath, Ohio.

"Mr DAHMER states that he is still willing to

cooperate with us and if we have any more photos or people that are missing and that we may have identification of them, he will be glad to view photos to try to make an identification of the other unknown victims.

"As of this report, we have ID tentative identifications with some being positive and possibly an 11th, that being victim #5, who has the tattoo of Cash D on his chest with pitchforks going up. A check of the Gang Crimes Unit revealed that they had stuck up an individual identified as Mark Lee BROWN-M/B, dob-8/10/63 with an address of 2110 W. State St. or 1025 N. 24th St. and this individual is a BGD Gang member from Chicago and that he does have the tattoo Cash D on his right chest area. Detective BARBER will attempt to locate this individual during his tour of duty. Further investigation is pending."

Report per Detective Dennis MURPHY.
DM: jaj 7/25/91

"On Wed., 7/24/91, I Detective KENNEDY on Squad 126, while interviewing the suspect in this offense, that being one Jeffrey DAHMER, spoke to him in regards to the fact that he had knowledge to whether or not the acts he was committing were right or wrong. At this time, Mr DAHMER stated that he was fully aware that the acts he was committing were wrong and that he feels horrified that he was able to carry out such an offense.

"He stated that it is obvious that he realized that they were wrong because he went to great time and expense to try to cover up his crimes. He stated that he used quite a bit of caution by setting up alarm systems in his apartment, that being in the outer door, the sliding door leading to his hallway bathroom and bedroom and his bedroom door. He stated that he set up a fake video camera and told other homosexuals that he had brought to his apartment that it automatically turned on if his door opened up without the

279

alarm being turned off. He stated that this was all done in order to keep people from entering into his apartment and discovering the evidence of his criminal act.

"He also stated that he drank excessively to try to forget the nightmare he felt he was living, as he remembered the horror of some of the acts that he performed. He stated that he is deeply remorseful now for what he had done and wished that he had never started. He states that he is not sure why he started committing these offenses and feels that in order to make restitution to the families of those he has killed, that he would like to help the police in any way that he can by trying to identify his victims."

Report dictated by Detective Patrick KENNEDY.
PK/rc 7/24/91

"On Thursday, 7/25/91, I, Detective KENNEDY, along with Detective Dennis MURPHY, did receive information from LUCAD that the suspect in this offense, that being Jeffrey DAHMER, had requested to speak with us. At this time, I proceeded to the LUCAD and retrieved the suspect, Mr DAHMER, from his cell, and returned with him to the fourth floor, CIB, where he was placed into an interview room, and we again began to talk.

"At this time, Jeffrey DAHMER began speaking regarding his early teenage and high school years in Bath, Ohio. Jeffrey stated that as a teenager of 15 or 16, he realized that he was a homosexual. He stated that he has never been interested in women and he had no idea why he was a homosexual, but that he distinctly remembers that in high school, and during his teenage years, he became acutely aware of the fact that he was only attracted to men.

"He also stated that it was at this time that he began to have fantasies of killing human beings. He stated that at this time, he also began picking up animals that he had found on the road, which had been killed apparently by vehicles and he would bring them home to his house, and he would use a knife in order to cut them up and cut them open to see what was on the inside of them and what they looked like. He stated that several of the animals that he cut up, he would completely strip down the flesh and meaty areas and then use bleach and various other liquids, which he found around his household, and experiment to see which ones would clean the bones the best.

"He stated that it was also at this time that he actually found a large dog that had been hit by a car and that he brought this dog home, cut it up, looked at its insides, completely cleaned it and then soaked the bones in a bleach solution, and that he eventually planned to reconstruct the bones and mount the skeleton, much the way a taxidermist would do it. He stated however, that he never got around to doing this.

"He also stated that during this time that he was cutting up animals, he would fantasize what it would be like to cut up a human being. He stated that he realized at this early age that his homosexual fantasies and his fantasies of killing and dismembering human beings were interlocked and that he received gratification from these fantasies and they occurred many times. He stated that whenever he had fantasies of homosexual activity, he also had fantasies of killing and dismembering. He goes on to state that he felt that the retrieving of road killed animals and the cutting of them up, satisfied his urges and his fantasies of killing and dismembering human beings.

"He goes on to state that after leaving home in Bath, OH to join the Armed Forces, that while in the Army, he was stationed in Germany. When asked why his behavior of cutting up animals and killing and dismembering of human beings did not occur while he was in the Army, he stated that he believes the reason he did not kill or dismember any one while he was serving his tour of duty in

Germany, was because he enjoyed the structure of the Army. He states that during the entire tour of duty, he lived on base and was in a dorm with three other men.

"Although he did not have any homosexual or heterosexual relationships while he was in Germany, or in the Army, he did satisfy his urge for sexual excitement by masturbation. He stated that he enjoyed the Army and wished that he could have finished his entire tour of duty; however, his abuse of alcohol made that impossible as the Army decided to let him go six months before his tour of duty was up. Next 7 lines (blacked out).

"Jeffrey stated that when he was released from the Army, he stated that he was tired of the cold winters that he had endured in Germany and when he was growing up in Ohio, and with the voucher given to him by the Army, he could go anywhere in the United States that he wished, so he stated that he took a voucher for Miami, FL. because he thought it would be nice with the warm weather all the time. He indicated that the entire time that he was in Miami, FL., he did not engage in any homosexual activity, nor did he kill or dismember anyone while he was down there. He stated that he was continually busy trying to make ends meet financially while in Miami, and this is the reason why he had no time to engage in this activity.

"Jeffrey stated that he, at one time, was actually living on the beach because of lack of funds, and this was eventually the reason why he moved back to the Midwest. He first moved in with his grandmother in West Allis and he decided to make a concentrated effort to find some direction in his life. He went on to state that he constantly felt lonely and empty without direction and that there was no meaning in life for him. His grandmother was a religious woman, that being a Protestant and a regular church goer and talked to him several times about religion and how it could turn his life around.

"He went on to state that when he first moved to West

Allis, he had continual fantasies again about homosexuality, and that along with the homosexual fantasies came the urges to want to dominate, to kill and to dismember other men. He stated that he constantly fought this urge by attending church with his grandmother, by reading the Bible and by trying to live his life in an orderly fashion; 'to walk the straight and narrow' are the words that he used.

"He said he constantly had the interlocked feelings and fantasies of homosexual behavior, killing and dismembering and that they finally overcame him as he was finding it more and more impossible to continue with the lifestyle of 'church going and right living,' as he put it.

"At this time, I questioned Jeffrey regarding the skeleton bones which were found in the file cabinet in his bedroom. He stated that this was victim number seven, the black male that he met in December of 1990 by the bookstore on North 27th St. He said that this is the only victim that he stabbed in the neck in order to kill him. He stated that the reason he did this is because the potion that he had given him of sleeping pills and alcohol was beginning to wear off and that the individual was rather strong and muscular, and he did not feel that he would be able to strangle him successfully without putting up a fight; so he took a knife and stabbed him once along the jugular vein in order to kill him.

"He stated that because this individual was the most attractive that he had met up until that time, he decided to clean and boil the entire skeleton in the solution of water and soilex and to save it. The reason he did this was to keep this individual with him as long as possible.

"Regarding victim number ten, tentatively identified as Errol LINDSAY. Jeffrey stated that this is the only one of his victims that he completely took the skin off of. He stated that this was done with a very small, very sharp paring knife and that it took him approximately two hours to completely take all the skin off this victim, while leaving intact the cartilage, ligament and fleshy muscular areas.

"When talking about his personal relationships, Jeffrey stated that he really has no close friends and that he is basically a loner. He states that he is a loner by choice and that he has never had any success in continuing any long-range relationships. He stated that he has had friends while he was in high school, but never any best friend that he would continually hang around with. He stated that he likes to be alone and he especially likes to be alone when he kills people and cuts them up, because it makes him feel more secure and more dominant.

"At this time, he went on to say that he realizes what he has done warrants the death penalty; however, he is not sure that he really wants to die as punishment for his offenses. He stated that when he was younger, he started cutting up animals and he enjoyed the excitement of cutting them up, and that he wished now that he would have just continued to cut up animals and would have stopped with them and not have moved onto human beings. He felt that he originally only started it for the curiosity. Next 5 lines (blacked out).

"Regarding smaller children, Jeffrey states that although he has been convicted of exposing himself to younger children, and that he has tried to take pictures of minors, that he has no sexual desires to be with a younger child, that he has never attempted to entice a smaller child for sexual purposes, and that he was strictly sexually excited by, and attracted to, young men of any race or ethnic persuasion from the early teens to the late twenties.

"It should also be noted that during this interview and the interview that took place on 7-24-91, several photographs taken from our Identification Division were shown to Jeffrey and he was asked if he has ever met these individuals, or if they were in fact any of his victims. These photographs were picked specifically because the individual in the photograph was known to still be alive and it should be noted that each photograph that was shown to him where the individual in the photograph was still alive, Jeffrey stated, 'I've never seen this man before, and he is definitely not one of my victims.' It was at this time that the interview was terminated."

Report dictated by Detective Patrick KENNEDY.
PK/rc   7/25/91

"On Thursday, 7-25-91, I, Detective Patrick KENNEDY, Sq. 126, was notified by LUCAD that the suspect in this offense, Jeffrey DAHMER, had requested to see me. At this time I proceeded to the fifth floor, LUCAD, where I did meet Jeffrey and he in fact stated he did wish to speak with me. I brought him down with me to the fourth floor CIB interview room, at which time I asked him what it was he wished to speak about. It was at this time that he requested a cigarette and a cup of coffee, which I gave him. He stated that he just wished to talk about the feelings he had regarding the confession that he had made about all of his victims and his apprehension as to the court appearance he was to make later on in the afternoon.

"At this time I stated that I would be willing to listen to any comments that he had to make. He states that he realizes that there is no way he can change anything in regard to what he did to his victims. He also states that he realizes it would be impossible to make amends for the crimes and offenses he has committed towards these people. However, he feels that the only way for him to make a new start in his life is to make a clean breast of things and to be fully honest. He states that he feels this is what he did and he knows it is the only way he can change his life.

"He states that he knows that this will not change any of the things that he did but that <u>maybe by telling the truth</u>

285

he can start to make things right and put at ease the minds of his victims' relatives. He also stated that the only way he could start to change his self was to admit exactly what he had done, to state that he is sorry for what he has done and to swear that he will try to change his life in the future.

"At this time I was advised by Detective Dennis MURPHY that we were to transport the suspect Jeffrey DAHMER to the Milwaukee County Sheriff's Dept. jail area, and we then walked him to the jail area and turned him over to Deputy SCHUH (Phonetic) at the Milwaukee County Sheriff's Dept. for his court appearance.

"It should be noted that in previous conversations regarding his court appearance, the suspect Jeffrey DAHMER expressed apprehension at appearing in court in the paper jump suit provided him by the City Jail. At this time, I advised him that if he wished I could bring some old clothes from my home and give them to him so that he would have some presentable clothes to wear for his court appearance. To this Jeffrey DAHMER stated that he would be most appreciative if we could bring some clothes in for him, and on the date of his court appearance we did in fact provide him with a button down collared shirt and a pair of pants which fit him, for his court appearance. Upon taking him over to the county jail and turning him over for his court appearance, we also requested that they provide him with some county foot apparel, which they did."

Report dictated by Detective Patrick KENNEDY.
PK: rd 7/26/91

"On Friday, 7-26-91, I, Detective Dennis MURPHY, met with Detective KARABATSOS, who is from the Summit County Sheriff's Department in Akron, Ohio, and with Lt. Richard MUNSEY, who is from the Bath County Police Department in Akron, Ohio. These two individuals flew to Milwaukee to interview the suspect, Jeffrey

DAHMER, in regard to the homicide that had occurred in Ohio in 1978, which DAHMER had confessed to. I informed the detectives that a meeting was set up for 11.00am at the Milwaukee County Jail, in which we were going to meet an associate of Gerald BOYLE; namely, Attorney, Scott HANSON, who would be present for the interview.

"At 11.00am, we proceeded to the Milwaukee County Jail where we did meet with Attorney Scott HANSON, and we proceeded to the County Jail where we met with Jeffrey DAHMER. Attorney Scott HANSON requested that he talk with the defendant prior to our questioning him. Attorney HANSON conversed with Jeffrey for approximately 10 minutes, and then we all sat in the Library Room in the County Jail. I personally informed Jeff that he still could invoke his "Miranda Rights" if he desired, and I again asked him if he wanted to talk with us regarding this homicide investigation.

"I stated to him that even though his attorney is here, I still had to advise him of his various rights, and he stated that he 'understood' his rights. He had told them numerous times, and he did not wish to invoke his rights, that he would "waive" them, and he would cooperate and talk to us because he wanted to clean up everything.

"I then introduced him to Officers KARABATSOS and MUNSEY, and informed him that they were from the Akron, Ohio Police Department and that they were investigating the homicide he had previously confessed to, at which time he stated he would co-operate with them. We then showed him area photographs of his previous residence at 4480 W. Bath Rd., in Bath, Ohio, and he pointed out the area where he had disposed of the bones in the photographs. This was a heavily wooded area and he was asked if he could make a diagram indicating same, at which time, Jeffrey drew a diagram of Bath Rd., the driveway, the garage and the house area, and a small wooded area just to the side of the house. He indicated that this was the area in which he had disposed of the victim's bones.

"We also asked him if he knew the name, Steve HICKS and he stated that that was the name of the victim in Ohio, and the reason he remembered it was because it was his first one and he stated, 'You don't forget your first one.'

"We then showed him a reproduction of the photograph of Steven HICKS, and upon looking at it he stated that this looked like the individual. He was subsequently shown the regular photograph of Steven HICKS, which depicts the entire body, and he stated, 'I'm almost positive that's him. Yeah, that's him. That's the individual that I killed in Ohio'. He was then questioned regarding how this transpired, and he stated that he was driving southbound on Cleveland and Maslin Rd., (phonetic) and he figured it was warm out because the victim did not have a shirt. He stated he thought it was early Fall but he cannot be sure. He stated that as he was driving southbound on Cleveland and Maslin Rd., he saw the hitchhiker, and picked him up at Ball and Cleveland and Maslin Rd. He states that he discussed with the individual about buying or smoking 'pot' and drinking. They decided to go to his residence, and he stated that this was in the later afternoon or early evening hours. He stated that he made a U-turn and drove back to his residence because no one was home.

"He states his father was living in a motel complex about 5-10 miles away, and his mother had already left for Chippewa Falls, WI and he was living in the residence alone. He states that when they arrived home, they went into the bedroom and they were drinking beer, and after a while the victim wanted to leave. Jeff states that he wanted the victim to stay. The victim was sitting either on the bed or in a chair in a bedroom, and he approached him from

288

behind and hit him with a barbell in the head, and then he used the barbell to strangle him. After this occurred, he states he put him in a crawl space under the house and subsequently dismembered him in the same crawl space. He states that after he dismembered him he put the body in plastic bags and put the bags in the back seat of a blue, 4-door auto that was in the garage. He stated that this was about 3.00 am, and as he was driving he was stopped by officers who stated he was driving left of center. He stated he was given a drunken driving test, which he passed, and was then allowed to drive away. He states he thinks he may have gotten a ticket, but he is not sure.

"He states he then returned home and put the bags in a drainage pipe behind the house, and let them sit there for a couple of weeks. After this time he took the bags out, broke the bones up in little pieces and proceeded to a rocky cliff area to the back side of the house and just to the rear, which about 10ft. above the ground, and he spread the bones around this area. He states that he then burned the victim's identification and clothes. Mr DAHMER states that he believed the victim had been wearing a necklace, something with what appeared to be teeth braces on this necklace. He states that he disposed of these by throwing them in the river by the sewerage plant.

"We then questioned Mr DAHMER as to whether or not he continued his education. He stated that he did start Ohio University in August of 1978, and that he had committed this homicide prior to registering for school. He then thought, 'Well, it was at least 2 weeks prior to going to school in August.' He states he cannot be sure of the exact time or month that this occurred, but he does readily admit committing the homicide, and upon viewing the photographs and hearing the name states, that that was in fact the person he did in fact kill.

"We then asked Mr DAHMER if he would draw a diagram depicting where the crawl space was, the drainage pipe, and the cliff area where he disposed of the body. He proceeded to make a drawing on the reverse side of the previous drawing indicating these locations and where he disposed of the bones. This drawing was signed by Jeffrey DAHMER and initialed by myself, Detective KARABATSOS, and Lt. MUNSEY. This will be retained by Lt. MUNSEY for his investigation in Ohio.

"I then informed Mr DAHMER that I had numerous questions from previous statements he had given me, and he stated he would answer anything.

"At this time I asked him where he bought the chemicals used; namely the muramic acid. He stated that he bought them at Ace Hardware on 4th St. by Lapham Lighting. He states he bought the 4 boxes a few days before his arrest, just after the last homicide, and he was going to use these chemicals in the 57 gallon barrel. He states he bought the ether, chloroform, and others at Laab's Pharmacy on 27th and Kilbourn. He also stated that the jewelry he had sold at work; namely a necklace with an Italian horn on, was his personal jewelry and he did not sell or keep anything from any of his victims.

"He was also questioned regarding the bones and skeleton that were found in the drawer in his residence, and he stated that these belonged to the same person whose arm was in one freezer, and he stated that this was from the victim by the bookstore who he stated he killed approximately 1 year ago.

"I then questioned him where he had worked when he moved to Miami Beach from the service, and he stated that he had worked at Sunshine Subs Shop, which was privately owned and it was on Collins Ave., approximately ½ mile from his motel.

"Mr DAHMER was then thanked for his co-operation and subsequently returned to the County Jail. It should be noted that during the start of our interview Mr DAHMER had requested to have cigarettes. He was given coffee, but he was unable to smoke in the County Jail, so at approximately 12.15pm., I Detective Dennis MURPHY, proceeded to get an order to produce, which was signed by Judge RANDA, and Jeffrey DAHMER was taken to the CIB Interview Room along with Detective Lt. MUNSEY, Detective KARABATSOS and Attorney Scott HANSON.

"The remainder of the interview was conducted at that location, and Mr DAHMER was subsequently returned to the County Jail. Just prior to his return, Attorney HANSON had requested that we not talk to Mr DAHMER regarding anything unless we contact their agency. I informed Mr HANSON that Mr DAHMER had been requesting my presence every day and stated he did not wish an attorney present when I arrived to interview him.

"In the presence of Attorney HANSON, I informed Jeffrey of his attorney's request, and he stated he "understood" it, but stated that he wanted to get everything out in the open. I informed Mr HANSON that if Jeffrey calls to talk to me and he does not wish the attorney present, I will conduct my interview. Mr HANSON stated that he understood, and requested again to Mr DAHMER that he contact him prior to contacting the police. Mr DAHMER was then returned to the County Jail."

Report per: Detective Dennis MURPHY.
DM/slb   7-27-91

"On Friday, 7-26-91, prior to returning the defendant, Jeffrey DAHMER, back to the County Jail and after the interview with Detectives Richard MUNSEY and John KARABATSOS, I, Detective Dennis MURPHY and Detective Lt. Ken RISSE and Detective Guy NOVAK, met with DAHMER at the CIB to question him regarding the homicides that he alleged to have committed in West Allis, WI.

"Mr DAHMER stated that he possibly killed his first

victim at the Ambassador Hotel because he stated he took him up there, gave him a portion and passed out, but he did remember beating him about the chest. He stated that when he woke up the victim was dead; he put the victim in a suitcase that he had picked up at the Grand Avenue Mall, and took a cab to his grandmother's house at 2357 S. 57th St., where he subsequently dismembered the body and disposed of the bones and the tissue in the garbage.

"He stated that the 2nd victim, whom he had met at the '219' Club, was conveyed with him in a City Vet Cab, and he readily admitted killing him the same way as the other victims. He states he believe this individual may have lived on 10th & National, because he thinks that's what he told him. He also stated that he offered him money for sex, and that's the reason this individual went with him.

"Victim #3, whom he also states he killed in West Allis, he recalls that about 2 weeks after the homicide, he was reading the personal section in the paper and there was a small photo of this victim and it listed him as missing and requested information regarding the individual. He states he cannot recall the name, but he does recall seeing this photo in the personal section of the paper.

"Mr DAHMER states that when he returned these victims to his grandmother's house, it was usually in the middle of the night, and usually on a Saturday night. He stated when he brought victim #1 back it was in the middle of the night, and the next day, Sunday, when his grandmother went to church was when he dismembered the body, cut it in little pieces, removed the flesh, muscle and tissue before breaking up the bones. He stated that he never kept any parts of these. He states he also did this with victim #2; he brought him over on a Saturday night and dismembered the body on a Sunday morning.

"He also states that when he took victim #3 over to the house, he had also taken a cab there and was dropped off 2 blocks away, usually up by the Mai-Kai Tavern, and then

292

he would walk to the address. He states that way no one would know where his grandmother lived or where he was staying.

"He states that the pills used to put these individuals to sleep were called 'Halcion' and they were prescribed to him by a Dr OLSON, of West Allis Memorial Hospital.

"He also states that there was one more occurrence that happened, but this time the individual woke up prior to him being able to kill him and he was also seen by his grandmother with this individual in the basement and he decided not to kill him. He stated that he did walk this individual to the bus stop and returned to the residence. It was shortly after this that his grandmother had asked him to leave.

"A check with West Allis revealed that there was a 'theft' complaint filed on 4-4-88, by Ronald FLOWERS, who was this alleged victim, case # 841212, file # 88-07829.

"Regarding victim, #4, who was subsequently identified as Anthony SEARS, he stated that he met this victim a few weeks before he went into the Work Release Center, and with him he was dropped off by the Mai-Kai Lounge around Easter of 1989. In fact, he stated it was the night before Easter. He stated that this did happen after his arrest, but he was at his grandmother's house. He states that after bringing him to his house on Saturday night, he did have sex with him, cut him up, disposed of the body in the same manner except for keeping his head, scalp, and genitals. He stated that he did dispose of this body on Easter Sunday.

"West Allis officers questioned him regarding any other information he may have in relationship to these alleged homicides in their jurisdiction, and he stated he could not think of anything at this time, but if he does recall he will contact me so that I can inform them of any further information.

"Mr DAHMER was then returned to the County Jail. I, along with the Ohio Police officers and West Allis Police officers, then subsequently went to the West Allis Police Department where we interviewed the father of Mr DAHMER; namely, Lionel DAHMER. While we were conducting this interview, I received a phone call from Captain Domagalski informing me that the subject, Jeffrey DAHMER, had requested that I come to the jail because he had something important to tell me.

"After our interview with his father, I subsequently returned to the County Jail, where Mr DAHMER informed me that he forgot to tell me about an incident that occurred about 1 year ago where one of them had gotten away. I asked him what he meant, and he stated that he had picked up a Spanish male for the purpose of taking photos and having sex, and he brought him over to his apartment at 924 N. 25th St. He stated that this had occurred prior to victim #7. He states that when he brought this individual over, he did not have any more sleeping pills left so he attempted to knock him out by hitting him in the back of his neck with his fist or hand.

"He stated this did not work and the Hispanic male fought with him, and after a while they kind of made up and he stayed there the remainder of the night and left in the morning. Mr DAHMER stated that he had forgotten about this, but he wanted to get it out. I asked him if he recalled any other incidents where this had occurred and he stated he 'did not'.

"I then informed him that we had just spoken with his father, and we had received information that he may have had a sexual experience when he was 14 or 15 years of age, with a person who lived across the street. Mr DAHMER stated that this did occur, and he had gotten undressed and did some body rubbing and kissing. I asked him if he recalled the [blacked out], and he stated this was the individual. He stated he did not consider this a homosexual

294

experience at the time, but he stated, 'but I guess it is'.

"I then asked him when he had acquired his fish tank and he stated it was about 6 months ago because he had developed an interest at that time.

"I then informed him that there were numerous allegations made against him by people calling and went through a stack of them, at which time he denied all of them. I asked Mr DAHMER if he had anything more to tell me, and why he did not request to have his attorney prior to talking to me, and he stated that he did not want his attorney there; he just wanted to tell me about this other thing that he had forgotten and he didn't need his attorney present for that. I asked if he felt he needed the attorney for any other questioning, and he stated he felt he did not because he has been truthful with me the whole time and he does not feel he needs his attorney present when I'm there. I again informed him of his attorney's request, that he contact the attorney prior to contacting me, and he stated he understands and if he feels he has something important enough to tell me, he will call me. I then informed him again that his attorney had requested his co-operation, and he stated he would consider it."

Report per: Detective Dennis MURPHY.
DM/slb   7-27-91

"On Monday, 17-29-91, we, Detectives Dennis MURPHY and Patrick KENNEDY, received a call from the Milwaukee County Sheriff that the subject, Jeffrey DAHMER requested to speak to us.

"At this time we obtained an order to produce and proceeded to the Sheriff's Department where upon presenting it we were informed that he was presently with the psychiatrist for Attorney BOYLE. An attempt to locate Attorney BOYLE met with negative results and we then informed the Sheriff to contact us when his interview was over.

"At approximately 12.05pm, we received a call from the County Jail indicating that DAHMER was finished with his interview and was available for us. At that time we proceeded to the Milwaukee County Jail.

"We picked up Jeffrey DAHMER and asked him if he had contacted his attorney regarding his request to see us. He stated he did and that his attorney would meet us at the CIB. We proceeded to the CIB where Jeffrey stated he would talk to us and wanted to talk to us even though his attorney wasn't present, because he stated that he told us everything already. He stated that he's not involved in any other crimes and he will talk to us regarding anything or answer any questions we may have relative to this investigation. We asked him if had wanted to again call his attorney and he again stated, 'No,' that he would wait until she arrives.

"I then asked him several questions regarding a statement he had made regarding the homicide in Bath, Ohio in regards to a call I received from Lieutenant Richard MUNSEY relative to the investigation. I asked him what he had done with the knife he had used to cut up the victim, namely Steven HICKS, and he stated that he believes he threw it in the river. I questioned him as to whose car he used when he stated that he was driving down the road when he picked up the hitchhiker and subsequently in a car later on in the evening after the death and he stated he used his father's blue 4-door, which his father had let him use to go to a movie.

"He indicated that his mother had already left for Chippewa Falls and his father was still living in the motel at this time. He stated that when he killed Steven his mother was gone. I also questioned him regarding how much time he had spent with the victim prior to killing him and he stated that they were together for a couple of hours and they were just drinking beer.

"I also went back to his earlier childhood when he had been cutting the dogs and I asked him if he did, in fact, ever cut up a dog and hang it up in the tree in Ohio and he stated that he only hung one dog in the tree and doesn't know why he did this. He also stated that he does not, nor did he have, any girlfriends in Milwaukee or in Ohio. He did admit going to the prom, but stated that he only went to see what it was like because he was junior and the girl he went with was a senior and they just went more or less to accompany each other to the prom.

"He stated that he does not recall any other thing regarding the Bath, Ohio homicide and if we have any further questions regarding it he would be glad to answer them for us."

Report dictated by: Detective Dennis MURPHY
DM: dls 07-29-01

"On Monday, 7-29-91, we, Detectives Dennis MURPHY and Patrick KENNEDY, after walking Mr DAHMER over to the CIB from the Milwaukee County Sheriff's lock up and informing that he had the right to have his attorney present during questioning. He stated that he did not need to have his attorney present and, in fact, he had called her and she was on her way but he would talk to us until she does arrive.

"I informed him that we had a call from Carlos CRUZ who stated that he had been in the service with Mr DAHMER while in Germany. Mr DAHMER stated that he does remember him and, in fact, he has nothing to hide regarding Germany. He stated that he does remember spending Thanksgiving at Mr CRUZ'S residence. He stated also present was an individual with the last name of DAVIS, another girl who was with DAVIS and also Mr CRUZ'S wife. He indicated that he did have Thanksgiving dinner at that location and he did become involved in an argument with Mr DAVIS regarding where they were going to spend the evening because there were not that many bedrooms.

"He stated that he was drunk because he had drunk heavily and it was snowing hard, similar to a blizzard, but he stated that he did not leave the house. He related that he remembers staying there and leaving in the morning, but he doesn't remember leaving at night, nor does he remember being covered with blood or having blood on any type of clothing. He stated that Mr CRUZ'S wife should be able to verify his statement that he did not leave that night or at any time once he arrived.

"He again denies being involved in any homicides in Germany and stated that he could not recall any other occurrences where he may have been away from the post other than when he went to Oktoberfest for three days in Munich, which he believes was in August of 1980. Again Mr DAHMER denies being involved in any homicides in Germany or in any other place other than the ones he has already confessed to."

Report dictated by: Detective Dennis MURPHY
DM: dls 07-29-91

"On Monday, 07-29-91, we Detectives Dennis MURPHY and Patrick KENNEDY while interviewing the subject, Jeffrey DAHMER at the CIB in the presence of his Attorney, Wendy PATRICKUS, we showed him numerous photographs of missing black males, one white male and one Hispanic male. Next 7 lines (blacked out).

"I then proceeded to show him another B of I (Bureau of Investigation) photograph #200484 (David C. THOMAS) and he stated, 'This looks like the victim who I possibly killed after the man in bookstore,' (who was subsequently the 8th victim… if you go in order). This follow up was given to Detective O'KEEFE to take this photograph, along with photographs that had been taken by the suspect of this homicide victim to the family in order to make identification.

"The next B of I photograph shown to him was #190872 (Richard GUERRERO), and he stated that he could not be sure, but the victim (who was victim #3 in Milwaukee) was a Hispanic male and had had his photograph in the personals in the Milwaukee Journal. A copy of this paper was obtained from 01-07-89 and upon viewing this photograph in the personals he stated, 'Yes, this is the Hispanic male I killed at my grandmother's house.'

"He further stated this occurred sometime in March of 1988 in West Allis. Both the identifications of THOMAS and GUERRERO were subsequently made as positive identifications and were listed as homicide victims.

"On Tuesday, 07-30-91, again while questioning DAHMER at the CIB in the presence of his attorney (PATRICKUS), we showed him a photo array consisting of four Hispanic males, B of I numbers: #209415, #234074, #234356 and #227440.

"Upon viewing these four photographs, DAHMER picked out B of I #234356 and stated this photograph looks like the first Hispanic male he met on South 2nd St., (victim #2), which occurred approximately in January of 1988. This is a photograph of Jay E. DOXTATOR, I/M, DOB 03/01/73 of 1010 W. Pierce St., and reported missing on 01-18-88. Further investigation was passed on to Detective MCHENRY and they will attempt to make positive identification on this individual.

"Further investigation is pending."

Report per Detective Dennis MURPHY
DM/htf   07-31-91

"On Monday, 07-29-91, I, Detective KENNEDY,

along with Detective Dennis MURPHY, were contacted by Deputy MALLICK (phonetic), of the Milwaukee County Jail. He stated at this time, which was approximately 9.45am, that the suspect, Jeffrey DAHMER, had requested to speak with us.

"We proceeded to the jail after obtaining an order to produce and returned with the suspect to the 4th floor CIB and placed Mr DAHMER in an interview room. At this time Mr DAHMER stated that he did, in fact, wish to speak with us regarding the offense.

"I advised Mr DAHMER that I had some further questions regarding the Asian male he stated that he met while he was walking around the Grand Avenue mall. He indicated that after introducing himself to the victim, he offered him $50 to accompany him back to his apartment to pose and have some drinks and watch videos. He stated that he advised the Asian male that the posing would be in nude or semi-nude states.

"The Asian male agreed to accompany him back to his apartment and they returned to his 25th Street address by bus. He feels that they returned home at approximately 5.00pm and once in the apartment, he had the victim disrobe down to his black bikini panties and that he posed for several photographs, which he took with his Polaroid camera. These photos can be found on Milwaukee Police inventory. He stated that during the time of the posing he also mixed his drink of rum, coffee and sleeping pills and offered it to the victim who drank it.

"He went on to state that during this entire time the victim spoke in perfect English and was completely able to understand English and spoke it fluently. He indicated that at about this time the rum/coffee concoction with the sleeping pills in it began to take effect and as the victim became drowsy he walked him into the bedroom area. During the time that he walked him to the bedroom area and sat on the bed DAHMER, stated that the victim, Tony

HUGHES, whom he had killed several days earlier, was lying naked on the floor of his bedroom.

"He stated that he believes that the victim saw Tony HUGHES' body; however, he did not react to it. He feels that this was because the rum/coffee/sleeping pill mixture was beginning to affect him. He went on to state that he put a video on and they watched it until the victim fell asleep. He related that during this time he began kissing and body rubbing the victim and he feels that he may have had oral sex, mouth to penis, on the victim. However, he denies at this time that he had penis to anus sex with the victim.

"He stated that after he realized that he was unable to arouse the victim by mouth to penis sex and by body rubbing and kissing, he continued to watch the video and to drink beer until he himself fell asleep. He indicated that after a few hours of sleep he woke up and it was quite late out, approximately 11.00 or 12.00, maybe later. He looked about and realized that the victim was still sleeping from the effects of his drink and he decided to go to the tavern located on 27th Street known as the Gare Bear Bar to continue drinking.

"He stated that he left the apartment, went to the Gare Bear Bar and drank beer until closing time. At closing time, after leaving the tavern, he stated that he began to walk eastbound on West State Street and observed the victim sitting completely naked on the southeast corner of 25th and State. He stated that the victim was sitting on the curb. He related that there were two black females standing by him and they appeared to be hysterical.

"He walked up to the victim, whom he realized was speaking to the black females in Asian. The victim was disoriented and appeared to be intoxicated. However, he realized that he must still be under the influence of the drink containing the sleeping pills he had given him. At this time he advised the ladies that the victim was, in fact, a friend of his and that he attempted to pull the victim in the

301

direction of his apartment. He stated that the women continued screaming at him, 'We don't know if you really know this guy and we've called the Police. Why don't you wait until the police get here?'

"He stated that he continued pulling the victim towards his apartment and that the victim did offer some slight resistance to this. When he got to the alley behind the Hong Fat Company, he noticed that the Fire Department had approached from the east end of the alley. He indicated that at this time he noticed that the victim had a slight laceration above his left eye and was bleeding from this. He stated that at this time there were no other signs of blood on either the anal or genital area of victim.

"As the police and Fire Department arrived, he stopped with the boy. He noticed that the Fire Department personnel simply stood by and did not make any efforts to attend to the victim. He stated that he feels that the police officer took a yellow plastic type blanket and wrapped it around the boy and he noticed that the black females who he had seen with the boy on 25th and State appeared to still be hysterical and were screaming at the police officers.

"At this time he stated that a police officer approached him and asked him what was going on. He stated that he handed the police officer his Ambrosia Chocolate Company personnel ID and stated who he was and gave a fake name for the victim. He stated that he believes he told the police that the victim was 19-years-old and he thought this was appropriate, as although the victim was young, he believed him to be approximately that age. He stated that he told the police that the victim, was in fact a close friend of his and gave him a fake name. He indicated that the victim had stayed with him several times in the past and that whenever he drinks he gets crazy and has been known to walk out of the apartment in the nude.

"He stated that the officers attempted to speak with the victim. However, he stood there speaking only in Asian dialect and appeared to be intoxicated and smelled of alcohol.

"He stated at this time he feels he convinced the police that this was some type of homosexual relationship that had some alcohol problems and that he would take care of the victim if he was allowed to return with him to his apartment. He stated at this time two officers escorted both he and the victim back to his apartment building.

"He went on to state that during the time that the officers were speaking with him regarding the Asian boy, the black females who had been screaming hysterically in the beginning of this, left the scene. However, he is unsure where they went to.

"He related that the victim was in no way an acquaintance of his before this evening, that he had never seen him before and had absolutely no idea that he was, in fact, the brother of the minor he had taken pictures of on an earlier offense. He indicated that it was a chance meeting at the Grand Avenue Mall and that to his knowledge, besides this offense and the offense where took pictures of an Asian boy, that there have been no other encounters, either personally, casually or sexual, with any other oriental males.

"At this time I again questioned Jeffrey DAHMER as to the bleeding from the anus of the victim and whether or not the bleeding would be visible to police officers. He stated emphatically that there was no blood coming from the anus or genital area of the victim as he had not had any anal intercourse or injured the victim in any prior to this meeting with the Police. He stated that the night was pitch black and the alley was also dark. He feels the police attempted to interview and investigate the incident to the best of their ability at the time. However, he feels he was able to convince police of the homosexual nature of the incident and that, in fact, all would be well if he was allowed to assist in taking care of the victim."

303

Report dictated by: Detective Patrick KENNEDY
PK: dls 07-29-91

"On Mon., 7-29-91, I, Detective KENNEDY, on Squad
126, along with Detective Dennis MURPHY, was in an
interview room located in the CIB on the fourth floor. At
this time we had the suspect in this offense, Jeffrey
DAHMER, who had previously requested to speak with us
regarding this offense.

"I advised Mr DAHMER that I had a series of
questions I would like to ask him regarding the offense, to
which he stated he was willing to answer them. At this time
I asked him regarding the patties of meat, which we found
in the lower freezer in his apartment. To these he stated
they were not exactly patties, however, they were strips of
muscle and flesh, which he had taken from his thirteenth
victim. He stated he met this victim in front of the bus
station and the reason these were not thrown out, along
with other parts found with the so called 'patties' was
because he had placed them on the bottom of his standing
freezer and that they had become frozen to the bottom and
he was unable to get them out.

"He stated his usual routine after cutting up his victim,
was to only throw out two and possibly three bags of
human flesh and bones at a time and at this time he would
hide the bags underneath other bags of garbage, which were
located behind his apartment building on 25th St. He stated
the remainder of flesh, chunks and strips of body parts
which he had cut off the victims, he would place in plastic
bags and freeze until a more appropriate time to throw them
out. He stated this was done in order to help stop detection
of his crime. He felt that if he would throw out entire cut up
body parts at one time, it would be easier for people to
detect his activities, so therefore he would freeze, or keep
refrigerated, body parts until he was able to more discreetly
dispose of them through the trash.

"Regarding the computer which was found in his apartment, Jeffrey stated he became interested in computers while he was doing his tour in the House of Correction. He stated he thought it would be fun and interesting and that he would use it for personal finance, daily planning, games and personal business. He stated there will be several discs found in his apartment, however, that he never recorded or put anything into his discs regarding the offenses that he has been questioned about. He stated the computer did not turn out to be as interesting to him as he felt it would and that he barely used it and that slightly before his arrest he was attempting to sell the computer and had an offer regarding so.

"Regarding whether or not he had ever been in Columbus, Georgia, or Fort Bennings, Jeffrey stated that while he was taking his military police training at Fort McClellan, Alabama, he kept getting drunk on base and ended up getting beat up by several other members of his unit. He stated they did this because he had caused the entire platoon to suffer extra physical training and punishment because of his abusive drinking pattern. He stated that one day after the entire unit was disciplined because one of his infractions, a large black private and a large white private took him into the men's room and physically beat him bloody. He stated that during this beating he received a concussion and the ear drum of his left ear was fractured. He stated that from this injury he was transferred to Fort Bennings in Georgia for treatment. He stated he was there for only two days and then returned to his barracks at Fort McClellan. He stated that after washing out of the MP training school, he was transferred to Fort Sam Houston, Texas, where he was trained as a medic. He stated this training agreed with him more and he felt he did well while there.

"Regarding questions as to whether or not he belonged to a health club, he stated he was a lifetime 'President's thus he was eligible to attend any Vic Tanny Health Club throughout the nation. He stated he frequently visited the Vic Tanny Health Club on North Hawley Road and that he went regularly for about a year. However, after that, time constraints and his job, along with his drinking problem prevented him from going any longer.

"Regarding having a locker at the Ambrosia Chocolate Company, he stated that while he was employed at Ambrosia Chocolate Company, he did have a yellow painted locker; he believes the number was '214.' He stated that to the best of his knowledge, there was nothing of value or of personal belongings in that locker at the time of his termination. However, he is not sure.

"Regarding how long ago he bought the standing freezer found in his apartment, he stated that he bought the standing freezer several months after he had killed the victim known as "Cash D." He stated the reason he bought the freezer was to store the flesh. This he said is because he was having difficulty storing the cut off flesh and bones, which he had cut from his victims. He stated he felt that by buying the freezer, it would be easier for him to store the cut up flesh and bones until he was able to dispose of them discreetly through the garbage to the rear of his apartment.

"Regarding the penis from the black male, which he kept and which he painted white, he stated he bought skin color paint and painted the penis simply because it seemed like a fascinating idea and he wanted the penis to look more natural. He was unable to give any further reason as to why he painted this penis. Regarding the head of the victim, BRADEHOFT and why it was partially decomposed when found in the freezer, Jeffrey stated that after he killed the victim, BRADEHOFT, he placed him on the bed in his bedroom and covered him with a blanket and left him there for approximately two days. He stated he remembers it was hot during those two days and that the air conditioning in his apartment does not really cool off the bedroom that well. He stated it had been at least a day and a half before he checked on his victim and that when he pulled the blankets back after approximately two days, he noticed that decomposition had already begun and that the head had acquired some maggots. He stated he quickly cut up the victim and disposed of him in the same way, except for keeping the head and placing it in the freezer.

"Regarding the black nylon strap, which he stated he used to strangle several of his victims and which was photographed by himself hanging one of his victims from his shower in his bathroom, I questioned Jeffrey as to the whereabouts of the strap and he stated he was unsure with which victim he got rid of the strap. However, he stated it became soaked with blood and he decided to throw it out and that he disposed of it through his garbage located in the alley at his building.

"Regarding the knives which he used, he stated that the large knife with the six inch blade and the black plastic handle, he bought at the knife shop in the mall and he had returned to the mall at least two or three times in order to get it sharpened, as the store would sharpen the knife for free. He stated this is the knife he used most often when cutting up his victims. However, there were the two small three inch bladed parry knives with the black plastic handles, he stated he bought at Lechtner's Kitchen Mart in the Grand Avenue Mall. He stated he did use these knives. However, they were not very strong. The smaller of the two parry knives, one of which is photographed and a copy of which can be found on MPD inventory, is the knife which he used to carve the skin off. This happened to the one victim that he totally skinned.

"Regarding the battery complaint, which he filed with the Milwaukee Police Department in November of 1988, he stated he met an individual and asked him if he would come back to his apartment for pictures. He stated that although he was no longer living in the apartment on North 24th St.,

Correction: he was no longer living in the apartment on North 24th St., he had just moved out in October and felt it would still be vacant. He stated he still had the key for that apartment and that he and the suspect went back to that apartment. However, upon attempting to enter, he realized it had been rented out and a female was living there.

"He stated that upon realizing this, he and the suspect walked down the stairwell of the apartment building at 808 North 24th St. and continued to drink beer. He went on to indicate that after all the beer was gone, he bent over and received a blow from behind. He is unsure what he was struck with. However, because of his intoxication and the fact that the blow was so hard, he knows he passed out. He stated when he became conscious, he was at the police station and that officers, after taking his complaint, took him to West Allis Memorial Hospital, where he was stitched up.

"He believes the suspect, who was a black male, also stole about $350 from his pockets and he does remember coming to the third floor of the Police Administration Building and viewing photos regarding this offense, however he was unable to pick anyone out of the lineup. Next 3 lines (blacked out).

"At this time I questioned Jeffrey regarding the fact that he apparently left the victims, who were already killed, lying about his apartment. He stated he never left anyone for more than two days. However, he did leave several of his victims uncut up and naked, lying about his apartment, either in his bed or on his bedroom floor. He stated there are several reasons why he did this. The first reason was because on several of his victims he intended and did return at a later date and had oral and anal sex, and kissing and touching of the body, after they were dead. He also stated that sometimes because of time constraints and work, he was unable to proceed with cutting up and disposing of the bodies at the time, so he simply left them. He stated also that there were other times, because of his drinking and the late hours he was keeping, that he was just too exhausted to try to cut up the body and dispose of it, so he left them there.

"Regarding the letter which was written to Judge GARDNER while he was in the House of Correction, he stated that he remembers talking to a white male inmate in the House of Correction regarding his predicament and wanting to get out. He stated that this inmate put the idea in his head to write a letter to the judge regarding a change in his sentence. He stated the inmate appeared to be knowledgeable in such matters and actually wrote out a letter, which he copied in his own handwriting. He stated the words and the ideas in the letters which he wrote to Judge GARDNER were not even his. However, he thought that they sounded all right and decided to use them to see if they would work. He stated that although he did write the letter, the ideas, words and composition were the work of another inmate.

"At this time I questioned Jeffrey regarding the long period of time which lapsed between his first homicide, which he committed in Bath, Ohio and the first homicide, which he committed here in Milwaukee. At this time we established that the first homicide, which he committed here in Milwaukee, occurred probably in November of 1987. This was the victim that he took to the Ambassador Hotel. Jeffrey stated he feels that the first homicide that happened in Bath, Ohio, was unplanned, somewhat of an accident. He stated this haunted him terribly for many years and that he had nightmares and was troubled by it during the entire time he was in the service. He emphatically denied committing any crimes while he was in the United States Armed Forces and stated he feels that one of the reasons that he did not get involved in criminal activity was because of the structure of the military and the fact that he never had a residence or an apartment of his own.

"He feels he was continually surrounded by other

309

soldiers and did not have an opportunity to commit any offences. He stated that after leaving the military and moving to Miami, Florida, that he was short of funds and was living on the beach after he ran out of cash. He stated he lived on the beach for approximately two months in between hotels and that there too he did not have an opportunity to commit an offense. He stated he busy working in the sub shop trying to make money or trying to find a place to stay and that Miami did not turn out to be the opportunity that he felt it would be when he left the service. He stated after calling his father and advising him of the financial trouble he was having in Miami, he was given a plane ticket to return to Ohio, and eventually moved to his grandmother's house in West Allis.

"He stated when he first moved to West Allis with his grandmother, it was at this time that he decided to try to put behind him the nightmare he had constantly re-lived regarding his first homicide. He stated his grandmother was a religious woman and at this time he began attending church with her and apparently was looking into religious ideals in an attempt to change his life. He stated he recalls reading the Bible and attempting to look for a job and to live the so called 'straight and narrow life.' He stated that although he constantly tried to delve into the religious aspects of life, he constantly had fantasies of homosexual activity and mutilation of human beings. He stated that eventually during this period of time the fantasies and the urges for, as he called them, 'the darker side,' bothered him and that he decided to quit attending church and looking into religion, and for awhile he delved into the occult.

"He stated he felt he did this because he felt that since religion wasn't working, maybe he should just delve into the occult and to Satanism. However, after reading several books and dabbling in it, he realized this was not for him and then he again gave in to his homosexual tendencies. He stated he began by going to the bookstores where he

310

obtained information regarding gay areas in Milwaukee. He stated he also started reading gay and homosexual pornography and eventually became acquainted with the bars in the homosexual areas of town.

"From there he began to frequent the gay baths and was a regular member of the gay baths and spent the night several times. He in fact stated that several times he used a liqueur, which had been tampered with by his sleeping pills in the gay baths. However, he did not commit any violent acts while there. He only drugged some of his gay friends who he had met and spent the night with in the gay baths. He stated he believes this is the reason why there was such a long span between homicides, as he was going through all of these mental changes, trying to leave the old life behind and that once he finally again gave in to his homosexual desires, that it slowly began to escalate over years until he finally gave in to his fantasies of killing and dismembering men after homosexual acts and culminated in his first homicide here in Milwaukee, at the Ambassador Hotel.

"At this time he was given several other questions regarding his tour of duty in Germany and a chronological explanation of the events of his life and Detective Dennis MURPHY will file a detailed supplementary regarding this part of the interview. It should also be noted that during this interview, I asked Jeffrey if in fact all the information he has been giving us regarding this offense is true and correct. At this point Jeffrey was very adamant, stating, 'What would be the point of lying now? You realized that the whole purpose for me cooperating with you and giving you this information is for me to clear my conscience so that I can go on with my life. What I've told you is the truth. Why should I lie now?' At this time the interview was terminated."

Report per Detective Patrick KENNEDY.
PK/lh   7-29-91

"On Tue., 7-30-91, I, Detective KENNEDY, along with Detective Dennis MURPHY, was called by Deputy COOPER of the Milwaukee County Sheriff's Jail and he informed us this time that the suspect, Jeffrey DAHMER, had requested to speak with us. At this time we proceeded to the 5th floor Lock Up of the Milwaukee County Jail and returned to the 4th floor of the C.I.B., with the suspect, Jeffrey DAHMER, and placed him into an interview room.

"At this time I was informed by Jeffrey DAHMER that he would like to speak with me some more regarding the above offense. At this time Jeffrey DAHMER stated that during the time that he was committing these offences, he had been incarcerated in House of Correction for the offense of taking photographs of a minor. He stated that during his incarceration he was given a 'day pass' on Thanksgiving Day. He stated that during his day pass he was ashamed to face his family who were gathered at his grandmother's house in West Allis for Thanksgiving dinner and that after dinner he left the residence and went to a local West Allis tavern where he began to drink heavily. He stated after he became intoxicated, he ended up down in the homosexual area of Milwaukee, that being 200 South 2nd St., and he bar hopped. He stated he is unsure, but he feels that this time he entered the 219 Club where he ended up sitting next to an older white male, approximately 35 – 40-years-old, who had dark curly shoulder length hair and a beard. He stated the two talked and drank heavily, and that he (DAHMER) apparently blacked out because of overindulgence in alcohol.

"He stated he recalls waking up the next morning and he was in a strange apartment. He states that at this time he was hogtied. He describes this as being tied behind his back and then suspended by hooks and ropes from the ceiling

312

and that both his legs were separated and tied and also elevated and that the suspect described earlier that he had met in the 219 Club, was using a white striped candle and placing it in his anal area. He stated that when he realized what was happening, he began screaming and swearing at the suspect, demanding that he be cut down and let go. He stated the suspect did cut him down and he quickly grabbed his clothing and attempted to leave the apartment when the suspect attempted to stop him and stated, 'What's your hurry? Let's stop and talk about this.' He stated at this time he was in no mood to speak with the suspect and quickly left the residence and made his way back to the House of Correction.

"He stated that approximately a day or two after this encounter, he was sick. He had a bowel movement and a six inch portion of candle was ejected from his anal area at this time. He stated he was highly intoxicated at the time of this encounter and that he is unsure whether or not he would be able to identify this suspect through photographs. He stated he chalked this up to being an experience that he had to endure because of his high-risk life style and the homosexual areas of town. He stated that at this time he was actually the victim.

"At this time I questioned Jeffrey DAHMER regarding the blood which he found splattered around the walls surrounding his bed in his bedroom of his apartment on 25th St., and regarding the blood which was found dried and soaked into the mattress of his bedding. He stated this blood was the result of the seventh victim, who had been identified as Ernest MILLER. He stated he met Ernest MILLER in front of the bookstore on 27th St. and that after taking him home to his apartment and drugging him with his sleeping pill rum concoction that the victim apparently began to wake up from the potion as he was lying on his bed. He stated the victim had a muscular build and he felt he would be unable to strangle him as he was coming out of

313

his daze, so he used his knife to cut him in the carotid artery. He stated that by cutting the carotid artery of the victim, the blood began to splatter all about the bed and the walls. He stated he did not do a very good job on cleaning up the blood afterward and this is the remaining blood which is located on the wall and the bedding in his apartment. At this time I questioned him regarding the apparel, that being clothing, that he would wear during the time he was dismembering his victims. He stated that whenever he dismembered his victims, he was always completely naked, that he wore no shoes, socks, or any clothing of any type. He stated this was not in fact done because of sexual gratification, but simply for necessity because the job of cutting and dismembering his victims was quite messy and he did not wish to get blood and body fluids about his clothing.

"At this time I was informed by Lt. Kenneth MEULER that detectives from the Chicago Police Department wished to speak with the suspect, DAHMER, regarding possible connections in offenses they were investigating in their jurisdiction. It could also be noted that Attorney Wendy PATRICKUS, from Gerald BOYLE'S Office, appeared and sat in on this interview.

"At this time Detective CARROLL and Detective KEENAN, from the Chicago Police Department entered the interview room and questioned the suspect, Jeffrey DAHMER, regarding this frequent excursions by bus to the Chicago area. At this time Jeffrey DAHMER stated that he had visited the Chicago gay area on approximately ten or eleven different occasions and that while he was there, he usually frequented the gay taverns located on Clark St. or Halsted St. He specifically mentioned men's bathhouses, one by the name of Man's Country Bath Club located on Clark St. in Chicago and the Unicorn Club, which is also a gay bathhouse located on Halsted.

"At this time the detectives from Chicago also asked

Jeffrey DAHMER if he had made any personal acquaintances while he was in Chicago, to which the suspect answered that all the male homosexuals he met in Chicago were strictly one night stands and he did not become personally involved with any of them. He also stated he never left the gay area or the gay bathhouses with any of his acquaintances and accompanied them to their personal homes or apartments. He stated that the males he met in Chicago were of all different racial backgrounds. The same is true of their ethnical backgrounds, including both black and white males.

"He also stated that on several occasions while he was visiting bath houses in Chicago, he brought his sleeping pills. He used them in a rum concoction to drug several of his 'gay pickups' (as he called them) during the one night stands. He stated that only one of them realized he had been drugged and the following morning accused him of putting something in his drink and struck him about the face before leaving. He stated he was never reported to any of the owners of the bath houses or to the Chicago Police regarding his activities.

"Upon being questioned further regarding his gay activities in the Chicago area, he stated to the detectives that he received his information regarding gay bars, gay bathhouses, and gay functions in the Chicago area by reading gay publications, which can be picked up readily in various locations both here in Milwaukee and in Chicago. At this time Jeffrey DAHMER denied being involved in any violent or homicidal acts while he was in the Chicago area and stated that the only two males that had met in Chicago, brought back to Milwaukee and subsequently murdered are the individuals whom he has already discussed with the Milwaukee Police, and those incidents have been documented thoroughly.

"At this time the detectives concluded their interview.

"At this time I, Detective KENNEDY, along with

Attorney Wendy PATRICKUS, was informed that detectives from the West Allis Police Department would also like to speak with Jeffrey DAHMER and they were admitted into the interview room. At this time Detective NOVAK and Detective RISSE, entered the interview room and questioned the suspect Jeffrey DAHMER regarding the possibility of any bones or materials left over from the victims that he had murdered at his grandmother's house located in West Allis.

"The purpose of this was to determine whether or not a search warrant would be needed in order to dig up areas around his grandmother's house. At this time Jeffrey DAHMER stated that there would be no need to get a search warrant because all of the bones were disposed of in the trash and carried from the home. He denied burying any of the bones or personal effects of his victims that he killed in the West Allis home, anywhere on the property in West Allis and he denies spreading the bones around any other area in West Allis. He stated that all of his victims were disposed of through the trash and taken away by the West Allis public trash collection.

"At this time they also questioned Jeffrey DAHMER regarding the instruments he used to cut up his victims in West Allis, to which he stated he is unsure what type of knife he used. However, he is positive it was not a kitchen utensil from his grandmother's kitchen and that he bought the knife and disposed of the knife the same way he did the body, that being through the trash.

"Regarding the GUERRERO identification, The West Allis detectives were interested in how he was positive that the victim that he had killed was in fact GUERRERO and he stated that after viewing the ID photos provided by the Milwaukee Police, he was also given newspaper pictures dated during the time element in which GUERRERO was missing and stated that he distinctly remembered reading the newspaper article and seeing the picture of his victim in the newspaper and realizing that was in fact the victim he had brought back to his grandmother's house and this is why he is sure that GUERRERO is in fact one of his victims.

"Lastly the detectives inquired regarding his victim, SEARS. He stated he met the victim, SEARS, at the door at closing time at LaCage, which is on 2nd and National. He stated he had been drinking and the victim, SEARS, was standing with a white male. He stated he was actually approached by SEARS and that in the conversation that followed, he asked if SEARS would be interested in accompanying him back to his grandmother's house for some homosexual activity and drinks. He stated SEARS was more than eager to accompany him and was actually more the aggressor in this encounter.

"He stated that the friend of SEARS, a white male, drove them back to his grandmother's location in his vehicle and that he and SEARS sat in the back on the way to his grandmother's house and on the way the victim, SEARS performed an act of oral sex on him (DAHMER).

"At this time the detectives from West Allis concluded their interview."

Report per Detective Patrick KENNEDY.
PK/ln   7-30-91   #2

"On Tuesday, 7-30-91, we detectives Dennis MURPHY and Patrick KENNEDY while interviewing the subject, Jeffrey DAHMER in the presence of his attorney Wendy PATRICKUS asked him numerous questions regarding the Bath County Ohio homicide which occurred in 1978.

"I asked Mr DAHMER where was the trash barrel he used to burn the victims' clothes by his house, and he stated behind the cliff where he threw the bones near the property line; the trash container was on his property, but the cliff was mostly on the next property just to the west of his residence. He stated he burned all of the victims' clothes, plus his I.D in this trash container.

"We also questioned him regarding the location of the tree where he hung the dog, and he stated it was in the lot next to his residence, namely the woods after the lot. He stated this would probably be east of his house in the wooded area past the next lot. He further stated it was the same wooded area, where a girl had committed suicide in 1977. Regarding the dog, he stated it was a road kill and he cut it open and removed the insides and hung it in the tree.

"I then questioned him further regarding where he had disposed of the knife in the river which was used in the homicide, and he stated the river ran along the treatment plant and the bridge ran across the river. He stated it was the closest bridge to the treatment plant, near the landfill site. He then drew a map for me indicating this location. He then stated that he parked the car on this bridge, got out and threw the knife and the victim's necklace about 10 ft. out into the river, which was approximately 50 ft. wide. He stated the name of this town may be Cuyahoga Falls in Ohio; he said it was like the town.

"We also questioned him regarding the time he was stopped by the police in June of 1978, and he stated the police stopped him around 3:00am, because he was driving left of center. He stated when he was stopped he was detained for approximately ½ hour and was given a drunk test. He stated he was made to walk the line, do the finger to nose test; he passed both tests and was eventually given a ticket. He further stated when the police stopped him that there was one car and one officer, but this officer called for backup and another car and officer arrived.

"I asked him if he had been drinking and he stated he had not. I asked him how he acted when the police stopped him and he stated he was very nervous, but he tried to act calm. I then asked did the police look in the car and he stated, yes with their flashlights and they then asked what was in the bags that were on the rear seat. He stated there were three bags on the back seat and he informed the police that it was garbage and that he had not had the chance to take them to the landfill and he was going to do that the following day. I then asked him if there was an odor coming from these bags, which he stated had contained the body parts of the victim.

"DAHMER stated there may have been a slight odor he is not sure; the windows of the car were rolled up to the best of his recollection. I asked him 'What was the reason you told the officers that you were out to drinking around?' To this he stated he told the officers that his parents were recently divorced and he couldn't sleep, so he just went out for a drive to get this off his mind. I then asked him if he was arrested previously and he stated to the best of his knowledge he had not been arrested prior to this stop and he subsequently received a ticket for driving left of center.

"I asked him what were his intentions with the three bags containing the body parts and he stated he was going to take them and throw them down the gully in the road, but before he got to that location he was stopped by the police. He stated once he was issued his ticket, he then made a u-turn and then proceeded back to the residence and placed these bags in the drainage pipe behind the house.

"I then asked him how long it had been since the murder and he stated it was possibly the next day or so after the murder that he did this with the intentions of disposing the body in this manner, but being that he was stopped, he left the bags in the drainage pipes for a week or two, removed them and subsequently broke them up with either a large rock or a sledgehammer and then spread them around the first cliff in his yard.

"DAHMER stated at the time the police were talking to him he was near the side of the car and they made him walk to the rear of the car to take the drunken driving road field sobriety test. DAHMER further stated he could not recall the type of knife he used to cut up and dismember the body, only that it was possibly one from his house and he threw it in the river with the victim's necklace.

"I contacted Lieutenant Richard MUNSEY (phonetic) regarding these statements and informed him that I would fax a copy of the diagram DAHMER made for me indicating where the treatment plant, river and bridge were located, along with a revised copy of the diagram he had made for us on a previous interview indicating where the second cliff area was and where the trash barrel was."

Report per Detective Dennis MURPHY.
DM/htf   07-31-91

"On Tue., 7-30-91, we, Detectives Dennis MURPHY and Patrick KENNEDY, re-interviewed the defendant, Jeffrey DAHMER, at the CIB in the presence of his attorney, Wendy PATRICKUS. At this interview which began at approximately 11:30am, we asked him several questions regarding some of the victims and regarding various calls that had come in to our department.

"We questioned him regarding victim #1 whom he stated died at the Ambassador Hotel and he related that he met this individual about one week before Thanksgiving in 1987. He stated he had rented a room at the Ambassador Hotel and had previously prepared sleeping pills in glass by breaking the pills down to a powdery form in the glass. He stated that when he and the victim returned to the hotel, he made a rum and coke in the glass with the pills. He stated he gave this drink to the individual and the individual subsequently passed out. Mr DAHMER that stated he had also drank a lot and was lying in bed with this individual and he passed out.

"When he awoke, he discovered the victim dead and blood coming from the side of his mouth. He stated that he also noticed on the victim, severe bruising on his chest and that he (DAHMER) had bruising on his forearms, so he surmised that he had beaten the victim about the chest, possibly killing him. After this occurred, Mr DAHMER took the room for another night, proceeded to the Grand Avenue Mall, where he purchased a large suitcase from Woolworth's. He stated the suitcase had a zipper with a leather buckle going around the suitcase. He stated he placed the victim in the suitcase and conveyed him to his grandmother's residence via a cab. Once at his grandmother's residence, he used a knife to dismember the body and he disposed of the body parts in the trash. He stated he did not use his grandmother's knife, but used one of his knives that he possibly bought at the mall, but he is not sure. He also stated that he did dispose of the suitcase.

"We questioned him further regarding his use of the sleeping pills and he stated that in all of the cases, he would have the sleeping pill broken down into a powder form in the bottom of either a glass or a cup and when he would prepare the drink for the individual, using either coffee or rum and coke, he would use the glass or cup that contained the powdered sleeping pill substance. He stated this would dissolve readily and the victim was unable to determine that anything was in his drink. Next 9 lines (blacked out)."

Report per Detective Dennis MURPHY.
DM/lh   7-31-91

"At this time Mr DAHMER was questioned regarding recent newspaper stories that stated that as an eight-year-old boy in Ohio, he was sexually assaulted by a neighbor. To this Mr DAHMER stated this is untrue, that the first time he experienced any sexual behavior was when he was approximately 14-years-old and that was with the young man who lived across the street by the name of (blacked out). He stated that Eric was one or two years younger than him and that they mutually consented and got together on several occasions in a tree house where they simply kissed and touched each other's body.

"I then questioned Mr DAHMER regarding a possible victim of his, that being P. (blacked out). At this time I showed Mr P's photo, which was a family photo, to Mr DAHMER and after viewing it, he stated that this in fact is the individual. This is the individual whom he fought with in his apartment on approximately 7-8-90. Regarding the incident with Mr P, he stated the day previous to the fighting with Mr P, he had met Luis P at the Phoenix tavern and had asked him to accompany him home to his apartment for some homosexual activity and offered him money to pose for nude photos. He stated that on this occasion Mr P readily accompanied him home to his apartment and they had "normal homosexual sex." He stated at this time they spoke of meeting again in the following night at the Phoenix. He stated that Mr P left on his own accord that night.

"Mr DAHMER stated that the following night they went to the Phoenix tavern. It is located on South 2nd St., where he again saw Mr P He stated at this time Mr P again voluntarily decided to return with him to his apartment and at this time they took a taxi from the Phoenix tavern to 23rd and Wells, where they got out and walked. At 23rd and Wells, Mr DAHMER stated he stopped and bought himself some cigarettes and from there they walked to his apartment building.

"He stated the reason why he would have the taxi drop him off several blocks from his apartment was in order to keep the taxi driver from knowing exactly where he lived at and to see if anyone had been following him, as he did not want anyone to detect his activities. He stated that after buying the cigarettes, they walked to his apartment and once inside, they had conversation; however, he cannot recall the words. He stated that at this time he asked Luis if he would get undressed and allow him to take several photos of him in the nude, which (blacked out) complied with.

"He stated (blacked out) lay on the bed and he took several photos; however, they did not come out, so he asked (blacked out) to turn on to his stomach so he could take some back shots of (blacked out) with his Polaroid camera. Mr DAHMER stated at this time he was starting to become intoxicated and had run out of sleeping pills to put into his rum coffee potion in order to give to the victim. He stated that in preparation for this evening and knowing he was out of sleeping pills, he had gone to the hardware store and purchased himself a rubber mallet hammer. He stated he did this because it was cheaper than filling his prescription which cost approximately $30.

"He stated his intention was to strike the victim on the head with his hammer and knock him out so that he would be able to strangle the victim while he was unconscious. He stated at this time as Mr P was lying on his stomach, he retrieved his hammer and struck the victim on the back part of his neck. He felt that by striking him on the back of his neck, he would cut off blood going to his brain and cause the victim to pass out. However, this only made (blacked out) angry and at this time they got into a physical fight. He stated that during the fight he tried to explain (blacked out) he only struck him because he thought he was going to take the money, rob him and run out without giving him photos.

"After fighting for a while on the front room floor, the victim promised he would not call the police and was allowed to leave the apartment. He stated the victim left the apartment and apparently went to the corner phone booth in order to call for a ride home and after discovering he had no cash, he returned to the apartment, knocked on the door. Mr DAHMER stated he opened the door and admitted Mr (blacked out) back into his room and that they sat on the bed in his bedroom and spoke about the incident all night. Mr DAHMER stated there was no homosexual sex between them for the rest of the evening and they simply sat up all night talking about the fact that Mr DAHMER had struck him with a hammer and whether or not Mr P was going to report him to the police.

"Mr DAHMER stated he felt comfortable that the talk he had with Mr P regarding the entire incident had calmed down to the point where Mr P was not going to complain to the police about him and that early the next morning he allowed Mr P to leave the apartment. He stated he does not recall seeing Mr P again after this incident and this was all the information he was able to give me regarding this offense."

Refer to Lacy follow up Number:

"On Wed., 7-31-91, we, Detectives Dennis MURPHY and Patrick KENNEDY, along with Defense Attorney Wendy PATRICKUS, were present at the Criminal Investigation Bureau in an interview with the defendant, Jeffrey DAHMER, who had requested our presence to attempt to identify other victims, and to answer any questions we may have relevant to this investigation.

"Mr DAHMER was shown a couple of photographs of individuals regarding this investigation and a supplementary report will be called in by Detective KENNEDY regarding these photographs. We then asked Mr DAHMER numerous questions regarding our investigation and he answered them freely. Next 12 lines (blacked out).

"He also stated that the spray paint that he used, which was a fake granite type, blueish color, should have a pamphlet in one of his drawers in the residence. He stated that he does not recall the brand name, but the can was light complexion. He stated that he bought this in Pallet's Art Store on Water St. This will be checked out by Detective Randy BAIER.

"Regarding the makeup he used to color the genitals that he kept of one of his victims, he stated that he bought a skin tone type make up at Sears at South Ridge and this was a specialized makeup that is used for hiding marks or discolored skin. He stated that the reason that he colored this is because he wanted it more of a flesh color.

"We then asked him questions regarding where he may have gone on vacation out of the States and he stated that in 1976, he went with the family to Puerto Rico on a two week vacation, and that's the first time that he had ever drank rum. He stated that he was with his parents and that nothing happened while he was in Puerto Rico. He also stated that during all the initial meetings with his victims, he always offered money for sex or taking photos or watching videos, or a combination of these; but stated that it was not for heavy sex, he just hoped it would lead to that.

"We questioned Jeff regarding some of the victims, and one of the victims, namely Ed SMITH, who was the bald headed guy, victim number six; we asked him if he knew this individual by the nick name of "Sheik". He stated that he did not know his real name neither his nick name, but this individual did wear a headband like an Arab type headband. He stated that he did take photographs, but he tore them up and threw them out.

"He stated that most of the homicides took place either on weekends or when he had time off from work. He also stated that he does not drive a car, never owned a car in Wisconsin, and that he did accept rides home from the Ambrosia Chocolate factory a couple of times from his supervisors, but he never used his car, nor anyone else's while in Wisconsin.

"DAHMER at this time again stated that he was not involved in any other homicides and that if he can recall any information that would help us with our investigation. He will contact me, Det. MURPHY, or Det. KENNEDY with this information.

"Mr DAHMER did bring along with him a book that he had received by mail from the Vanity Fair Magazine, and this book's title was " Killing for Company," written by Brian MASTERS. This book depicted the case of a suspect, Dennis NILSEN, who would kill people, dismember them, and throw them in plastic bags and dispose of them.

"This case is possibly similar to Mr DAHMER'S and Vanity Fair requested an interview from him. This information was given to his attorney in our presence, and she kept the copy of the book. Appointment was set up that we obtain an order to produce on Thursday, 8-1-91 and have a meeting at the Criminal Investigation Bureau at 1:30pm with Mr DAHMER, his attorney and Wendy PATRICKUS to show him additional photos we expect to arrive today of possible victims. Also to ask any additional questions that may arise through the evening."

Report dictated by Detective Dennis MURPHY
DM/rc 7-31-91

"On Wed., 7-31-91, we, Detectives Dennis MURPHY and Patrick KENNEDY, in the presence of Attorney Wendy PATRICKUS, who is the attorney for Jeffrey DAHMER, interviewed Jeffrey at the CIB, Room 421. Mr DAHMER was interviewed regarding a teletype we had received from the German Federal Criminal Police, requesting we ask certain investigative questions which may help them determine if Mr DAHMER was in their country at the time some homicides had occurred, or whether he was stationed in the Army at this time. This teletype was sent to our department by a Legat BONN. This teletype requested we ask approximately eleven questions relative to our investigation.

"Next I requested the background of Mr DAHMER, including his blood type and whether or not he has any knowledge of German. At the present time in this investigation, we do not know his blood type and he stated he does not speak any German. Mr DAHMER was born on 5-21-60, in Milwaukee, Wisconsin, at Deaconess Hospital. He attended and graduated from the Revere High School in Akron, Ohio. He attended from September of 1975 until June of 1978, and he received his high school diploma.

"He then went on to Ohio State University in Columbus, Ohio, where he attended from September of 1978 until December of 1978, but he did not graduate. He then immediately enlisted in the Army on December 29, 1978. He was rated as Private E1 and enlisted in Cleveland, Ohio. Following his enlistment, he was sent to Military Police School in Ft. McClellan, Alabama, for an eight week course, which he did not complete. On May 11, 1979 he was sent to the Army Hospital School at Fort Sam Houston, Texas, in San Antonio, where he attended a six week course to become a Medical Specialist. Upon completion of this course, he was assigned to Headquarter Company, 286 Armor Division 2nd Battalion 68th Armor in Baumholder, Germany. He was stationed at that post from June of 1979, until March 24, 1981.

"Upon his discharge, he was sent to Fort Jackson, in South Carolina, where he was discharged on March 26, 1981, from the United States Army, at which time he took a plane to Miami Beach, Florida, where he remained until approximately September of 1981. He then returned to his Bath, Ohio, where he had been living prior to joining the service. He remained in Bath, Ohio until approximately December of 1981, when he moved to Milwaukee, Wisconsin, and lived at 2357 South 57th St., in West Allis, Wisconsin. He remained there with his grandmother until approximately 1988, when he moved about May of 1988, or in that vicinity, to 808 North 24th St.

"He then was arrested for taking the pictures of a minor, charged with Second Degree Sexual Assault, and subsequently sentenced to a year under the 'work release program' and five years' probation. Approximately June of 1989, he began serving his term and was released in March of 1990. He moved back in with his grandmother until May of 1990 when he moved in to the apartment at 924 North 25th St. He remained in location until his arrest.

"He stated that while he was stationed in Germany, he went to Munich for October Fest of 1980, and went to the Lansthole (phonetic) for about two months of training. He also stated he would go to Ideroberstein, Germany, for dinner, but never would remain overnight. He stated these were the only places he would travel to in Germany. Next 5 lines (blacked out).

"Mr DAHMER did leave Germany as soon as his military duties ended. He stated he has not visited Germany since he left the Army, nor did he have a passport. He also stated he does not have any relatives living in Germany and that he has been a homosexual all his life. He stated he is not interested in women or not intentionally in juveniles, and he stated the age group he participated with the homosexuals range from the late teens, 13- 19, to the middle to early 20's. He stated if the individual is younger but looks older, he will attempt to have a relationship with him.

"With regard to the number of victims in the United States, Mr DAHMER admits to killing seventeen people. Of these, one is from out of Wisconsin; that was his first victim in June of 1978 and that was a white male who he killed in Bath, Ohio. The next victim was in November of 1987, and that was a white male, 25 years of age, whom he killed in Milwaukee. The next victim was a Hispanic male, about 16 or18, whom he killed in January of 1988. The next victim was a Hispanic male, about 25 years of age, whom he killed in approximately March of 1988. The next victim was a black male, about 25 years of age, whom he killed in March of 1989. The next victim was a black male about 33 years of age, whom he killed in May of 1990. This individual was killed after he was released from serving his time for the sexual assault complaint. The next victim was a black male about 28 years of age, whom he killed in July of 1990.

"The next victim was a black male about 23 years of age, whom he killed in September of 1990. The next victim was a black male about 23 years of age, whom he killed in October or November of 1990. The next victim was a black male about 17 years of age, whom he killed in February of 1991. The next victim was a black male, 18 years of age, whom he killed in March of 1991. The next victim was a black male, 31 years of age, whom he killed in May of 1991. The next victim was a black male, 14 years of age, who was also killed in May of 1991. The next victim was a black male, 20, whom he killed in June of 1991. The next victim was a Puerto Rican male, 23, whom he killed in July of 1991. The next victim was a black male, 23, whom he killed in July of 1991. The last victim was a white male, 25, who he killed in July of 1991. The exact dates of these homicides cannot be determined at this time. As far as the sexual preference and/or race, religion, or education of the individuals that the suspect preferred, the suspect stated it was not a matter of race, religion, or education, it was just a matter of opportunity. He stated that he offered each one of these individuals money to be photographed, to view videos, or to have sex, and he persuaded them to come into his apartment.

"Then he would give them a sleeping potion, namely Halcion, and once they went to sleep, he would strangle them either manually or with a strap, photograph most of them after death, sometimes have sex with them after death, and then subsequently dismember them and, on

329

approximately eleven of the victims, kept the skulls and approximately four torsos, the hands, a couple of hearts and other inner organs.

"On Wednesday, 07-31-91, we, Detectives Dennis MURPHY and Patrick KENNEDY re-interviewed the defendant, Jeffrey DAHMER, at the Detective Bureau. This interview was conducted with his attorney, Wendy PATRICKUS present. After his attorney had left and we were about to convey Mr DAHMER back to the County Jail, he requested another coffee and a cigarette. We provided him with these and upon sitting with him we asked him whether or not he would be willing to answer some questions regarding the last offense, the attempted homicide, file #91-51770, which had led to his arrest.

"Mr DAHMER stated that he did not need his attorney present, that he has cooperated with us fully and he will continue to cooperate with us. He wished to tell us what he recalls of the incident. Mr DAHMER stated that about a week prior to this offense, which had occurred on 07-22-91, he met the subject, Tracy EDWARDS, at the bus stop in front of the Eagles Club at 24th and Wisconsin. Mr DAHMER stated that he was just sitting there drinking a beer and thinking when the victim asked DAHMER for a cigarette. There was small talk and then the victim got on the bus.

"Mr DAHMER stated that about a week later, 07-22-91, he was having pizza and some beer at the Grand Avenue Mall. After he finished this he walked down to the 3rd St. front entrance and he saw the victim with two other of his friends. He stated that he approached them and they had small talk; this was about 5:00 or 6:00pm. He stated that he then asked the victim if he wanted to make approximately $50.00 to $75.00 to go home with him so that he can take some pictures of him and watch some videos. He indicated that the victim then went over and talked to his friends and they agreed to go to his apartment.

330

He stated that they all walked over to the liquor store, the victim and both of his friends, which is located at 6th and Wisconsin. He stated that he went into the liquor store, bought a bottle of rum and coke and, he believes a 6 pack. He related that as he walked out, his two friends were gone so he and the victim proceeded to the Greyhound bus station where they took a taxi.

"He stated that he got out of the taxi in front of the Eagles Club so that nobody would know where he lived and they walked to his residence. He indicated that they walked through the back door because that's the way he always went. It's the door closest to his apartment. He stated that once he got into the apartment he made a drink of rum and coke and he did not have any sleeping pills left, so it was just rum and coke.

"He stated that they were sitting there talking about going to the gay bars in Chicago and they started watching videos, namely Exorcist II. He then started talking about taking some pictures, namely bondage pictures, and he told the victim that he wanted to handcuff him. He stated that he got the first cuff on him as they were sitting on the edge of the bed in the bedroom.

"Mr DAHMER stated that then things begin to get fuzzy and he does not remember having a knife or putting a knife up to the victim. He stated he must have blacked out. He also stated that he does not remember telling the victim anything about showing him things that he would not believe. Mr DAHMER stated that he then recalled hearing a knock at the door, which he answered, and he observed two police officers along with the victim standing in the hallway. He related that he invited them in and the victim still had the handcuff on his wrist. The next thing he can recall is that one of the police officers went into the bedroom and then he heard him say, "Cuff him," at which time the other officer placed handcuffs on him. He indicated that when he placed the handcuffs on him he began to struggle. He stated that he continued to struggle even when the officers opened the refrigerator door.

"I asked Mr DAHMER whether or not he told the officers where the handcuff key was because the officers could not remove the cuffs and stated that he might have said they were in the bedroom, but he doesn't remember. He also related that he didn't remember showing any photos to the victim, nor does he remember threatening the victim with a knife. He did state that the reason he uses handcuffs is so that he can keep control of the victim.

"He stated that he keeps the knife in the bedroom. I asked Mr DAHMER if he remembered stating anything to the victim about threatening him or about cutting his heart out and he stated that he does not recall doing this. I asked Mr DAHMER why he fought with the police and he stated it was probably because he did not want to be arrested, and that he did not want them to see what was in the refrigerator. Mr DAHMER stated that he cannot recall everything regarding this due to the fact that he had been drinking and thought he was intoxicated.

"Mr DAHMER does recall when the police arrived, but stated he does not recall the victim leaving nor does he know when the victim left his apartment. I asked him where the handcuff key was, and he stated that he threw the handcuffs and the key in the garbage earlier and retrieved the handcuffs and not the key. He states that he would have been unable to remove the cuffs if he had placed them on the victim unless he removed the hands from the victim."

Report per: Detective Dennis MURPHY.
DM/dls   8-1-91

"On Thursday, 08-01-91, we, Detectives Dennis MURPHY and Patrick KENNEDY proceeded to the Milwaukee County Jail after receiving a call at 1:00pm from Deputy MALEK indicating that Jeffrey DAHMER

332

was requesting to talk to us. Upon obtaining an order to produce, we escorted Mr DAHMER to the CIB, along with his attorney, Wendy PATRICKUS. At the Detective Bureau, in an interview room, we interviewed Mr DAHMER with regard to his activities in Bath, Ohio in June of 1978, as to the location where he had disposed of the knife.

"Lieutenant MUNCEY of the Bath, Ohio Police Department had faxed me a map of the area by the Sewage Treatment plant locating where the bridges were and requested that I show this to the defendant and have him point out where he disposed of the knife.

"At this time Mr DAHMER drew an " X " in the middle of the Cuyahoga River, approximately in the middle of the Bath Road bridge and stated that he threw the knife about 10 feet out into the water. I then faxed this map back to Lieutenant MUNCEY.

"I also asked him several questions regarding the homicide scene. This, as to whether or not he had broken the knife he used and dropped it where the bones were recovered. He states that he did not recall doing that. I asked him if his parents knew anything about this homicide or any of the other homicides and he stated that they did not know anything regarding this. I also informed him that pruning shears were found at the location where the bones were being recovered and he stated that he did not use pruning shears, nor does he know anything about it. I was also informed that there was a tool box in the crawl space under the house. I asked him if he knew anything regarding this tool box and he stated that the time he was living there and the time he dismembered the body under the crawl space, there was no tool box there. This was passed on to Lt. MUNCEY."

Report dictated by: Detective Dennis MURPHY.
DM: dls 08-01-91

"At this time Mr DAHMER stated that he wished to speak again regarding his relationship with the individual known to this department as (blacked out). He stated that there were a few facts he forgot to mention regarding his relationship with Mr P and he wished to reiterate them. Mr DAHMER stated that he had seen Mr P working at the 219 Club as a cleanup helper for some time before he actually got to know him. He stated that he observed Mr P cleaning up glasses and sweeping up floors in that tavern several times late in the evening. He stated that the first time he met Mr P was in the Phoenix tavern and that he found him attractive, so he approached him and offered him $200.00 to return with him to his apartment to pose nude for some pictures and to have some homosexual sex.

"He stated that they took a cab to his apartment on North 25th Street where they mutually consented to engaging in sexual activity, which involved kissing, masturbation and oral sex. He stated that he also took several pictures of Mr P. However, he did not like the way they turned out so he tore them up and threw them out. He indicated that Mr P willingly spent the night with him on that evening and before leaving in the morning he advised Mr P that if he met him at 12:00 the next day he would, in fact, give him money for the previous night's activity. Mr DAHMER stated that they agreed to meet at 12:00 and that he took that to mean 12:00 noon and decided that he would, in fact, make Mr P one of his victims.

"He stated that at this time he was out of his sleeping pills, which he had used in previous potions to knock out his victims and did not have the $30.00 in order to refill his prescription. So early in the morning he went to the Army/Navy Surplus store on West Wisconsin Avenue where he bought a plastic hammer. He stated that he bought this hammer and planned to use it to strike Mr P on the head in order to render him unconscious so that he could strangle him and make him one of his victims.

"He related that he returned to the Phoenix bar at 12 noon. However, Mr P was not there so he went about his business for the day. He stated that later on that evening he again returned to the gay area of town, that being 200 S. 2nd Street, where upon bar time, that being approximately 2:30am, he again saw Mr P standing inside the Phoenix tavern. At this time Mr P again agreed to accompany him back to his apartment and they took a cab. He stated that once at the apartment they again engaged in sex which involved kissing, masturbation and oral sex. Then Mr DAHMER stated that he wished to take a few more pictures of him in the bedroom. He stated that it was during this picture taking session when Mr P was lying on his face with his back and head exposed, while lying on the bed, that Mr DAHMER took out his plastic hammer and struck Mr P in the back of the neck in an attempt to render him unconscious.

"Mr DAHMER stated that upon striking Mr P he became angry and he got up, at which time a small argument ensued. Mr DAHMER then stated that the only reason he struck him was because he felt Mr P was going to take the $200.00 and leave without spending the night. He stated that Mr P did not buy that explanation and he left stating that he was going to call the police. Mr DAHMER stated that Mr P in fact, left the apartment building. However, approximately 10 minutes later he heard pounding on the outer building entrance/exit door and when he went to investigate, Mr P was standing there requesting to get back in and was asking for money. Mr DAHMER stated that at this time Mr P followed him back to his apartment and once inside Mr DAHMER grabbed him by the neck and attempted to strangle him and a fight ensued. He related that they fought for a couple of minutes when Mr DAHMER simply stopped fighting and decided to calm the situation down by stating, 'Let's talk.' He stated that Mr

P agreed, although he was highly agitated and they went into the bedroom where they sat down. Mr DAHMER stated after calming him down he asked Mr P if he would, in fact, allow him to tie his hands behind his back and Mr P agreed.

"Mr DAHMER stated that he tied Mr P'S hands behind his back, albeit, not very tightly and they continued to talk. He indicated that during the next ½ hour or so Mr P wriggled free from the extension cord he had tied on his hands and attempted to leave the apartment, when Mr DAHMER, in fact, grabbed his six inch blade, black plastic-handled, knife. He stated that he believes that Mr P thought this was a gun and decided to sit down again. He related that they again began to talk and talked approximately until 7:00am. Mr DAHMER stated that during the talk he was trying to convince P not to tell the police about the night's activities and he continued to apologize for striking him with a hammer.

"Mr DAHMER stated that although he did intend to kill P and make him one of his victims, because of the previous night's sexual activities and the fact that they had spent hours talking, he began to sober up and know Mr P on a more personal level and had decided that he would not kill him. He indicated that at approximately 7:00am in the morning, he walked Mr P to the bus stop on 24th and Wisconsin and gave him money for cab fare. He indicated that was the last he saw of Mr P until about 5 or 6 months later. As he was walking in the Grand Avenue mall, he observed Mr P walking in the mall as well. He stated that Mr P approached him and said, 'Hi.'

"He related that there was no further conversation, but approximately March of 1991 as Mr DAHMER was sitting in the mall eating ice cream Mr P observed him, walked up to him and initiated a conversation. He stated that they had small talk for a while and then both went their separate ways.

336

"This is all the information that Mr DAHMER stated he had regarding the incident with Mr P and this part of the interview was terminated.

"Other questions were asked of Mr DAHMER regarding the night that he was arrested and a detailed supplemental regarding this portion of the interview will be filed by Detective Dennis MURPHY."

Report dictated by: Detective Patrick KENNEDY
PK: dls 08-01-91

"Below is a list of the homicide victims that Jeffrey DAHMER has confessed to and he states this is the order in which he had killed each individual. Included in this list is his description of the subjects, the approximate time when he killed them and how he had lured these individuals to his residence. Also, the identity of each one if they had been identified and what part of the body he kept of the individuals, if any.

DETECTIVES' FINDINGS AFTER INVESTIGATIONS

"1. White male, 25 yoa, 5'6", 130 lbs Fair complexion, smooth skin, blonde shoulder length straight hair. He stated he met him approximately 1 week before Thanksgiving, in November, 1987. He states he met him around the 219 Club on South 2nd St. and he offered this individual money for sex. He states when he got him to the Ambassador Hotel, where he rented a room, he gave him a drink mixture of rum and coke with approximately 5-7 crushed sleeping pills (Halcion). He states they both went to bed in the nude and when he awoke he observed this individual to have a black & blue chest and blood was coming from his mouth. DAHMER also states that his

337

forearms were black and blue. Therefore, he figured he had killed him by beating him.

"He then kept the room for another night, proceeded to the Grand Avenue Mall where he purchased a large suitcase at Woolworth's, returned to the Ambassador, placed the victim in the suitcase and took a cab to his grandmother's residence at 2357 S. 57th St., where he was living. He dismembered the victim in the basement, placed him in various garbage bags and threw them in the garbage. He did not keep any remains. As of this time, this victim has not been identified.

"2. Hispanic male, 16-18 yoa, 6'0", 150 lbs, slim build, dark complexion, regular cut hair, clean shaven, lives in the vicinity of 10th and National. He states he met this individual in front of the 219 Club on South 2nd St., around 1:00am and the individual was waiting for a bus. He stated he offered him money for sex, he accepted, and they took the bus to his grandmother's house at 2357 S. 57th St. He stated they had light sex, kissing, body rubbing and masturbation. He states he gave him the drink mixture of rum and coke with approximately 5-7 crushed sleeping pills (Halcion).

"He states that after the victim fell asleep he strangled him, dismembered him, smashed the bones with his sledgehammer and disposed of the bones inside garbage bags and into the trash. He viewed a photo array and tentatively picked out ID #234356, which is the photo of DOXTATOR, James E, Indian male, 03-01-73, 1010 W. Pierce St., reported missing on 01-16-88 and the report came in on 01-18-88. DAHMER states he met this individual in approximately January, 1988. There were also no remains of this victim.

"3. Hispanic male 19-21 yoa, 5'8"-5'10", slim build, light complexion, short straight black hair, wearing a long knee length coat. DAHMER states he met him in March, 1988 in a bar called the Phoenix. In the doorway he offered him money for sex, at which time they took a taxi to his grandmother's house at 2357 S. 57th St. While there, he gave him the drink mixture of rum and coke and sleeping pills, they had oral sex, the victim fell asleep, he strangled him, dismembered him, broke up the bones, threw them in garbage bags and into the garbage. He did not keep anything of this victim. This victim was subsequently identified by DAHMER, as GUERRERO, Richard, a Hispanic male, 12-12-65, 3332 N. 1st St., 263-5512. GUERRERO was missing since 03-29-88.

"4. Black male, 21-22 yoa, 5'9", 150 lbs, slim build, light complexion, short curly hair with a small ponytail, with a rubber band on it. He stated he met this individual the night before Easter, at closing time at the LaCage, on 03-25-89. He states that a friend of this individual, a white female, drove them and dropped them off near a tavern by his grandmother's house, the Mai Khi Tavern (phonetic). He states they walked to his grandmother's house, he gave him the drink and the reason he got him there was money for sex. He states they had sex, he fell asleep and he killed him. He dismembered him on Easter Sunday, but kept his scalp, genitals and skull. He subsequently painted the skull and genital area and preserved the scalp. This victim has been identified through photo by the suspect and also through dental records, as last name SEARS, Anthony L. black male, 01-26-65, 1657 N. Astor was reported missing 03-25-89.

"5. Black male, 22 yoa, 5'8"-5'9", 140 lbs, curly black hair, slight mustache. He states he met this individual in May, 1990. He offered him money for sex and for posing for him and watching videos. He states he met him in the area of the 219 Club, about two months after he had been released from the House of Correction. DAHMER states they took a cab from the 219 Club to his apartment. He gave him the drinking potion and took pictures. After he died, he had oral sex with the victim, took photographs of him, dismembered him, kept his skull and painted it. This victim was also identified by the suspect, as SMITH, Raymond L. black male, 08-10-57, a/k/a BEEKS, Rickey Lee, black male, 08-10-57, with a nick name of "Cash D". This individual had not been reported missing.

"6. Black male, 24 yoa, 6'2", 170 lbs, medium build, dark skin, prematurely bald, close cut hair, clean shaven and he used to dance with the Milwaukee Ballet. He states this victim wore a headband like an Arab. He states he offered this individual money for sex and posing and that he had met him approximately in July, 1990. He states he met him at the Phoenix Bar, they took a cab to his apartment, had oral sex, gave him the drink mixture of rum and coke or coffee and sleeping pills, strangled him, dismembered him and also took 4 or 5 photos of him and disposed of the body by placing it in garbage bags and putting it in the trash. He states he also disposed of the pictures of this victim. This victim was identified by the suspect, to ID Photo # 244654, that being a SMITH, Edward W. black male, 08-02-62, 3606 N. 11th St., reported missing on 06-23-90.

"7. Black male, 24 yoa, 6'0", 160 lbs, medium build, medium complexion, chin whiskers, short black hair. He states he met this individual around September, 1990. It was in the 800 block of N. 27th St., in front of the bookstore. He states he offered him money for sex and for posing. This individual agreed and they proceeded to his residence where he gave him the drink mixture, had sex and then when he fell asleep he cut his throat. He photographed the body, cut it up and kept this individual's skull, his

340

biceps and heart. He states he painted the skull and kept his biceps and heart to eat. He also kept the entire skeleton and bleached it down. He also took numerous photographs of this individual. This individual was identified by the suspect and through dental records as MILLER, Ernest, black male, 05-05-67, of Chicago, IL. He had been missing since 09-03-90.

"8. Black male, 25 yoa, 150 lbs, slim build, medium to dark complexion, short dark hair. He states he met this individual around October, 1990, on 2nd and Wisconsin and they walked to his residence. He states he offered him money for sex, to pose for him and view videos. When he got to his apartment, he gave him the mixed drink with the sleeping pills in it, they talked, but didn't have sex, because he wasn't his type. He states after the individual fell asleep, he killed him because he had already given him potion and thought when he woke up he would be 'pissed off.' He states he took two pictures of this individual, but he didn't keep anything because he wasn't his type.

"The suspect, DAHMER, viewed a photograph of the victim and identified him to this photograph. This victim was subsequently identified by relatives, through photographs. He has been identified as THOMAS, David C. black male, 12-21-67, 6432 W. Birch, and has been missing since 09-24-90, ID # 200484.

"9. Black male, 18 yoa, 6'0", 140 lbs, slim build, medium complexion, three inch perm, mustache. He states he met this individual approximately February, 1991. He offered him money for posing, sex and videos, while this individual was waiting for a bus near Marquette. He states they proceeded to his residence, where he gave him the drink mixture containing the sleeping pills. They had oral sex, the victim fell asleep and then he killed him and photographed him. He then cut him up, kept his skull, hands and genitals. He states he used a strap to strangle this victim. He also stated this victim was wearing an earring, but he disposed of it. This victim was subsequently identified by the suspect, and by dental records, as STRAUGHTER, Curtis, black male, 04-16-73, 3628 N. 19th St., and he has been missing since 02-18-91. He states that he disposed of this individual in two barrels, one for bones and one for flesh and used acid to melt down the bones and flesh. He did take pictures of this victim also.

"10. Black male, 20 yoa, 5'9"-5'10", 150 lbs, short black hair, medium build, medium complexion. He states he met this individual approximately March, 1991, on the corner of 27th and Kilbourn. He states he offered this individual money for posing and to view videos. He states when they got to his residence, he gave him the drink mixture with the sleeping pills and when he fell asleep he strangled him, had oral sex after death on the victim, took pictures of him, dismembered him and saved his skull. He also disposed of this individual by putting the bones and the flesh in the two barrels with the acid. This individual was subsequently identified by the suspect, and with dental charts. He was LINDSEY Earl, black male, 03-03-72, 2510 W. Juneau, Apt. 4, ID #220831.

"11. Black male, 25yoa, 6' 0", 150 lbs, and a deaf mute. He states he met him approximately early May, 1991, in front of the 219 Bar on South 2nd St. He states the victim was with friends who were also deaf mutes and these friends drove them to 23rd and Wells where they got out and subsequently walked to his apartment.
"He states he had them drop him off there, so they would not know where he lived. He states he communicated with this victim by writing notes to him and that he offered him $50.00 for sex. He states he does not remember whether or not they had sex, but upon going to

his apartment, he gave him the drinking potion and the victim subsequently passed out and so did the suspect. Suspect states that when he woke up this victim was dead. He said he dismembered him and kept his head. He states he disposed of the body and flesh in the two barrels of acid. He did not take any photos of this individual. The victim was identified by the suspect, and through dental records, as HUGHES Tony Anthony, black male, 08-26-59, reported missing in Madison, WI. on 05-31-91, and last seen on 05-30-91.

"12. Asian male, 18-19 yoa, 5'5", 120 lbs, slim build, black hair. He states he met him in late May, 1991, in the Grand Avenue Mall. He states he offered money to take pictures of him and to view videos, but not for sex. He was hoping it would lead to sex. He states they took the bus back to the apartment and the individual posed for two photos while he was alive. He states he gave him the drink mixture and the victim passed out. Suspect states he then had oral sex on him, after he passed out and finished watching a video and then he ran out of beer. He then went to the Gare Bear Tavern, in the 900 block of N. 27th St., drank beer until around closing and returned to the apartment.

"As he was returning to the apartment, he saw the victim sitting on the curb at 25th and State in the nude. He was taking him back to the apartment when the police and Fire Dept., showed up. Someone put a yellow blanket around the victim and he told the police that the victim always acted like this when he got drunk and that the victim could not speak English, because the victim was not speaking English. Police questioned him, subsequently escorted him back to the apartment, at which time he convinced the police it was his homosexual lover. The police left and later on he subsequently strangled the victim, had oral and anal sex with the victim after death, took numerous photos of the victim, dismembered him and kept his head. He put the bones and the flesh of the victim in the acid barrel. This victim was subsequently identified through photos and dental charts, as SINTHASOMPHONE, Konerak, Asian male, 12-02-76, 2634 N. 56th St., and he had been reported missing on 05-26-91.

"13. Black male, 22 yoa, 5'8", 140 lbs, medium build, dark complexion, having a high top fade to the left side. He states he met this individual on June 30th, after the Gay Pride Parade, at the Chicago Bus Station. He states he offered him money for sex, posing and to view videos. This individual accompanied him back to Milwaukee on the Greyhound Bus and then took a cab to his apartment, namely a City Vet Cab. He states he then gave him the drinking potion and they were nude and playing with each other.

"He states this victim fell asleep, so he strangled him, possibly with a strap and did not have sex with him. He then took photos, dismembered him and kept his head in the freezer and the body in the blue 57 gallon barrel, which he had purchased a short while before this. The victim was identified by the suspect, through a photo from Chicago. He was also identified by friends from Chicago. This individual has been identified as TURNER Matt, black male, 07-03-70, a/k/a Donald MONTRELL. DAHMER states that he disposed of this individual's flesh in the trash.

"14. Puerto Rican male, part Jewish, 23-24, 5'10", 140 lbs, slim build, light complexion, short black hair, thin mustache. He states he met this individual around July 6th, at Carol's in Chicago (gay bar). He states they left about 4:00am, returned to Milwaukee with the victim, via the Greyhound and took a cab to his apartment. He states they spent two days together. He states they had oral sex the first day and on the second day the victim wanted to leave, so the suspect killed him, by giving him the drink mixture with the sleeping pills and when he fell asleep he strangled him, took photos, dismembered him, put his head in the freezer and his body in the 57 gallon barrel. This subject was identified by the suspect, through pictures, as WEINBERGER Jeremiah, Puerto Rican male, 09-26-67, 3404 N. Halsted, Chicago, IL., 929 -2478. DAHMER states that he threw the victim's flesh out in the barrel.

"15. Black male, 24 yoa, 5'9", 160 lbs, muscular build, short hair. He states he met this individual on 27th Street., between State and Kilbourn, which would be the 900 block. He states he met this individual about the second week in July. He states that he offered him money to pose for pictures and watch videos with him and have a drink. He states the victim proceeded with him to his apartment, he gave him the drink mixture, they did some body rubbing, the victim fell asleep and he killed him. He states he had anal sex after death. He then took photos, kept the victim's ID., and two other personal photos, because he wanted more pictures of him.

"He dismembered this individual, placed his head in the bottom of the refrigerator in a box, kept his heart in the freezer to eat later and ate his right bicep. He also put his body in the freezer. He states the victim was wearing a white shirt and blue jeans at the time he met him and that the victim told him he was a weight lifter and a model. The suspect identified the victim to his I.D., which was found in his wallet and he was also identified through dental records and prints, as LACY Oliver, black male, 06-23-67, 3237 N. 24th Pl. The suspect stated that he disposed of the victim's flesh in the trash, but that he kept his head, body, heart and took photos and he also ate the bicep. This victim was reported missing on 07-15-91, last seen on 07-12-91.

"16. White male, early 20s, 5'9", 140-150 lbs, brownish blonde hair, short mustache. He states he met this individual approximately 07-19-91, at around Wisconsin Ave., near the Marquette University. This victim was waiting for a bus, with a '6 pack' in his arms. He states he offered this individual money to pose for pictures and to view videos. He agreed and they took a bus to his apartment. He gave this individual the drink mixture, had oral sex before he fell asleep. When he fell asleep he strangled him with a strap, then dismembered him, put his head in the freezer and placed the body in the 57 gallon barrel. He states he disposed of the flesh in the trash. He identified this victim from a photo in his apartment, as BRADEHOFT Joseph, white male, 01-24-66, 426 E. Spring, Lot 11 Greenville, IL.

"17. White male, 18-19, 6'0", 150 lbs, light hair. This victim was killed in June, 1978. After further questioning he identified him as wearing a necklace with braces on. He states this individual did not have a shirt, but had jeans and shoes. He states he met him hitchhiking on Cleveland Massing (phonetic) Rd., in Ohio, picked him up and took him to his home to drink beer. Once they got there they were drinking beer in his bedroom and the victim wanted to leave. He states he hit him in the head with a barbell and then strangled him with the barbell. He states he did not have sex with the victim. He states he then put him under the crawl space under the house. He subsequently dismembered him and put him in three garbage bags. Two weeks later he broke up the bones and threw them in the woods behind his house. He disposed of the knife he used to dismember him and the victim's necklace in the river. This victim was identified by the suspect, through a photo, and by the suspect recalling his last name, that being HICKS Steven M. white male, 06-22-59, 2993 Pryor Dr Ohio, 644-5600. He stated he recalls the name HICKS, because he states, 'you don't forget your first one'.

DAHMER states he gave the drinking potion to most of his victims, therefore being easier to control them and he could kill them without having them fight with him. He stated the reason he killed them was because there was excitement and gratification in it and he wanted to keep the victims. Further investigation is pending."

Report dictated by: Detective Dennis MURPHY
DM: hvs   08-02-91

"At this time we showed family photographs regarding a possible victim of DAHMER, that being Steven W. TUOMI, W/M, DOB 12-19-62, lna 1315 N. Cass Street. Mr DAHMER viewed this photograph and positively identified him as being the individual who he first murdered in Milwaukee at the Ambassador Hotel.

"It should be noted that Detective James DEVALKENAERE will file a detailed supplementary regarding this identification.

"At this time the interview was terminated and DAHMER'S Attorney, Wendy PATRICKUS, left the building.

"As I was attempting to take Mr DAHMER to the 5th floor of the Sheriff's lock up, we again began to speak regarding the second victim in Milwaukee and the fact that we have been unable to identify this individual through photographs. Mr DAHMER stated that the photo that he had viewed, which has been provided by the ID Division, does have similarities of the person who he was with during this offense. However, he stated that he cannot be sure and that it would be helpful if he could receive other family photographs. At this time I advised Mr DAHMER that the only family photos available of this possible victim would have him considerably younger, approximately 14 or 15-years-old. To this Mr DAHMER stated that even younger photographs would be of help and stated he would be glad to view them.

"At this time I asked Mr DAHMER if he would like to again go over the offense regarding the second victim here in Milwaukee and he stated that he did. He stated that to the best of his recollection he remembers him as being a light tanned-skinned male and he assumed he was 18 to 20-years-old as he met him in front of the Phoenix Club at approximately 1:00am in the morning. He stated that he may have been younger than this. However, because he was out at this hour and in front of a tavern, he assumed him to be slightly older. He indicated that he believes he offered him $50.00 to return with him to his apartment, to watch videos and have sex.

"He related that at this point they took the bus to 57th and National and they then walked to his grandmother's house. He stated that they did not have any conversation on the bus as they sat in separate seats, because the bus was slightly crowded. He stated that once at his grandmother's house they sat in the front room and had some light sex, which he described as hugging and kissing and that at this time he told the victim that it would be quieter down in the basement.

"He related that they proceeded to the basement where there was a large easy chair and they continued to hug and kiss and mutually masturbate one another. He indicated that it was around this time that the victim stated that he would have to be home in the morning. Upon hearing this, Mr DAHMER made him a drink of coffee Irish cream and the sleeping pills. He stated that after the individual fell asleep, he pulled out an old sheet and laid it on the ground of the basement. He indicated that he did this because the basement floor was chilly. He laid the victim on the sheet and at this time he strangled him. After strangling him, he lay on top of the victim and kissed and hugged and held him and then wrapped him up in the sheet and placed him in the fruit cellar. He stated it was approximately 7:00am in the morning at this time and his grandmother awoke. He indicated that he went upstairs and had breakfast with his grandmother and after she left for church he returned to his victim and decided to dispose of his body.

"At this time I asked him how he went about disposing of his victims. He stated that he generally placed them near a drain or in a tub, that he took off all of his clothes and took off all of the clothes of the victims if they were not already completely undressed. He stated that he would then take a sharp knife and start at the top of the sternum and make a single cut down the middle of the upper torso of the victim.

"He stated that once the initial cut was made, he would spread the wound and remove all the internal organs. He stated that he would place the internal organs that he would cut up into fist size pieces, into a plastic bag. He related that then he began to cut the flesh off the arms and biceps, then the chest and then slowly work his way down the leg until he got to the feet. He stated that at this time he would slice up all the strips of flesh into small fist like pieces and place them into approximately 3 bags, that being plastic garbage bags. He indicated that he was careful not to place too much into each bag. Approximately 25 lbs worth was in each bag. He would then triple bag the garbage bags.

"He stated that at this time he rewrapped up the skeleton and head of the victim in the sheet and then used a sledgehammer to smash the bones until they broke into smaller pieces. He related that he would then place the upper part of the torso bones in a plastic bag and the lower part in another bag. He stated that this was his usual pattern and it usually took about five 25 lbs bags to dispose of his victims.

"He stated that during the time that he was cutting up his victims and attempting to dispose of the bones that he was feeling several different emotions. He indicated that the emotions were a combination of fright, for fear of being caught, and excitement knowing that he had done what he had done. He stated that he also had the feeling that the victims could not leave him anymore because he had complete control over them. He stated that when he would place the plastic bags into the garbage after cutting up his victims he felt an intense sense of loss and stated that as he placed the bags in the garbage, he felt that the individual's life was such a complete waste and at one time they were a full human being and now they were reduced to 4 or 5 bags of plastic garbage, which he has placed in the trash. He also stated that at this time he felt deep remorse for his actions. However, it did not last.

"He went on to state that he feels that one of the triggers that started him on this path of murder happened shortly after he had moved to Milwaukee and was living with his grandmother. He feels that sometime in 1983 he was attempting seriously to find some religious meaning in his life and he was attending church with his grandmother and doing a lot of religious reading. He related that he did have fantasies of dismemberment and strong homosexual urges.

"He stated that one time while he was sitting in the West Allis Library, an individual walked by and threw a note in his lap and continued walking. He stated that upon opening the note he read that if he wanted a blow job he should go to the second level bathroom. He stated that at this time he thought, 'It's going to take more than this to make me stumble,' as he was continually fighting his homosexual urges. However, he stated that it was shortly after this incident in the library that he again began frequenting the gay bookstores and gay bars and he feels that this was the catalyst that started him again in his homosexual lifestyle, which eventually lead to the killing and dismembering of his victims.

"At this time Mr DAHMER was turned over to the

Milwaukee County Sheriff's on the 5th floor."

Report dictated by: Detective Patrick KENNEDY.
PK: dls 08-05-91

"On Monday, 8-5-91, at 2.00 P.M., I, Detective James
DEVALKENAERE, along with Detective Patrick
KENNEDY, interviewed Jeffrey L. DAHMER in an
interview room on the fourth floor of the Police
Administration Building. Also present at that time was
Jeffrey DAHMER's attorney, Attorney Wendy
PATRICKUS. By the time of this interview, a photo of a
possible homicide victim, namely Steven W. TUOMI,
W/M, 12-19-62, of 1315 N. Cass Street, had been obtained
from his family.

"In previous interviews, Jeffrey DAHMER had related
to Detectives KENNEDY and MURPHY that he believed
he had encountered this individual in November of 1987.
Jeffrey DAHMER viewed the photos that had been
received of Steven TUOMI and he positively identified this
as being the person he had encountered in November of
1987.

"DAHMER related that at that time he had been in
front of the 219 Club, is a tavern on South 2nd Street, at
about bar closing time. At that time he had encountered
TUOMI while TUOMI waiting at a bus stop. He had
already obtained a hotel room at the Ambassador Hotel,
which he believes is located around 24th and Wisconsin. He
had gotten the room earlier with the plan that if he had
encountered someone, he would take him back there for the
purpose of having sex with him. He had already purchased
some sleeping pills, which he had at the hotel room, for the
purpose of rendering anyone he brought back there,
helpless, so he could have sex with them.

"He spoke with TUOMI and asked him if he wanted to
spend the night with him at a hotel room. TUOMI agreed.

DAHMER does not recall if he offered TUOMI money to come with him, or not.

"On arrival at the hotel, both DAHMER and TUOMI got undressed and laid on the bed. At that time they had what DAHMER called 'light sex'. He described this as hugging, kissing and mutual masturbation. After about an hour or two, DAHMER made a drink for TUOMI in which he put the sleeping pills. TUOMI drank this and fell asleep. DAHMER kept drinking and eventually fell asleep himself. DAHMER related that when he woke up he was lying on top of TUOMI and DAHMER'S forearms were visibly bruised. He then saw that TUOMI was obviously dead. He was bleeding from the head and his chest was crushed in and some of the bones were broken. DAHMER then carried TUOMI and placed him in a closet in the hotel room. DAHMER sat around the hotel room for a couple of hours, trying to figure out what to do.

"At about noon he went to the Grand Avenue Mall. He bought a large suitcase with wheels on it and returned to the Ambassador Hotel. During that time he may have had some beers and he left the hotel room to get a bite to eat. At about 5:00pm he returned to the hotel room and placed TUOMI into the large suitcase. DAHMER related that it was a very tight fit, but he was able to get him into the suitcase.

"DAHMER related that he had purchased the room for another night and he remained in the room that night until 1.00am. At that time he left the room with the suitcase, taking an elevator to the ground floor. He got a cab and upon approaching the cab, had the cab driver help him place the suitcase in the back seat of the cab. He then took the cab to his grandmother's house on S. 57th Street.

"Upon arrival at his grandmother's house, DAHMER put the suitcase in the fruit cellar beneath the house. He left the suitcase there for about a week. He said he did this because it was Thanksgiving time and it was cold in the basement and he knew this will slow the decomposition of

352

the body. After about a week, he got the suitcase out of the fruit cellar and removed the body from it. After removing the body from the suitcase, DAHMER used a knife to open the body and then stripped the flesh from it. He placed the flesh in plastic bags. DAHMER then used an old sheet that had been in the basement to wrap the bones and he then crushed the bones with a sledgehammer. DAHMER related that he wrapped the bones in a sheet so that when he was crushing them, the splinters and fragments of bones would not fly all over the basement. He then put these items in the trash.

"Regarding the Ambassador Hotel, DAHMER related that on four or five times previous to this encounter with TUOMI, he had rented a room at the Ambassador for the purpose of having sex with someone he would meet. He indicated that at no previous time had he killed anyone there and nothing had happened.

"On 8-5-91, information was received from the Bath Township, Ohio Police Department that they had recovered a receipt from Don Stricker Guns located at 2465 S. 84th Street, Milwaukee. The receipt showed that Jeffrey L. DAHMER had purchased a Colt Lawman 357 Magnum revolver, serial #20301U, on 1-23-82. DAHMER was questioned regarding the ownership of this gun. DAHMER related that while working at the Plasma Center he had purchased a 357 snubnose revolver. DAHMER thinks he bought the gun in 1982 or 1983. He related that he only owned this gun for about one year and he used it for target shooting at a range. DAHMER related that he bought this gun at a gun shop in the area of 83rd and Lincoln. He paid about $350.00 for same. He does not remember the cost for using the range.

"DAHMER was shown a faxed copy of the receipt, which Don Stricker's had given for the purchase of the gun, bearing the signature of Jeffrey L. DAHMER. DAHMER identified this as a copy of the receipt he had received when he bought the gun, that the signature at the bottom of the sheet was, in fact, his. DAHMER further related that when his grandmother found out he had a gun in the house, she did not like it. He showed her the gun. Shortly after that, his father visited from Ohio and his grandmother told his father that he had a gun and his father took the gun from him. DAHMER believes that his father took the gun back to Ohio and sold it.

"DAHMER further related that he only bought the gun because he had enjoyed shooting while he was in the Military and felt that it was something he might like to do. DAHMER also related that he had stated he never owned a gun, in previous interviews, because he did not feel the gun had any connection with any of the victims in the homicides for which he was being questioned. He had never used the gun for anything other than target shooting."

Report per Detective James DEVALKENAERE.
JD gb 8-5-91

"On Wednesday, 08-07-91, I, Detective KENNEDY, was informed by the Milwaukee County Sheriff's Dept., that the suspect in this offense, Jeffrey DAHMER, had requested to speak with me. At this time, after obtaining an order to produce, I went to the 5th fl., Lock Up, of the Milwaukee County Sheriff and returned with the suspect, DAHMER, to the 4th fl., interview room of the CIB. At this time we were joined by DAHMER'S attorney, Scott HANSON and I questioned DAHMER, regarding information we had received from Bath, Ohio Police Department, that while he was staying in Miami, that he in fact had a girlfriend who lived with him and that he had intended to marry her. To this, DAHMER stated that while he was in Miami he was working at a submarine shop called Sunshine Submarines. He states he met another employee there. He states she was a white woman, with long curly, thick black hair and that she was originally from England. He states that she was in this country illegally and that they had become friends. He states that he is unsure, but he thinks her name was Julie. He states he did go out to dinner with her several times and walk along the beach with her. However, he, at no time had any inclination for sexual activity with her and never felt attracted to her. He states they were merely friends.

"He goes on to indicate that many times she advised him that she would be willing to marry an American, as a marriage of convenience, in order for her to obtain her naturalized citizenship. He states to the best of his recollection she was attracted to the manager of the Sunshine Submarine Club. However, she did mention to him, DAHMER, several times, that she would be willing to marry him in a marriage of convenience, if he could help her to become a citizen. He states they did talk about that several times. However, he never in fact took it seriously and because he was not interested in her sexually, or as a lifetime partner, he never actually encouraged this conversation.

"He states after moving back to Ohio, he believes that she did either call him once or twice or write him a letter. However, he did not respond, as he had stated previously he was not interested in pursuing a relationship with her. He denies that at no time he considered her a girlfriend, or had any relationship with her, other than a work relationship and he also denied that she ever lived with him in any of the motels that he had while he was staying in Miami.

"Regarding information we received that he had (blacked out), who lived in the Milwaukee area during the time he stayed with his grandmother, he states that this is true and that he felt he always had a good relationship with his (blacked out). He states that he saw her several times during the holidays, as he was living at grandma's house and he felt that it was usually [blacked out] who reported to his father activities that got him somewhat in trouble while he was living at grandmother's house. He states that he believes that she was the one who informed his father that he had a gun in the home and that several times she complained about the foul smell emanating from the basement at grandma's house.

"He states that he told grandma and (blacked out) that the smell was because of the cat that grandma had by the name of Jody, had fouled the kitty litter box, which was located in the basement and it had not previously been emptied. He states one time his Aunt Unis pressed him further, stating that was not a kitty litter smell and at this time he made up a play story stating that he had found a dead raccoon and had cut the raccoon up in the basement, in order to save the bones. He states he told this, because he realized that there was the smell of dismembered bodies that came from the basement.

"At this time I asked him how this could be. He states that was because several of his victims, although he cut them up and dismembered them over the drain pipe in the basement, he states after hosing down the basement floor and washing all the blood down the drain he was careful that none of the body parts or chunks of flesh got into the drain. He states after disposing of the body parts and the bones and hosing down the blood, he would pour a full gallon bottle of bleach down the drain in order to try to get rid of the smell, but the dismembered bodies would give off an awful odor and it would linger in the basement for one or two days before it would go away.

"He states this is the smell that his Aunt [blacked out] smelled and that she was the one that brought up the foul smell to his grandmother and to his father. However, he was usually able to dissuade them from investigating further, by his explanations of the raccoon and the kitty litter box.

"At this time I showed DAHMER another photo array of several individuals that may be the second victim who is still unidentified and after viewing all of these photos, he stated that none of the photographs resembles the victim he in fact killed at his grandmother's house.

"At this time I informed DAHMER that these were all the questions that I had to speak with him about on this occasion and at this point his Attorney, Scott HANSON, left the interview room. I then advised DAHMER that I would be returning him to the Milwaukee County Sheriff's Jail, at which time he requested a cup of coffee and another cigarette. To this request I complied and he asked me to again sit down with him. He stated that he wished to know some of the information regarding the events happening in Milwaukee at this time. At this time I lightly advised him that the news' media was reporting daily bits of information they had received regarding this case.

"At this time DAHMER started to talk about the movie that we found in his apartment, that being the Exorcist II. I asked him at this time why he in fact purchased the Exorcist II and he stated that he had seen the movie when it was first released and that he was fascinated by it. He stated that he enjoyed the movie so much, that when it was first released on video cassette he spent approximately $100.00 in order to purchase a copy of it. I asked him what his fascination was with the movie, to which he stated he was unsure, but he knows that he felt a tremendous amount of guilt, because of his actions.

"He stated he felt evil and thoroughly corrupted, body and soul, because of the horrible crimes he had committed against people. He stated that every time he would try to overcome his feelings of wanting to kill and dismember, they would haunt him and overcome him, almost like an addiction. He states he felt that he could not fight that feeling and wondered if in fact the devil had anything to do with his evil thoughts.

"He states because of this he watched the movie Exorcist II on almost a weekly basis, for approximately 6 months and sometimes 2 or 3 times a week. He states that in the movie he could tell that the devil was angry for being condemned. He went on to state that the main character in the movie appeared to be driven by evil.

"At this time I questioned DAHMER regarding the heads that he had kept in his apartment. I asked him how in fact he got the brain matter out of the skulls and why the skulls looked so completely clean and dried when we discovered them. He states after killing his victims and decapitating them, he would use a small drill to drill several holes on various areas of the head and then he would boil the head.

"He stated during the boiling process he would use a large plastic syringe, which he had purchased at an Ace Hardware Store and that he would fill the syringe with a Soilex cleansing solution and boiling water and inject that solution into the holes, which he had previously drilled into the skulls. He states that this solution would help to turn the brain matter into a mushy substance and that after approximately 1 hour of boiling, the upper vertebra, located in the neck area, would become loose and he could dislodge them. He states at this time he would use a large serving spoon or utensil to dig into the back part of the skull and scoop out the brain matter, which had turned into mush.

"He states after scooping out the brain matter and discarding it in the toilet, he would again place the skull into the boiling water and boil it thoroughly until it was completely clear of any flesh, hair, mucus or brain matter. At this time I asked him why he kept the heads and if in fact he considered them to be a trophy. He stated that he did not consider them to be a trophy, but he wanted to keep the skulls of his victims, because to him the skull represented the true essence of his victims. He states that he felt by at least keeping the heads, the death of his victims would not be a total loss, because the heads would be with him. He stated he eventually planned to paint all of the skulls in order to keep them from being detected but, he never got around to doing that.

"At this time DAHMER stated to me, 'It's hard for me to believe that a human being could have done what I done, but I know that I did it. I want you to understand that my questions regarding Satan and the devil were not to defuse guilt from me and blame the devil for what I've done, because I realized what I've done is my guilt, but I have to question whether or not there is Devil in the world and whether or not I have been influenced by it. Although I am not sure if there is a GOD, or if there is a devil, I know that as of lately I've been doing a lot of thinking about both and I have to wonder what has influenced me in my life .'

"To this I again asked DAHMER if there were any other victims that he had neglected to tell me about, to which he stated, 'Pat, what good would it do for me to admit to just half of my victims or to a few of my victims, or to not tell you of a couple, when I know that in the long run it will be me that has to stand before GOD and admit to my wrong doings and He'll know if I was truthful and honest when I finally was caught, and if I helped to try and clear this whole matter up. I'm telling you the truth now, because I want to clear my conscience and all that I've told you is the truth and I've not left anything out.' At this time DAHMER finished his cup of coffee, cigarette and I returned him to the 5th floor where he was locked up."

The Oxford Apartments, Milwaukee, Wisconsin

Sopa Princewill inside his office at the Oxford Apartments

Sopa Princewill's friend, Amadu Bangura